ETHIOPIA & FOOD SECURITY

ETHIOPIA & FOOD SECURITY

WHAT WE KNOW, HOW WE KNOW IT, AND FUTURE OPTIONS

Logan Cochrane

TSEHAI
Publishers & Distributors

TSEHAI
Publishers & Distributors

Ethiopia and Food Security: What We Know, How We Know It, and Future Options.
Copyright © 2021 by Logan Cochrane. All rights reserved.

TSEHAI Publishers books may be purchased for educational, business, or sales promotional use. For more information, please contact our special sales department.

TSEHAI Publishers
Loyola Marymount University
1 LMU Drive, UH 3012
Los Angeles, CA 90045

www.tsehaipublishers.com
info@tsehaipublishers.com

Paperback ISBN: 978-1-59-907279-1
Hardcover ISBN: 978-1-59-907280-7

First Edition: 2021

Publisher: Elias Wondimu
Cover and interior designer: Sara Martinez

A catalog record data for this book is available from:
U.S. Library of Congress, Washington, DC, USA

10 9 8 7 6 5 4 3 2 1

Los Angeles | Addis Ababa | Oxford | Johannesburg

TABLE OF CONTENTS

LIST OF FIGURES

LIST OF TABLES

LIST OF BOXES

ACRONYMS

AIDS	Acquired Immune Deficiency Syndrome
CSA	Central Statistical Agency
DDT	Dichlorodiphenyltrichloroethane
DFID	Department for International Development (UK)
ECX	Ethiopian Commodity Exchange
EPRDF	Ethiopian People's Revolutionary Democratic Front
ETB	Ethiopian Birr
FAO	Food and Agriculture Organization
FDI	Foreign Direct Investment
FEWS NET	Famine Early Warning Systems Network
FTC	Farmer Training Center
GM	Genetically Modified
GDP	Gross Domestic Product
GNP	Gross National Product
GoE	Government of Ethiopia
GPS	Global Positioning System
HIV	Human Immunodeficiency Virus
MSF	Medecins Sans Frontieres (Doctors Without Borders)
NGO	Non-governmental Organization
ODA	Official Development Assistance
PSNP	Productive Safety Net Program
SIDA	Swedish International Development Agency
SNNPR	Southern Nations, Nationalities and Peoples' Region
TPLF	Tigrayan People's Liberation Front
USAID	United States Agency for International Development
WHO	World Health Organization

INTRODUCTION

Dawn, and as the sun breaks through the piercing chill of night on the plain outside Korem it lights up a biblical famine, now, in the 20th century. This place, say workers here, is the closest thing to hell on earth (BBC, 1984).

On October 23rd, 1984, the British journalist Michael Burek reported on the Ethiopian famine. The images televised across the world altered the way Ethiopia and Ethiopians would be viewed for decades (Gill, 2010). Thereafter, Ethiopia became known for hunger. The experience of famine also left deep imprints on the country and its citizens. When the late Prime Minister Meles Zenawi unexpectedly died in 2012, one of the accomplishments that was attributed to him and proudly proclaimed on state-owned television and radio stations, was that Ethiopia was no longer the example given in *The Oxford English Dictionary* for the entry on "famine." This was not a message for the international community, nor was it a public relations strategy to change global opinion. The message that famine in Ethiopia had ended was for the domestic audience. Throughout Ethiopian history, extreme food insecurity events have contributed to the rise and fall of governments in the country. That Ethiopia had nearly eliminated deaths due to famine during the Meles Zenawi's era was a victory, of sorts.

When I first started working in Ethiopia in 2006, much of the imagery of the 1984 famine colored my vision and expectations of the country, including assumptions about insufficient agricultural production that were apolitical and ahistorical. As someone who was working as a development practitioner, these assumptions influenced my perspectives about the causes of food insecurity and famine. However, understanding food security, as well as Ethiopia itself, requires grappling with many

1

complex and interconnected factors. Often this requires unlearning as much as learning. With each lesson learned there are new questions.

From a historical perspective, extreme food insecurity is not new. Some areas of the country have faced recurring drought and chronic food insecurity throughout much of the last two centuries. Regional crises have become national in scope several times since the 19th century (Pankhurst, 1985), including the large-scale famine events of 1888-1892, 1958, 1966, 1973 and 1984 (de Waal, 1991; Graham, Rashid and Malek, 2012; Sen and Dreze, 1999; UN, 2011; 2015; Wolde Giorgis, 1989). These famine events took the lives of hundreds of thousands of people. In addition to these large-scale famine events, Wolde Mariam notes that between 1958 and 1977, on average 20% of Ethiopia was experiencing famine conditions every year (1986: 147).

What is remarkable given the history and experience of severe food insecurity events in Ethiopia is what has happened more recently. While food security in Ethiopia remains a serious challenge, it has greatly improved since the famine of in the mid-80s. Despite the fact that Ethiopia's population has grown rapidly—18 million in 1950, 35 million in 1980, 65 million in 2000, and is approaching 115 million in 2020, making Ethiopia Africa's second most populous country—there has been a trend in declining deaths due to famine since 1984 even as population has increased (Figure 1). This has also occurred alongside the emergence of new challenges, such as parts of the country being highly vulnerable to the negative impacts of climate change. Indeed, several serious drought events have occurred since 1984, but these have not resulted in famine. Notable examples of this shift are that the droughts of 2002-2003, 2011-2012 and 2015-2016, each of which affected millions of people, but did not result in significant losses of life (de Waal, Taffesse and Carruth, 2006).

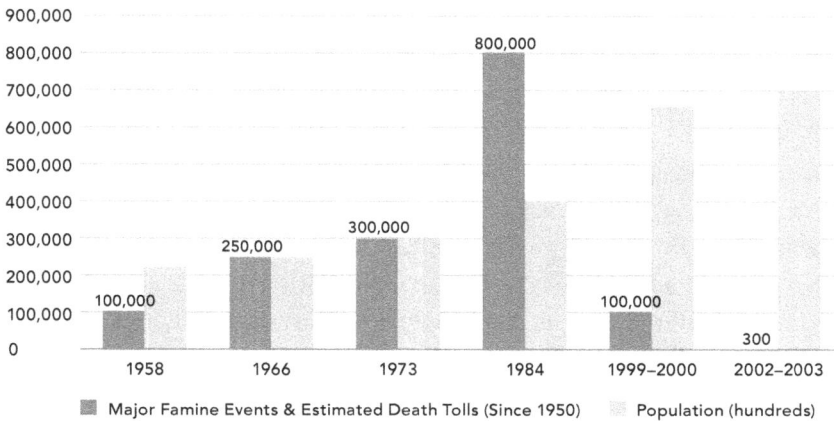

Figure 1. *Key Events Related to Population Growth and Death due to Famine (1950-2020)*
Source: de Waal, 1991; Devereux, 2009; Dorosh and Rashid, 2012; Gill, 2010; Graham, Rashid and Malek, 2012; Sen and Dreze, 1999; Wolde Giorgis, 1989.

Improved management of drought and prevention of famine-related death is an important success, yet up until 2003 it was based on unsustainable and costly humanitarian interventions, often made possible by international support. In 2005, Ethiopia launched Africa's second largest safety net, the Productive Safety Net Program (PSNP), to support the most food insecure households with predictable multi-year transfers so that the reliance upon emergency aid could be significantly reduced and to protect against the loss of assets at the household level (Coll-Black et al., 2012; de Waal, 2018). The program has grown to support nearly eight million people and has reduced food insecurity and enabled farmers to retain assets during challenging, drought-affected years (Coll-Black et al., 2012; Debela, Shively and Holden, 2014; Fisseha, 2014; Kassa, 2013; Katane, 2013). However, despite the progress enabled by the PSNP, significant challenges remain. As indicated by the statistics on malnutrition in Ethiopia (e.g., in 2015 32% of the Ethiopian population was malnourished), the improvements in food security have not yet been able to address the "silent famine" of malnourishment and micronutrient deficiencies. To this end, one of the key challenges the fourth manifestation of the PSNP (launched in 2014) is attempting to address is child malnutrition (a deficiency or imbalance in the diet essential to good health) by becoming more nutrition sensitive.

Despite widespread coverage of the safety net, concerns have arisen that it is not enabling households to become food secure. Rather, it is stabilizing households from losing assets while leaving them vulnerable to extreme food insecurity (Maxwell et al., 2013; Rahmato, 2013; Siyoum, 2013). When the rains failed in 2015 in connection with an El Niño event, these concerns materialized: the government determined that the poorest households remained vulnerable to food insecurity despite the safety net program being well established and having operated for 10 years. Furthermore, in addition to the almost eight million people already being served by the safety net at the time, the drought resulted in an additional 10 million people requiring emergency food assistance in 2015 and 2016 (OCHA, 2016). Independent studies on the impact of the 2015/16 drought are not yet available, but the loss of life is expected to be lower than that of 2002/03 (Davison, 2015). However, the fact that almost one in five Ethiopians required food aid during 2015/16 demonstrates that the transition from emergency responses to sustained and targeted support is ongoing, and much more progress is required. Even as we acknowledge the positive changes that have taken place with regard to preventing famine through early warning systems and emergency response, we also need to be mindful of the serious challenges that remain—high levels of chronic food insecurity in many parts of the country and high rates of child malnourishment and micronutrient deficiencies.

This book addresses food insecurity in Ethiopia, with a focus on rural areas in the south of the country. The methodology employed, Stages of Food Security, enables us to rethink the measures we use to generate evidence, and this may enable us to better ensure that the right to food is realized for all Ethiopians. Building on a human rights perspective, this book explores diverse factors for understanding the complex problem of food insecurity. Based on these foundations, this book reflects on the broader questions of what methods we use to generate evidence about food security and how the measures shape our understanding of the complex factors involved. A rights-based perspective also considers the right to participate and have power in decision-making, which shapes how the evidence presented in this book was obtained.

The opening chapters introduce us to the context of Ethiopia and some of the commonly used metrics and measures of food security, as well as politicization of responses to extreme food insecurity. These ideas are continued in Chapter 4 when analyzing how food security concepts are defined and who determines in what ways they are measured. In questioning the ways we collect and analyze data, the book proposes an alternative approach to deepen our understanding of complex issues, such as food security. Building upon the findings of this new methodology, and drawing upon a wide range of research, Chapters 5 and 6 investigate how we measure food security and the implications these methods have for the design of programs, policies and services. Chapter 7 explores how participatory ways of knowledge might facilitate positive change, analyzing the underlying assumptions in development activities and the highly contextual nature of influencing positive change. Readers may find these lines of inquiry relevant to contexts beyond Ethiopia and for issues beyond food security.

Arriving at the question

I first began working in Ethiopia in 2006. At the time, HIV and AIDS were presenting serious challenges for the country. While a treatment for HIV was first developed in 1987 and combination therapy became available in 1996, these were largely unavailable in Ethiopia at that time. I spent the better part of my first two years in the country with local organizations supporting children living with HIV or those left without guardians due to the loss of loved ones. Drawing upon my anthropological training, I went on to partner with local organizations in Benin, Burundi, DR Congo, Tanzania and Uganda, where we worked to bridge biomedical knowledge and best practices with the socio-cultural contexts they worked within. In the years following my first visit, I kept returning to Ethiopia, and with each stay my ties to the people and country deepened. For several years, I continued working in the public health sector alongside the Ministry of Health to strengthen the healthcare system. Nutrition and food security were issues facing Ethiopia at this time but were not my primary focus. The more time that I spent in rural and remote areas, the more opportunities I had to learn about people's lives and livelihoods. This drew my attention to questions about food security and nutrition. I also heard about people's frustrations. The ways that governmental and non-governmental organizations supportive and service programs were designed and implemented, I was told, were ineffective or served objectives different from their stated purposes. My doctoral research sought to understand some of the questions people raised about government programs and services, particularly rural agricultural extension services and the safety net; it acts as a foundation for this book.

In the time since I completed my doctoral research I have explored additional issues related to food security and nutrition that rural Ethiopian communities face such as land certification, expropriation and large-scale foreign land deals. This research also informs this book. In addition to academic research, I conducted "operational research" or "learning initiatives" for several large projects run by the Ethiopian government or by NGOs. These evaluative activities aimed to help understand which of the activities were working well, and which were not; who the activities were working well for, and who not; for how long positive change was occurring, and potential challenges for sustaining such change. I have worked on such projects in the regional states of Afar, Amhara, Benishangul Gumuz, Oromia, and Southern Nations, Nationalities and Peoples' (SNNP). All of these experiences shape the types of questions I raise in this book and the ways I seek to find answers to them.

This book does not set out to necessarily present new empirical evidence of food security in Ethiopia. Instead, this book offers a synthesis of existing knowledge, revolving around a set of key questions regarding what we know, how we know it, and how new perspectives might provide insight for ways forward. Given the slow pace of book publication and the timeliness required for decision-making regarding food security, it seems to me reasonable to publish new empirical findings in reports and academic articles and thereby make them accessible on shorter timeframes. While I hope that subject experts may find some useful insights here, the intended audience is broader. I have tried to write a book that is accessible to those who are not already experts on Ethiopia or food security.

In 2015, I started teaching at Hawassa University, and became a faculty member in 2017, where I am a part of the Institute of Policy and Development Research. In partnership with colleagues and students, we have worked on wide range of research projects. I am indebted to these colleagues and friends in particular (alphabetically): Addiswork Tilahun, Fekede Menuta, Hirut Bekele, Melisew Dejene, Tafesse Matewos, Tesfaye Semela, Yeshtila Bekele and Yidekachew Ayele. I am greatly indebted to patient teachers who offered informal lessons which were much more instructive than I have experienced in any classroom. I recognize them here but do not imply they agree with all the ideas presented in this book: Dessalegn Rahmato, Daniel Taddesse, Teferi Abate Adem, Zerihun Mohammed and Asnake Kefale. I continue to be inspired by Dessalegn Rahmato, who showed me immense kindness and patience as a student beginning to learn about a field where he has been the preeminent scholar for decades. This book builds upon much of these teachers' work and it aims to make a contribution to their collective aim of improving the lives of the people of Ethiopia. My hope is that the book will support better decision-making such that all people in the country can live healthier, happier and freer lives, and everyone can fulfill their potentials.

Framing and bias

As Cronon (1992) has pointed out, all stories are shaped by their authors. I do my best to make my biases explicit while recognizing that I may have blinders that I am unaware of. The historian Eugen Weber reflected on why the obvious did not necessarily become apparent to him, concluding that when "one looks for different things, one sees different things" (1976: x). To see those different things, we must be looking for them. We are all, as Antonio Gramsci stated, "conformists of some conformism or other" (1975: 324). The ways in which we conform includes our modes of thinking, norms, perceptions and priorities, what Gitlin described as how we view "what exists, what happens, and what matters" (1980: 6). As a consequence of these conformities, what we view as important influences our narratives and the presentation of our ideas.

The discussions presented in this book could have been framed much differently. Exploring some of those alternatives helps expose some of my biases. Building on the work of Scott (2009), one could frame the entirety of smallholder farmer action from a political perspective whereby actions of the marginalized are primarily acts of resistance against elites. To do so, one could draw on historical examples of how farmers changed crops to avoid government controls and taxation (McCann, 1995) and analyze examples of resistance to rural programs and services (Cochrane and Tamiru, 2016). Alternatively, the focus could have been environmental, such as conducting research on the processes that influenced a transition from a sustainable agricultural system to one that is unsustainable, causing rapid soil erosion and depletion of soil nutrients. Such a study may have focused on alternative agricultural approaches such as agroecology and how farmers view the milieu of choices they face and where more sustainable practices fit within their livelihoods. The study could have taken a deeper ethnographic dive, as Yelemtu (2014) has done, into one specific aspect of smallholder farmer knowledge and practice. I did not take these paths, and I suspect it reflects my assumptions and biases.

Returning to rights and responsibilities

The protection of human rights, including that of the right to food, even if enshrined in ratified international conventions, is largely the responsibility of the nation state. The Government of Ethiopia was amongst the first nations that voted in favor of the Universal Declaration of Human Rights in 1948. It has also ratified the International Covenant on Civil and Political Rights, the International Covenant on Economic, Social and Cultural Rights and the African Charter on Human and Peoples' Rights. Although the Ethiopian government has limited capacity, having one of the lowest gross domestic products per capita globally, I do not believe that having insufficient resources justifies the abuse of human rights such as restrictions on freedom of expression and freedom of the press or the ability to engage in politics.

Rather than make an argument about the need for the protection of human rights in Ethiopia, I have taken a pragmatic approach in assessing how the past and current programs and policies have worked and how existing resources can be more effectively and appropriately utilized in an effort to strengthen food security for all. Farmer (2005: 9) argues that "pragmatism assuredly has its role even in utopian struggles," but Goldman (2005: 13) might suggest this legitimizes the "project of development, writ large, justifying it as a necessary, if flawed, uniform project." I believe Goldman's stance falls into the simplistic dichotomy of positive practitioners and negative academics described by Chambers (1983: 29), whereby "to some critical and intolerant academics, practitioners are narrow-minded philistines and at best naïve reformists, part of a system of exploitation of which they are largely unaware." I aim to work and act in the space in-between, the messy middle ground of critical engagement.

Taking a pragmatic and therefore largely incrementalist approach to human rights necessitates reflexivity about my theoretical approach to research (Eyben, 2014). As Farmer (1999: 15) argues, double standards must be forcefully questioned. Am I, based in my specific place and time, justifying the unjust? Is the pragmatic approach to human rights akin to Madrid's 1789 introduction of more humane laws of slavery (Anderson, 1983)? Inasmuch as I have discussed human rights as a foundational means through which recommendations are made, there are embedded assumptions about what manifestation human rights take, and more broadly what are the appropriate means to attain justice. I have been influenced by the work of Rawls (1971), who introduced the important idea of "justice as fairness," which demands dramatic changes to the way society is structured and resources are distributed. I am also influenced by Immanuel Kant (1781) and his idea of categorical imperatives, whereby justice is not determined by its outcomes, but rather right and wrong are determined by maxims that can be applied as universal laws. However, my own understanding of justice aligns closely with the realism and pragmatism of Sen (2009) and Farmer (1999). In recognizing the plurality of worldviews and one's inevitable conformity, as well as the plurality of ideas that inform how justice ought to be envisioned, I draw upon Smith's (1790) idea of the impartial spectator to evaluate my own work, whereby one reflects upon one's own ideas as if they were a neutral third party. In essence, this is a form of critical reflexivity.

In 1971, two ideas were proposed that challenged thinking about justice. One was Rawl's idea of "justice as fairness" and another was the work of Gustavo Gutierrez and liberation theology, which proposed the preferential option for the poor. What unites the work of Rawls and Gutierrez is the powerful argument that justice cannot be the result of minor adjustments (i.e., pragmatic incrementalism), but demands a reorganization of society and resource distribution. When my research is viewed from the perspective of either of these standards, my theoretical approach seems insufficient as it does little to confront the global injustice that entrenches poverty in Ethiopia. The recommendations that result from my theoretical approach may insufficiently expand the opportunities smallholder farmers have, thus limiting them to what Weber described as "hard labor without chains" to which they remain "bound by necessity" (1976: 14).

Cognizant of these criticisms and shortcomings identified by Smith's suggested perspective of the impartial spectator, I continue down the path that seeks to move toward justice in a way that I see as being the most practical and realistic, in line with the positions of Farmer and Sen, rather than await or demand a form of perfect justice that appears impractical or unrealistic. Starting "from where the world is, not as I would like it to be"

(Alinsky, 1971: xix), I optimistically take the position of Hardt and Negri (2004: 289), who explain:

> There is no conflict here between reform and revolution. We say this not because we think that reform and revolution are the same thing, but that in today's conditions they cannot be separated. Today the historical processes of transformation are so radical that even reformist proposals can lead to revolutionary change. And when democratic reforms of the global system prove incapable of providing the bases of a real democracy, they demonstrate even more forcefully that a revolutionary change is needed and make it ever more possible. It is useless to rack our brains over whether a proposal is reformist or revolutionary; what matters is that it enters into the constituent process.

In addition to positioning myself on the incremental-transformational spectrum, a brief note on the researcher-practitioner spectrum is worthy of mention. Li (2007: 2), an anthropologist who studies international development, argues that the practitioner and critical academic roles are distinct and separate, and that the former is not in a position to make development programming an object of analysis. I have spent nearly two decades working as a practitioner. I do not believe my role as a practitioner bars critical thought, and in many ways continued engagement has furthered my critical analyses. Li is someone whose work and opinions I greatly respect, and it was therefore encouraging to align myself with critical scholars who also disagreed with her stance on the researcher-practitioner dichotomy. Roy, Negron-Gonzales, Opoku-Agyemang and Talwalker explain: "we depart from Li on one significant matter of expertise and politics... we are reluctant to conclude such a firm separation between the trustees and recipients of development. Instead, we interpret the mediators and functionaries of development—from star economists to young volunteers—to be engaged in the battle of ideas. Instead of positioning critics as those situated outside of development, we seek to explore how those within the system can participate in such struggles" (2016: 46). I have continued to be a practitioner while also a researcher in order to proactively and purposefully engage not only the ideas but the processes, power and politics of development.

Structure of book

This chapter sets the scene for chapters that follow, dealing with more specific issues related to food security and government programs, policies and services. The first two chapters that follow discuss the idea of food security, and then contextualizes that for Ethiopia. Chapter 3 reflects on ideas of development, and how the theories and assumptions affect the decisions that are made. Specific attention is given to the roles of power and politics, as they are often underappreciated in food security studies but are critical in seeking to affect change. The book turns to questions of how we know in Chapter 4. The focus is upon the methods, metrics and measures used in food security research, and it presents a methodology for asking new questions as well as old questions in new ways. Chapter 5 assesses what makes people vulnerable to food insecurity in Ethiopia, and Chapter 6 assesses the existing policies, programs and services aiming to strengthen food security. Having outlined where positive change is required, Chapter 7 reflects on how change might actually occur, drawing upon insight from diverse theories of change. Despite the availability of significant evidence on the topics addressed in this book, there are no specific recommendations. Instead, Chapter 8 reflects on possible options. This framing is in recognition of the aspects affecting food security not considered in this book as well as a willingness to continue to learn and unlearn. An exploration of those options is presented in the concluding chapter of this book.

CHAPTER ONE

FOOD SECURITY

What is food security?

Food security is a complex, global issue. The most common definition of food security is that developed by the Food and Agriculture Organization (FAO) of the United Nations: "when all people, at all times, have physical, social and economic access to sufficient, safe and nutritious food that meets their dietary needs and food preferences for an active and healthy life" (2003: 28). The FAO suggests that more than 810 million people are chronically hungry and approximately two billion people lack food security (FAO, 2017; 2020). Yet, the conceptualization and assessment of food security varies greatly. There are at least 200 definitions of food security, and there are hundreds of indicators used to measure it (Hoddinott, 1999). Food "insecurity," or the lack of food security, is not assessed by a single measure, as one might use for the level of particulate matter in the air. Food security is an idea or a construct embedded within socio-political contexts that is assessed using a range of direct and proxy metrics (a comparison of tools is presented in Chapter 4).

As the FAO explains, there are "differences in methodologies—what to measure, how to measure it, and even how well to measure it—and therefore in the measurements themselves. And there are differences in complementary (and often competing) terms such as 'food safety', 'food sovereignty' and the 'right to food'—all of which further contribute to the challenges of communicating for and about food security" (FAO, 2012b: 20). While the lack of safe, sufficient and nutritious food is not altered by its definition, the way that it is understood and measured impacts the programs and policies designed to strengthen it. Understanding the entire history, as well as the breadth of definitions, policies, agendas, ideologies and programs, is beyond the scope of this book. The topic has been the subject of at least one doctoral thesis, which resulted in a 684-page book (Gibson, 2012). The following explores a selection of the trends and key ideas that inform much of the current thinking and practice concerning food security.

Hunger is not new, but our thinking about it has changed significantly over the centuries and decades. In 1798, Malthus proposed that the rate of population growth is faster (exponential) than agricultural growth (lineal), thus resulting in a situation of insufficient resources causing famine. The Malthusian theory did not stand the test of time, in part because he did not foresee advances in technology and production. Despite rapid population growth since his time, the world produces a sufficient quantity of food to feed the entire population (WFP, 2016). While Malthus was proved wrong, food insecurity continues to be a challenge, the causes for which continue to change (e.g., trade bans following the commodity price spike in 2008 created new potential causes of food insecurity, particularly for food importing states). In 2008, the FAO concluded that while "the world has grown richer and produced more food than ever," hunger has increased (FAO, 2008b: 4). Understanding the causes of food insecurity forces us to look beyond the algorithms of Malthus.

A set of facts set us in new directions of inquiry. First, there is enough food to feed everyone. Second, more than 800 million people—approximately one in ten people globally—are food insecure (FAO, 2020). Third, as the FAO definition indicates, food security is about access to food. Thus, food security cannot be viewed in isolation from other social and environmental issues. It intimately interacts with poverty, inequality, human rights violations, resources and capacity, agroecology and the climate, instability and conflict as well as overconsumption and waste.

This section takes a narrow view of the concept of "food security," and in doing so it neglects the centuries wherein challenges of food insecurity were encountered and grappled with (examples of this range from Biblical accounts of multi-year food stores to charitable foundations, known as *awqaf,* providing food during the Ottoman period, amongst many forms of public administration). The idea of having sufficient food has a deep history. As Gibson (2012: 481) notes, "the idea that food security emerged fully formed as a concept in the mid-1970s is frankly laughable were it not for the pervasiveness of its many believers." Indeed, when I first started writing about food security I also repeated the common narrative that the concept of food security arose out of the challenges of the 1970s: the global oil crisis and its related food crises, as well as large-scale famines, that drew worldwide attention (Ethiopia 1972-73, Bangladesh 1974, Cambodia 1975-79). However, these events of the 1970s resulted in the concept of food "security" gaining greater global attention, and as a result it was subject to much more discussion, which is the main reason so many point toward this period as its origin (e.g., IFAD, 2009; Maxwell and Smith, 1992; UN, 1975; World Bank, 2008). Since the crises of the 1970s, food security has remained a prominent global topic of discussion. Notably, the global rise of this concept grew in tandem with the increasing "securitization" of food, the latter having roots in the World War II "Food for Freedom" initiatives as well as the "War on Hunger" of U.S. President Lyndon Johnson's administration (see Rosenthal, 1974).

For those global discussions on food security to take place, evidence was needed. While this was not the first time that food security was measured, it was a moment when concepts related to food security were expanded upon and developed. As new aspects were considered in the definition, such as nutrition and appropriateness, metrics of measurement were proposed and applied to diverse scales—global, national, sub-national, household and individual. As the information landscape expanded, studies began to analyze broader food and agricultural systems that affected its security, such as international commodity prices and and national policies (Barraclough and Utting, 1987; Smith, Pointing and Maxwell, 1993; Wolde Mariam, 1986).

As the concept developed in the 1970s and 1980s, the bulk of the attention in the international community was paid to availability and national access to food, and specifically to increasing production and building food reserves (Adedeji, 1989; FAO, 2006). As the concept of food security developed over time, so too did its complexity. Food security began to address questions of equity, poverty and other barriers, in addition to production, storage and supply at the macro level. At the 1974 World Food Summit the focus was on food volume and stability of supply; in 1983 the FAO added the concept of access; the World Bank included sufficient individual consumption in 1986; and, at the 1996 World Food Summit "safe and nutritious" along with meeting cultural food preferences were added (FAO, 2013b). The culmination of these developments is the Four Pillars Model proposed by the FAO (2009b), which focuses upon four key areas: availability, access, utilization and stability/vulnerability.

Academics and activists began to develop new conceptualizations relating to food, taking different departure points and emphasizing other aspects in their framing and definitions. For example, in the same year that the World Food Summit was refining its 1996 definition, members of a grassroots coalition of peasant farmers called La Via Campesina proposed a new concept: food sovereignty. Rather than access, this definition focused upon rights and control. La Via Campesina and its member organizations argued that local production should prioritize local consumption and be shaped by local needs and what is defined locally as appropriate. Foundational to this reasserting of control was a protest against corporate control, industrialization and the globalization of agriculture, food products and food systems (La Via Campesina, 2011; 2013). Advocates of food sovereignty believe that food security can only be achieved with a radical restructuring of society, namely through localization and the prioritization of self-sufficiency (Holt-Gimenez and Shattuck, 2011; Pimbert, 2008).

The ideals of the sovereignty movement have been challenged by some critics as having the potential to result in undemocratic outcomes, such as the potential contradictions that emerge between the objectives of achieving national and local food self-sufficiency as well as between the ability of farmers to determine their own crops, and in which ways to farm, and prioritizing food crops (Agarwal, 2013). The possibility of a peasant-driven food system focused on self-sufficiency that also produces surplus to meet global demands has also been contested (Bernstein, 2013). As well, concerns have been raised about the extent to which nationalist policies emerging from the food sovereignty discourse can negatively affect global food security (Margulis, 2013). It has also been suggested that the food sovereignty movement needs to better integrate international trade within its discourse, as many smallholder farmers rely upon it (Burnett and Murphy, 2013). In response to these challenges, new approaches to food sovereignty shift attention to justice, individual rights and environmental responsibility (Kneen, 2012).

While the food sovereignty movement has put forward policy proposals, it should be viewed as being driven by ideology rather than primarily being driven by a reformist agenda to implement policy changes. Rather than propose policy remedies (see Holt-Gimenez and Shattuck, 2011; Pimbert, 2008), La Via Campesina offers a set of ideas founded on the notion that farmers rather than international corporations should control the means to food security, and that farmers should have access to the fruits of their labor rather than rely upon the market to meet their needs. This ideological contribution is based on the fact that markets "do not just allocate a good based on how much it is needed or desired by the buyer; they also allocate based on the consumer's ability to pay for it. And, in a world of huge inequalities, those with the greatest needs are often those with the least ability to pay" (Ferguson, 2015: 130). Thus, the movement offers an ideological alternative to market-based solutions. In advocating for specific policies, the food sovereignty movement has had limited success, or has simply shifted the discourse towards justice and human rights. As an ideology, it has fostered global activism.

For reasons specific to Ethiopia, this book utilizes the concept of food security. One of the reasons for this is that the food sovereignty movement has had a negligible impact in the country. Although I have written about food sovereignty in Ethiopia (Cochrane, 2011), the ideological and policy aspects of the movement have limited traction with farmers and policymakers. Food security is also used in this book because Ethiopian food security research has included important considerations of justice, rights and sustainability, and therefore encapsulates some of what the food sovereignty movement has introduced into the broader conversation about ensuring all people, at all times, have sufficient, safe and nutritious food (Cochrane, 2018). This framing also enables linkages to existing international conventions as well as Ethiopian constitutional law and policies.

Definitions of food security focus attention on different dimensions of a complex issue. This is demonstrated by the diverse manifestations of priorities, policies and programs based upon the level at which the concept is applied—global, national, regional, community, household or individual. The FAO definition, for example, is a global definition (all people, at all times). This global perspective does not address issues of equality or equity, whereas Powledge (2012) suggests a definition that includes equal and consistent access to food by all people. Another approach, rooted in social justice, is a human rights-based perspective, which includes international conventions such as the Universal Declaration of Human Rights, the United

Nations Convention on the Rights of the Child, the International Covenant on Civil and Political Rights, the International Covenant on Economic, Social and Cultural Rights, the African Charter on Human and Peoples' Rights, the Geneva Conventions and the Universal Declaration on the Eradication of Hunger and Malnutrition. Rights advocates also point to a non-binding American resolution passed in 1976 stating that every person throughout the world has a right to a nutritionally adequate diet (Messer and Cohen, 2007). International conventions do not stipulate responsibility if, and when, a state is unable to fulfill the rights of its citizens. Thus, the right to food, although utilized in the global discourse, often falls within national jurisdiction and as such respective national governments "are primarily responsible for instituting and maintaining this order and thus for protecting the right to food" (Li, 1996: 154).

I adopt a human rights-based approach primarily because it reframes food security as an issue of justice rather than assistance. Ferguson frames this as a "rightful" share, which casts "aside age-old presumptions about who 'deserves' to receive payments and severing the link between labor and income in a quite fundamental way" (2015: 188). Furthermore, Ferguson argues, a shift to rights, or rightful share, offers citizens new and powerful social identities as co-owners of national resources rather than deserving recipients of support. Strengthening food security is a means to establishing and protecting the right to adequate food, which was recognized in the 1948 Universal Human Rights Declaration, stating:

> Everyone has the right to a standard of living adequate for the health and well-being of himself and of his family, including food, clothing, housing and medical care and necessary social services, and the right to security in the event of unemployment, sickness, disability, widowhood, old age or other lack of livelihood in circumstances beyond his control (Article 25, Universal Declaration of Human Rights).

This right has been re-emphasized in subsequent international agreements, including the International Covenant on Economic, Social and Cultural Rights (Article 11), which offered the following definition for the right to food: "The right to adequate food is realized when every man, woman and child, alone or in community with others, has the physical and economic access at all times to adequate food or means for its procurement" (FAO, 2016). This right has been enshrined as governments adopt international conventions as well as craft their own constitutional rights to food. Ethiopia has protected the right to food in Article 90(1) of the constitution (although the responsibility of the state is "to the extent the country's resources permit," and therefore it is not a protected right that citizens can demand for all people at all times).

Within the Ethiopian context, the rights of rural residents have long been an area of critical importance. In analyzing individual and community vulnerabilities to famine, Wolde Mariam (1986) argued that there are numerous claimants calling upon the resources of rural residents, for which they receive little, if anything, in return:

> The government demands all types of taxes; the church has similar taxes on its land; the landlords want rent; the traditional elders want their dues; government officials require something; usurers want their money plus exorbitant interest; the dead cry for tribute; and spiritual and social needs impose expensive ceremonies. Subsistence producers have an impressive array of obligations, but hardly any rights (Wolde Mariam, 1986: 14).

Since Wolde Mariam's writing more than thirty years ago, undoubtedly much progress has been made—education, healthcare, agricultural support services, social services and the safety net. Yet, these positive developments have not yet shifted into the realm of rights. Rural residents are conditionally included in many of these services, primarily on the condition that they support the ruling political party and oblige it of all requests made. One might envision the provision of these services as favors and gifts bestowed in return for "correct" behavior and not as rights that citizens can demand.

Demands must also be considered in light of capacity, as the Government of Ethiopia faces limited capacity to protect the rights of all its people; as the Government of Ethiopia has reported, it does not have the finances, access to credit or the technical capacity required to meet the basic needs of all its citizens (NPC, 2017). The result is a situation where decision makers have to make less than ideal choices—and they recognize their inability to uphold the basic rights of all people. This forces decision makers to make difficult trade-offs when designing programs, policies and services.

Food security in global context

While this book focuses upon Ethiopia, the topic of food security exists within a global context wherein food insecurity continues to be one of the world's greatest challenges. The FAO (2020) estimates that more than 800 million people around the world are undernourished. The number of undernourished people has declined significantly over the last three decades but has begun to increase in recent years (particularly since 2015), largely driven by food insecurity in conflict zones (De Waal, 2018) The burden of this challenge is greater in developing countries, and particularly in sub-Saharan Africa, which has the highest prevalence of people experiencing chronic food insecurity. Furthermore, the challenges of food insecurity are encountered disproportionately by smallholder farmers, who constitute the majority of the global population experiencing poverty and food insecurity (CFS, 2018).

The Ethiopian experience differs from the recent global trends. The percentage of the population that is undernourished has declined from 71.4% in 1996 to 60.6% in 1999, then to 47.8% in 2004, and the rate was expected to be 32% in 2015 (NPC, 2017; World Bank, 2017). The Central Statistical Agency of Ethiopia also reports consistent gains in agricultural production for the last two decades (for summary and criticism, see Cochrane and Bekele, 2018a). Akin to their counterparts globally (Gibson, 2012), Ethiopian smallholder farmers cultivate the majority of the agricultural land, and do so on small plots, with the majority working plots less than 2 hectares in size (Taffesse et al., 2012). Ethiopian smallholder farmers, like their global counterparts (Gibson, 2012), are critical in their roles of supplying the nation with food, particularly cereal crops, and producing food for export (Taffesse et al., 2012). Because Ethiopian smallholder farmers share similarities with smallholder farmers in other countries, identifying pathways to strengthen food security in Ethiopia has the potential to offer direction for positive change elsewhere.

Globally, the rise of people who are food insecure has not been a result of a lack of food; rates of agricultural production have risen faster than population growth (FAO, 2012a). The distribution of food, however, is unequal. Agroecological factors, such as rainfall, soil types, land size and water availability, affect the production potential of individuals and countries. For example, while much of North and South America, Europe and South East Asia have per capita food production above 8,000 kcal/

day, per capita production in much of Africa, the Middle East and Asia is less than half or a quarter of that level (FAO, 2012a). Food insecurity is not solely related to geography, there are limitations and opportunities related to different systems of social support, politics, and infrastructure. At the individual and household levels, barriers to obtaining food primarily revolve around localized challenges that include what food is produced, in what quantities and at what times as well as socio-economic status that limit access to food.

Regions that currently have lower per capita food production, such as East and Central Africa, the Middle East and North Africa, and parts of Asia (specifically from Iran to Bangladesh) are also ones that have high population growth rates. These areas are where much of the projected global population growth is expected to occur (FAO, 2012a; UN, 2011). Additionally, these regions face the greatest overall vulnerability to the negative impacts of climate change (CGD, 2014). Compounding issues of regional availability, the ways in which existing resources are utilized affect the distribution of food and food types, such as shifting the composition of diets to include more meat and dairy products, or shifting land use to grow crops for non-food use such as biofuels (Brown, 2012; Cotula, 2013; FAO, 2012a). These changes can increase production and improve nutrition for some while simultaneously entrenching or creating food insecurity for others.

High levels of chronic hunger, and expectations that the situation may worsen (Hallegatte et al., 2016), have resulted in a great deal more focus on food security. For example, climate change has the potential to weaken food security and increase vulnerability. Despite newfound enthusiasm to eliminate global hunger within the UN's Sustainable Development Goals (SDGs) and its 2030 Agenda to "leave no one behind," the recent rise of people experiencing food insecurity globally is a reminder that change is not always positive.

In order to have better policies, programs and services to achieve the bold new objectives of the SDGs, there is a need for more research to support evidence-based decision-making. A challenge for the research community is to address inequalities of research, particularly as countries most food insecure and vulnerable to the negative impacts of climate change receive less research focus (Cochrane and Thornton, 2018). Along these lines, the evidence presented in this book highlights how the global trends of food insecurity may worsen, with specific reference to processes that are occurring within Ethiopia. In doing so, this work emphasizes how definitions and metrics greatly affect the understanding of food security and thus the ability to appropriately and effectively design programs that reduce vulnerabilities and strengthen food security. One example of how metrics affect our understanding of food security is a focus on caloric intake. If food security is defined in caloric terms alone, the quality and variety of the food a population receives may be overlooked resulting in sufficient calories being consumed but also the occurrence of micronutrient deficiencies. The following sub-sections aim to clarify some of the concepts and metrics employed in the conceptualizations of food insecurity, namely malnutrition, seasonality, linkages to poverty.

Malnutrition

Food insecurity impacts the lives of people in many different ways, and assessments ought not to be limited to reducing famine-related deaths. Large-scale failures of food security are frequently recorded in history and reported in contemporary times, but the "silent famine" of chronic undernutrition and malnutrition often goes unnoticed and unnoted. Malnutrition can take diverse forms; too much of the wrong types of food as well as too little of the right types. This book largely focuses on the experiences of having insufficient food. However, Ethiopia is increasingly experiencing malnutrition related to poor food quality in urban areas, which is contributing to the rise of chronic non-communicable diseases like diabetes (Abebe, Kebede and Addise, 2017; Animaw and Seyoum, 2017). Understanding the manifestations of malnutrition and food insecurity related to too much bad food requires a book of its own (and is only an emerging area of research in Ethiopia that requires much greater attention).

A lack of sufficient food is one challenge. Insufficient food quality and diversity is another. Micronutrient deficiencies for infants and children can result in lifelong developmental consequences (Gibson, 2012; Martins et al., 2011; Rivera et al., 2003). In this regard, Ethiopia has also made some progress. Stunting of growth due to malnutrition for children under the age of five was reduced from an extremely high rate of 57% in 2000 to 44% in 2011 (UNICEF, 2013). However, the "silent famine" of chronic malnutrition due to food insecurity in Ethiopia remains far too common, and its consequences are severe: 38% of children are stunted, 24% are underweight, and 10% are wasted, defined as having a low weight for height ratio (DHS, 2016).[1] The impacts of this silent famine contribute to unacceptably high levels of loss of life: one in every 15 children dies before reaching the age of five (DHS, 2016). Tied to poverty and inequality, the scale of the problem is immense. Globally, it is estimated that each day more than 16,000 children under the age of five die due to diarrhea, malnutrition, tuberculosis, meningitis, hepatitis, malaria, respiratory infections (such as pneumonia) and childhood diseases (such as measles) (UNICEF, 2016). All of these causes of death are tied to food as the overall health of a person, and the strength of their immune system, impacts their potential for recovery and survival when experiencing ill health (Butterly and Shepherd, 2010).

How research on food security is framed is important. On the one hand, such research can be framed to highlight the desire to prevent the negative impacts of food insecurity. On the other hand, motivations for conducting food security research can also be framed in positive ways. For instance, food security has positive impacts on health, strengthens immune systems, and enhances educational outcomes as families are better able to send their children to school and children are better able to learn. Improved food security also has positive economic impacts. For example, farmers are less likely to sell their assets during periods of insufficient or irregular rainfall when they are food secure. They are also less likely to seek high-interest loans to meet their basic household needs during these times. This more positive framing of food security research encourages us to take a more holistic perspective that enables us to better see the broader positive impacts of strengthening food security. In other words, food security is a strength multiplier, meaning that better nourished people are healthier and therefore are better able to fulfill their full potential.

Seasonality

Food insecurity is best understood in rural agricultural contexts as a seasonal experience that reflects a dependence upon rain-fed practices that are vulnerable to unpredictable rainfall. Each year, during the lean season when food stocks run out, there is a spike in malnourished children

---

1   The World Health Organization defines wasting as a weight for height ration that is lower than 2 Standard Deviations based on the WHO Child Growth Standards median.

(Cochrane and Gecho, 2016). Because the vast majority of smallholder farmers rely entirely upon rainfall for their agricultural livelihoods (CSA, 2009), rainfall variability (too much, too little or at the wrong time) can result in crop losses or complete crop failure and cause significant increases in food insecurity. The failure of two consecutive rains in 2015 demonstrated the compounding impacts of these shocks to food security in Ethiopia. When farmers experience a series of adverse weather events, they are often forced to draw on household assets to survive. Even if future seasons are more ideal, these farmers continue to experience the impact of lean periods as they no longer can use liquidated assets to invest in future crops and livestock. The compounding and multi-year impacts of failed yields have been long noted in Ethiopia. Wolde Mariam, who conducted important assessments of rural vulnerabilities to famine in Ethiopia, argued that the "slow and grinding action of famine which perhaps originates in one poor harvest starts a process that reduces the harvest of subsequent years. Famine prolongs and intensifies famine" (1986: 63).

Later chapters in this book make clear the impact of seasonality and its key role in vulnerability to food insecurity. Yet, as Chambers has stated, the topic remains "grossly neglected" (2012a: xv). Hirvonen, Taffesse and Worku (2015: 2) state that despite the recognition of intra-annual shifts in health and nutrition "seasonality generally has received less research attention and has been largely neglected in the policy arenas." While research is available regarding the seasonality of child malnutrition diagnoses that result from insufficient food quantity (diagnosis requires significant wasting), less is known about nutrient fluctuations, in other words, the seasonality of the quality of diets, micro-nutrient deficiencies and malnutrition. Evidence indicates that in rural Ethiopia there are seasonal drops in average per capita caloric intake (10%) and declines in average diet diversity (7%) (Hirvonen, Taffesse and Worku, 2015).[2] Based on the available data, and drawing upon research from other countries (Devereux, Sabates-Wheeler and Longhurst, 2012; Devereux, Vaitla and Hauenstein-Swan, 2008; Gill, 1991; Sahn,

---

2   Hirvonen, Taffesse and Worku's 2015 study is important, but it has a number of limitations. The impact of seasonal changes varies significantly from year to year, and their study only draws upon one year alone (2010-2011). Additionally, the averaging of all rural households makes invisible the inequalities that exist between households, while quintile-based assessments of changes to diet quantity and quality would have been much more beneficial in understanding how seasonality impacts households in different ways.

1989), it is evident that an understanding of seasonality is crucial if food insecurity is to be reduced, and it must be taken into account in the design and implementation of programs and services.

Linkages to poverty

Food security is connected to, and often an expression of, wealth and poverty. Some explanation is necessary regarding what a food security focus can offer, in contrast to studies of poverty. In many parts of Ethiopia, food insecurity can be a primary manifestation of poverty. Many rural households meet all their household needs primarily in a subsistence manner and thus have limited engagement with the cash economy. Having limited dealings with the cash economy (i.e., no to minimal cash income) means they will be classified as poor regardless of their material circumstances, including whether or not they are food secure. While a number of measures of poverty align with those used for food security, an emphasis on food security highlights metrics that have not been included in studies of poverty alone. More importantly, a focus on food security enables an assessment of the programs and services that seek to strengthen food security specifically.

Furthermore, there are some indications that traditional poverty measures do not necessarily equate with those of food security. For example, Bhattacharya et al. (2004: 839) found that nutrition, poverty and food security are not always linked and that "researchers should be cautious about assuming connections." In a study of Vietnam, Mahadevan and Hoang (2016) found the linkage between poverty and food insecurity is strong in urban areas but less so in rural ones. As in the study by Mahadevan and Hoang (2016), my own research indicates that measures of poverty and food insecurity are not as linked as might be assumed. The linkages between assets (e.g., landholding size) and food security in rural communities are not always direct; a household with relatively large landholdings may be food insecure due to insufficient labor or ability, while a household may be food secure due to remittances while being landless (Cochrane, 2017c). For the majority of households, broad generalizations cannot be drawn. Averages and regression analyses based on household survey data that examine questions such as household assets tell only one of many potential narratives of food security. As every farmer will emphasize, there is no average household, average yield, average rainfall or average food security situation. Averages are imposed; they provide illumination but are not lived realities. Instead of focusing on averages, greater attention should be placed on the diversity of ways in which households encounter food insecurity (as discussed in Chapter 6).

These three factors—malnutrition, seasonality, linkages to poverty—are points that this study will return to when exploring how people conceptualize food insecurity themselves. As will be shown in later chapters, for rural households in Ethiopia malnutrition in the form of micronutrient deficiencies is chronic, food insecurity is often experienced during particular months of the year, but on a recurring basis, and the root causes of vulnerabilities are interconnected with access to markets, infrastructure, and information.

Looking forward

Progress made in reducing mortality, malnutrition and nutrient deficiencies will not necessarily continue. In fact, the trends suggest that existing programs and services in Ethiopia will be insufficient as rainfall becomes more unpredictable due to climate change and as landholding size decreases due to population growth, inheritance and fragmentation, dropping below levels that are able to meet the basic needs of households (Barker, 2007; Eriksen, 2008; UNEP, 2014; Vervoot et al., 2013; Wegner and Zwart, 2011). The eminent rural development and land researcher Rahmato (2007) suggested 0.5 hectares for a household as a minimum required for survival (based on his work in the root-crop systems in southern Ethiopia), however, in some areas of Ethiopia the average landholding size has already decreased to below half a hectare (Taffesse et al., 2012). The figure put forward as a minimum by Rahmato was not a recommendation, but a warning point.[3]

This book analyzes food security as existing in a complex system. While it seeks to assess a range of factors involved in food security, there are aspects that are not covered in as much detail. This includes international trade regulation, unfair competition due to subsidies and profiteering in

---

3   This point is also reflected in some regional land proclamations regarding land inheritance (which sets minimum land sizes acceptable for transfer, deterring fragmentation of land below certain sizes). For example, in Oromia region the land proclamation (No. 130/2007) sets 0.5 ha for annual crops and 0.25 ha for perennial crops as the minimum acceptable holding, and therefore the smallest holding size that will be officially recognized.

agricultural investments affecting commodity price variability, to name just three. While I am optimistic that positive change will continue to occur, the radical transformations of the global marketplace and the restructuring of the global community that are necessary for global food security appear unlikely in the foreseeable future. A single book cannot sufficiently cover all relevant issues. Fortunately, recent books have extensively covered aspects of the Ethiopian economy (e.g., Cheru, Cramer and Oqubay, 2019), and book-length analysis are available of crops relevant for Ethiopia (for teff, see Minten et al., 2018). There are important books that aid in developing a fuller understanding of Ethiopia, such as of its general history (Pankhurst, 1998), its agricultural history (McCann, 1995), its social history (Pankhurst, 1990) and the history of its peripheral areas (Pankhurst, 1997). There are also detailed books on land tenure (e.g., Ege, 2019) as well as the broader Ethiopian political economy (Aalen, 2011; Cochrane, 2019; Lyons, 2019). Books have been written on historical famine events in the country (e.g., de Waal 1991, 1997; Rahmato, 1984; Wolde Mariam, 1986), broader studies of famine (Devereux, 2006; Webb and Braun, 1994), and on the ending of famine (de Waal, 2018). Each of these works makes important contributions in providing insight into particular complex questions, and each provides important context for this study. My hope is that this book will help to advance the state of knowledge and practice of food security by improving rural programs and services, and in the process supporting smallholder farmers to enhance their livelihoods in a sustainable way. In focusing upon rural experiences of food security, where most Ethiopians live, I do not offer insights on urban food insecurity (although, with the launch of the Urban Productive Safety Net Program, lessons might be drawn from this study for the implementation of that new initiative). The following chapter presents an overview of Ethiopia and introduces a diverse set of aspects that are relevant to the lives and livelihoods of people throughout the country.

CHAPTER TWO

ETHIOPIA

This chapter begins by briefly providing an overview of Ethiopia's general history, with some reflections on historical food security. In the sub-sections that follow, a range of political, geographic, demographic, economic and agricultural characteristics are analyzed. These explorations provide important context for understanding the country context and how these broader aspects impact food security as well as initiatives aimed at strengthening it.

Ethiopia is located in Eastern Africa, within the region known as the Horn of Africa, between the Equator and the Tropic of Cancer. Much of the country is mountainous; the capital of Addis Ababa is more than 2,300 meters above sea level, one of the most elevated capital cities in the world. In most of the agricultural areas there are two growing seasons associated with the two rainy periods, the *meher* and *belg*. The former is the main production season, with harvesting generally lasting from September until February, while the latter runs from March until August. This generalization holds true for much of the highlands but excludes other regions. For example, in the Afar and Somali regional states, in the east of the country, there are low elevations, warmer temperatures and much less precipitation, while some of the western parts of the country have tropical rainforest environments and nearly year-round precipitation.

Ethiopia has a land area of 1.1 million km², which is about as large as France and Spain combined, or California and Texas combined, or the Canadian province of Ontario. Within that area, Ethiopia has a great variation in climate, temperature, elevation and terrain (Pankhurst, 1990). The country borders six independent states: Djibouti, Eritrea,

Kenya, Somalia, South Sudan and Sudan as well as territories whose independence are not widely recognized by the international community (e.g., Somaliland, Puntland). Following the civil war that culminated in Eritrea's independence in the early 1990s, Ethiopia became landlocked and much of its exports are transported via ports in Djibouti. Although the country exceeds a million square kilometers in size, 88% of the population lives in the highlands located between 1,500 and 3,500 meters above sea level, which accounts for approximately half its landmass.[4] The highland area is also home to 75% of all livestock and 95% of total cultivated land (Dalelo and Stellmacher, 2012).

As a result of these geographic differences, livelihoods and vegetation vary from region to region. The highland areas are cereal breadbaskets and are thought to be the original locations for plant domestication of teff (*Eragrostis teff*), nug/Niger seed/blackseed (*Guizotia abyssinica*) and dagusa/finger-millet (*Eleusine corocana*) (Pankhurst, 1998). Indigenous crops that are important for domestic trade and consumption include enset (*Ensete ventricosum*), the stimulant khat (*Catha edulis*) and coffee (*Coffea arabica*), the latter two of which are key export commodities. Other important cash crops include pulses, oilseeds and cereals. In the last 10 years, the fresh-cut flower industry has developed into one of the largest agricultural exports in the country. Livestock populations in Ethiopia are amongst the highest in Africa, and pastoral livelihoods are primarily located in the east and south of the country.

Due to the diversity of livelihoods, crops, and practices, few generalizations can be made about agriculture in Ethiopia (Box 1). Agricultural practices and crop types are strongly influenced by ecological zones, as the country ranges from less than 500 meters above sea level to more than 3,700 meters above. Below 500m there are low levels of rainfall, and agriculture of any type is only possible with irrigation. From 500-1,500m, sorghum, teff and pulses/oilseeds are grown; in the 1,500-2,300m range, wheat, teff, maize, sorghum, oilseeds, barley and enset are produced; from 2,300-3,200m, we see barley, wheat, and pulses/oilseeds; barley is grown in the 3,200-3,700m range; and, above 3,700m no regular crops are grown (Chamberlin and Schmidt, 2012).

---

4   Hurni (1988) posits 43%, when Eritrea was included; Hawando (1997) suggest 44% when it was not; both seem approximations given the highly varied terrain.

Box 1. Reflection

This chapter highlights some of the political, environmental, historical, socio-cultural and livelihood contexts that influence food security. Varying degrees of emphasis are given to each of these thematic areas by highlighting unique features that contribute to food security. Although this chapter is detailed, it is selective. For example, while relevant, the governmental and constitutional structure (formal and informal) are presented in brief; to sufficiently cover the details would require entire books (e.g., Abebe, 2016; Kefale, 2014). Other specific details, such as crop choices, are presented as they offer insight into the livelihood options or rural Ethiopian farmers, opportunities and limitations. In the selection of data presented in this book, I have aimed to provide a sufficient amount of relevant information for a comprehensive contextualization of the country to better understand the food security situation, without presenting a burdensome level of specificity. Determining what to exclude and what amount of background detail is required are challenging tasks; invariably some readers will feel important aspects are underrepresented, while others may find the book overly detailed. I have attempted to present a sufficient amount of context to provide an understanding of the conditions, politics, policies, programs and services that influence food security.

Although in some parts of the "developing" world, or "global south," livelihoods are becoming detached from farming (Rigg, 2006), agricultural practices continue to be important for the majority of Ethiopians (Bezu and Holden, 2014; Mengistu, 2006). Some studies of "traditional" agricultural practices suggest these are inefficient or harmful and require change (Coppock, 1993; Dubale et al., 2014; Mintesinot et al., 2004; Temesgen et al., 2007), while others suggest these practices are suited to the contexts within which they are practiced and may be more sustainable than their modern counterparts (Ciampalini et al., 2008; Ciampalini et al., 2012; Lemenih et al., 2004; Mesfin and Obsa, 1994; Nyssen et al., 2000; Tesfahunegn, Tamene and Vlek, 2011; Teshome et al., 1999). Yet, others find that no simple conclusions can be drawn; "traditional" practices may be better suited and more productive in some settings, while commercial operations and chemical inputs can be more appropriate in others (Kassie et al., 2010). The research presented in this book suggests that generalizations such as these do not align with the experiences of farmers and the decisions they make. More commonly, smallholder farmers selectively and purposefully integrate "traditional" and modern practices into different aspects of their agricultural system.

History

The borders of Ethiopia are a relatively modern phenomenon. The empires of ancient history were largely based in the northern and highland areas, from the D'mt in the 10th century BCE to the Solomonic Dynasty of the 13th century. It was not until Tewodros II in the 1850s and Menelik II in the 1880s that "unification" and expansion processes resulted in the forming of what would become the country of Ethiopia (Rubenson, 1966). Of note, however, is that those who were conquered in these processes do not view it as unification but rather as colonization. According to Aadland, the "state did not attempt to integrate, but to dominate the different peoples" (2002: 29). Since many regions are relatively recent additions to the nation-state, and its inhabitants faced marginalization once incorporated, tensions between loyalty to the country and to one's ethnic group continue to be one of the most challenging domestic issues. For example, during the run-up to the election in 2015 I was in Benishangul Gumuz regional state, wherein politicians from the majority ethnic group of that regional state promised that if elected they would kick out the "red" people, meaning members of the Amhara and Tigray ethnic groups, and take back the land that had been stolen from them, the Gumuz people.

The rate and scale of globalization that emerged in recent decades is unprecedented. Yet, the international exchange of goods and ideas has long been practiced, and the lands that would become Ethiopia have played an important role in this. Trade in ancient times occurred between the empires in the current area of Ethiopia with the Pharaohs of Egypt, to areas in present-day Sudan, and the Middle East and India (Pankhurst, 1998). In international trade markets, Ethiopia was known as a source of gold, ivory, myrrh and slaves, for which it would seek in trade weaponry and luxury goods for the elite, such as Mediterranean wines (Pankhurst, 1998). International interactions were not limited to trade, however. The Aksumite Empire conquered southwestern Arabia and Sudan between the 3rd and 6th centuries (Pankhurst, 1998), making it one of the most important political empires of the world, along with Rome, Persia and China (Munro-Hay, 2002). It also embraced Christianity as a state religion in the 4th century, making it one of the first Christian nations (Sulas, Medella and French, 2009). The Aksumite Empire was the only African empire to mint its own currency, which was valued on par with Roman and Byzantium coinage. The empire fell in the 10th century and was followed by the Solomonic line of rule, the leaders of which claimed lineage from King Solomon of Israel and the Queen of Sheba, whose meeting is described in a Biblical account, but whose supposed progeny are not (1 Kings 10:1-13).

The modern Ethiopian state took its form during the reign of Menelik II, who ruled from 1889-1913. Under his lead, the country expanded and conquered much of what is now southern and eastern Ethiopia, developed currency and postage stamps, introduced piped water, established a railway and telegraph line, and founded modern hospitals and schools (Pankhurst, 1998). Menelik II led the defeat of the Italian army in 1896 at the Battle of Adwa, which was the only African victory against a European power's attempting to colonize African lands. This victory would protect Ethiopia's sovereignty, giving the country a unique history in Africa. Menelik II was followed by Empress Zewditu in 1916 and then Emperor Haile in 1930, the latter of whom experienced a return of Italian forces, who occupied Ethiopia from 1936 to 1941. The Italian forces were later defeated with allied support as a part of World War II.

Around the time of the Italian occupation, new forms of social organization emerged, such as *iddir* (funeral societies), which originated as member-based funerary associations (Pankhurst 2008). Over time, these associations expanded and took root in urban areas, taking on a range of functions, from engaging in public health campaigns to influencing local politics as well as aligning with unions. It is thought that the urban *iddir* emerged in response to needs and changing contexts specific to the new urban setting (Pankhurst, 2008). However, nearly every rural community also has multiple *iddir* associations, yet less research is available on the origin of these. Unpublished research by scholars such as Svein Ege suggests the rural expansion appears less organic than what might be assumed. While these organizations are inclusive (e.g., in some *iddir* associations members contribute, and benefit, based on their ability), they often replicate existing power structures. As discussed in Chapters 3 and 7, there are questions about social differentiation that should be asked in seeking to understand the membership and beneficiaries of these associations. In posing such questions, it is not implied that these organizations are not important—they are—nor that they do not provide important services—they do. Rather, inquiring about inclusion allows us to see whose interests are being served through them, and who might be marginalized by them.

The Solomonic dynasty came to an end in 1974, when it was overthrown by the Marxist-inspired Derg government. A coalition of rebel groups, largely led by the Tigrayan People's Liberation Front (TPLF), which took power in 1991. Meles Zenawi, chairman of the TPLF and the Ethiopian People's Revolutionary Democratic Front (EPRDF), was the transitional President of Ethiopia following the fall of the Derg, and Prime Minister of Ethiopia from 1995 to 2012. The new EPRDF government organized the country around a concept of ethnic federalism, whereby ethnicities with large geographic areas and/or populations were granted regional status. This model, in theory, decentralized power to regions, although not all ethnicities were granted equal status, and this remains a point of serious contention. From the early 2000s forward, the government, led by Prime Minister Meles Zenawi, shifted direction and advanced a "developmental state" approach to governance, which emphasized the role of a stable, centralized government pursuing long-term planning.

After the unexpected death of then Prime Minister Meles Zenawi in 2012, the constitutionally mandated successor, Hailemariam Desalegn, took over as Prime Minister. The party won every parliamentary election since coming to power (along with its allied parties), including every single seat in the 2015 election (NEBE, 2015). The fairness of the 2005, 2010 and 2015 elections has been widely contested (Abbink, 2006; de Waal, 2015; Di Nunzio, 2014; HRW, 2016b; Tronvoll, 2010). The government heavily controls the media, telecommunications and the Internet, and tolerates very little criticism. Individuals who have attempted to speak freely—from bloggers to politicians—have been imprisoned (Committee to Protect Journalists, 2015; PEN International, 2016).[5]

---

5   Fortunately, most political prisoners were released in 2018, along with many imprisoned religious leaders, protesters, journalists and bloggers. This book was finalized amidst the transition from the EPRDF to the Prosperity Party; this description is reflective of the former, the latter offered an uncertain future at the time of writing.

Localized instances of discontent were expressed from the early 1990s, the causes of which ranged in type as did the forms resistance took. During the 2000s, when the repression of freedoms increased, discontent with the government and the way the country was being ruled spread beyond localized concerns. For the most part, however, this was a feeling that was quietly expressed because open opposition was not tolerated. However, starting in 2014, the mood began to change. Goliath no longer looked undefeatable, and across the country Davids began to call for resistance. It is estimated that as many as 500 protests occurred between November 2015 and March 2016, to which the government responded with lethal force and mass arrests (HRW, 2016a; 2016b). The mass movements began diversifying their tactics, moving beyond protest to include non-participation events, such as that which occurred in Gondar city in August 2016, when an informal strike took place as everyone stayed at home. Despite its stated objective of doing so, the Government of Ethiopia's transition to "minimalist" democratic processes (Norris, 2011) has been weak (Abbink, 2006; Tronvoll, 2010), and its movement toward inclusive and accountable democratic governance negligible (Kebede, 2013).

The year 2018 was an important one for Ethiopia. Protest and unrest resulted in the resignation of Prime Minister Hailemariam and the inauguration of Prime Minister Abiy Ahmed Ali. Hailemariam's resignation demonstrated the power of the popular movements to provoke change in Ethiopia. While within the ruling coalition, the new leader started processes of significant change, eventually culminating in his establishing of a new coalition, the Prosperity Party. Protesters and opposition politicians were released from prison. Peace was made with domestic opposition groups and many opposition members in the diaspora began to return. Peace was also made with Eritrea. Talk has begun about partial privatization of state-run sectors, and there is hope for freer and fairer multi-party elections. These were originally scheduled for 2020 but were delayed due to the COVID-19 pandemic.

A Note on the History of Famine

Agriculture played an important role in the early empires, with historical records suggesting that, at least for the landholding class, significant relative wealth could be obtained from crop yields and livestock (D'Andrea et al., 2008; Munro-Hay, 1991; Pankhurst, 1990). At the same time, however, regional droughts and famines have been recorded for at least a thousand years. Between the 15th and 19th centuries, for which greater data is available, historian Richard Pankhurst suggests that a famine (either regional or countrywide) occurred, on average, once per decade (Pankhurst, 1985). This apparent contradiction—wealth and famine—is best understood as a manifestation of inequality. The elite held large tracts of land, and their wealth insulated them from the difficulties faced by the majority.

In more contemporary times, a major famine occurred between 1888 and 1892, known as the "evil days," wherein a third of the population may have died (Sen and Dreze, 1999). Famine occurred in Tigray in 1958 and in Wollo in 1966, respectively resulting in the loss of an estimated 100,000 and 250,000 people (Graham, Rashid and Malek, 2012). Famine occurred again in Wollo in 1973 causing the death of between 40,000 (Gill, 2010) and 300,000 (Graham, Rashid and Malek, 2012) people, which was one of the first famine events to be shown on international media. The 1984 famine resulted in the death of between 400,000 (de Waal, 1991) and 1.2 million (Wolde Giorgis, 1989). Politics played an important role in the death toll of the 1984 famine, which occurred while the Derg government was fighting rebel movements in the north and east of the country. Their efforts to contain people from supporting and/or joining rebel movements restricted movement out of famine-affected zones and disrupted possible recovery when massive numbers of people were resettled in a large-scale villagization scheme. Alex de Waal (1991) suggests that 50,000 died due to the resettlement process itself, while Doctors Without Borders (*Medecins Sans Frontieres*, MSF) suggest the figure was closer to 100,000 people (Gill, 2010).

Politics & Policymaking

The Federal Democratic Republic of Ethiopia is composed of the federal government and regional states. The lowest level of government is the sub-district, *kebele*, followed by the district, *woreda*, and then the zone, which are administrative levels under the regional state. Article 50 of the constitution outlines that the regional states are "responsible" to residents of that state and that lower levels of government are granted "adequate power" to make decisions accordingly (GoE, 2014). The constitution gives the federal government power to "formulate and implement the country's policies, strategies and plans in respect of overall economic, social and development matters" as well as to "enact laws for the utilization and conservation of land and other natural resources" (Article 51; GoE, 2014). While the federal government "shall formulate and implement the country's policies," the regional states have jurisdiction in some areas (those not "given expressly to the Federal Government alone," Article 52 of the Constitution). Constitutionally, therefore, the regional states potentially have the power to create and implement policy. In practice, however, the federal government continues to centralize power, even through its decentralization initiatives (Chinigo, 2013; Mezgebe, 2015).

Within its constitutional scope, and within the space afforded to it by the federal government, regional states have exercised their power through the creation and implementation of development policy. Examples of this include the first pilot of the land certification scheme and unique regulations for land inheritance in Tigray regional state (land tenure systems have transformed significantly over the last century, which is discussed in detail in Chapter 6). Both of these processes, however, operate within the bounds of federal policies regarding land tenure. As such, the federal government remains the primary creator of policy, and delegates jurisdiction and responsibility, allowing regional states to tailor some of the details for their particular contexts.

When the EPRDF came to power they "understood the role that famine had played in its victory" (Graham, Rashid and Malek, 2012: 263). The members of the new government had lived through and fought amidst famine. Its members had also witnessed two governments weakened, if not toppled, as a result of their lack of action on addressing emergency needs and ensuring food security, and in the case of the Derg, its worsening of the famine (Bahru, 1991; 2014). When in power, the EPRDF set about to support the majority rural population, placing them at the center of their major policy documents, including in the Agricultural Development-Led Industrialization policy (1992), the National Policy on Disaster Prevention and Management (1993), the Sustainable Poverty Reduction Strategy (2002), the Plan for Accelerated, Sustained Development to End Poverty (2006), and the Growth and Transformation Plan (2010). The government also upheld, and created, a number of bodies to support the country's rural residents, such as the Agricultural Input Supply Enterprise/Agricultural Inputs Supply Corporation, the Emergency Food Security Reserve Administration, the Ethiopian Grain Trading Enterprise (1992), the Productive Safety Net Program (2005), the Ethiopian Commodity Exchange (2008), the Disaster Risk Management and Food Security Service (2008), the Household Assets Building Program (2009), and the Ethiopian Agricultural Transformation Agency (2010). While many of these policies were geared toward supporting rural residents and agriculture, the priorities did not always align with those of smallholder farmers. For example, promoted crops have tended to be those which are key for export, the safety net was not implemented in all regions, and the commodity exchange has set minimum commodity contributions at levels well beyond the capacity of average smallholders.

The making of agricultural policy is not only about agriculture. Governments are influenced by other factors, from socio-cultural to macro-economic ones (Dreze, 2018). Two of the pressing challenges with which Government of Ethiopia has to grapple are a severe shortage of foreign currency and insufficient financing to implement its plans. As a result, some agricultural policies are geared toward increasing the production of export crops for sale on international markets. This has resulted in a focus on high-potential areas and larger producers, leaving out the most vulnerable and food insecure farmers. Another avenue used to address these issues is the attraction of revenue through foreign investment in the agricultural sector (see discussion on large-scale land acquisitions in Chapter 6). These initiatives also often leave out the most vulnerable and food insecure farmers and pastoralists or are done at their expense. While it is easy to criticize the government for its choices on these matters, having sufficient government revenue enables it to provide a range of services, from building roads to expanding healthcare coverage. As mentioned, the Government of Ethiopia does not have sufficient financial capacity, or sources of credit, to meet the basic needs of all (NPC, 2017), resulting in difficult decisions and trade-offs.

Population

The most recent national census took place in 2007, and since that time population data has largely been based on projections, resulting in significant discrepancies.[6] For example, in 2015 the Government of

---

6   The Central Statistical Agency of Ethiopia planned to conduct a census in 2017/18, but this was delayed due to the mass protests and unrest throughout the country. The census was then planned to take place during 2018/19, but that too was delayed. As of April 2020, the national census had still not taken place.

Ethiopia projected that the population was 87.9 million (CSA, 2013), while the World Bank projected the 2015 population to be 99.9 million (World Bank, 2016). This discrepancy amounts to a larger population than neighboring Djibouti and Eritrea combined, and almost as much as the entire population of neighboring Somalia or South Sudan. While this specific demographic point is not an essential one with regard to questions regarding food security, it highlights the problematic nature of data in Ethiopia. In many instances, the figures provided by federal-, regional-, zonal-, *woreda-* and *kebele-*level administrations are best viewed as approximations, and, at times, they are used as political tools (for discussions of data quality, see Carletto, Jolliffe and Banerjee, 2015; Cochrane and Bekele, 2018a, 2018b; Jerven, 2013; Sandefur and Glassman, 2015).

Based upon available data it is clear that the national population has grown steadily over the last century, a trend that is expected to continue until 2050. In 1960, the national population was estimated to be 22 million, which had more than doubled by 1990, growing to 48 million, and doubled again by 2014, rising to 97 million (World Bank, 2016). The United Nations projects that the population will double again by 2055, reaching 200 million, and will stabilize by the end of the century at around 240 million (UN, 2015). Based on global population growth, by 2050 Ethiopia will be amongst the top ten most populated countries in the world and will remain so throughout the rest of the century (UN, 2015).

At present, the urban population is low (16%), and urbanization rates are relatively low compared to global and African rates, yet these urbanization rates are affected by how "urban" is defined (this varies by country, and changes over time) and some suggest the urbanization rate may be as much as double the government-listed rate of 4% (Chamberlin and Schmidt, 2012). In any case, the predominantly rural population engaged in smallholder agricultural livelihoods will encounter increasing pressure on land distribution as the population continues to grow. Due to limitations in the amount of unused land, existing family plots are being divided through inheritance, resulting in smaller landholdings. One of the reasons population growth has not resulted in urbanization (given the shortage of land) is the country's land tenure policies. Rural land cannot be bought or sold. Inheritance of land, therefore, ensures family members stay in rural areas to keep control of this valuable asset.

Religion and Ethnicity

Ethiopia is home to great religious and ethnic diversity. There are an estimated 80 ethnic groups, most of which are officially recognized by the Government of Ethiopia and recorded in national census data. The two largest ethnic groups are the Oromo (35% of the population) and Amhara (27%), followed by Somali (6%) and Tigray (6%) (CSA, 2007). Ethnic division is often aligned with linguistic groupings, with multilingualism being common, linking smaller linguistic groups with larger ones. For example, an ethnic Harari living in the city of Harar will speak Harari (called *Gey Sinan* by its own speakers, a name rarely known by non-speakers) at home and with fellows of their ethnic group, but they will also speak the national language of Amharic, have a basic knowledge of English from the public school system, and the elder generation able to read and write Arabic (this is less common amongst the youth today). In Wolaita, the linga franca is *Wolaitenya*, the local language of the Wolaita ethnic group. Outside of the towns, there are few speakers of Amharic. More than the national language, people in Wolaita speak Afan Oromo, an important regional language, and the dominant language of the Oromo ethnic group.

Religious affiliation is typically divided into three groups: Christianity, Islam and Traditional Faiths. However, divisions within these groups are also significant, particularly between Ethiopian Orthodox, Protestant and Catholic. Residents in rural areas will often avoid intermarriage amongst these different Christian sects. However, syncretism between Christianity or Islam with traditional faiths is common in Ethiopia and is manifested in diverse ways (e.g., Braukamper, 1992; Vecchiato, 1993). For example, someone classified as a Muslim may, in numerous aspects of their life, prioritize rites of traditional faiths over those of Islam.

Historically, Ethiopia was a Christian state, and government statistics continue to show that Ethiopian Orthodox Christians are the majority of the population. The statistics on religious demographics, however, are contested. Government statistics offer the only available nationally representative data, which suggests 33% of population was Muslim in 2000 (CSA, 2000) and 34% in 2007 (CSA, 2007). Although the source is not cited, a report commissioned by the United Nations in 2006 suggested that 45% of the population was Muslim (Barnes, 2006), which was a figure also listed by the U.S. State Department (2007), making it the largest religious group. However, recent U.S. State Department reports use Government of Ethiopia data (e.g., U.S. State Department, 2014). Like the population total, this religious demographic data does not directly affect the present study but again highlights the politics and politicization of data.

The intersections of religion, ethnicity and language and their impacts on daily life cannot be understated (Aalen, 2011). The boundaries of regional states are largely drawn upon ethnic line, which in some instances are reinforced through regional language policies.[7] Local languages are commonly the language of instruction in primary schools, after which the language of instruction is English. The result is that many children do not become proficient in the federal language of Amharic. As a consequence, in many parts of the country the federal language is not commonly spoken, written, read or understood. These ethno-linguistic choices, manifested in some regional state policies, have implications for national cohesion as well as the ability and opportunity for individuals to obtain employment outside of their regional state (Cochrane and Bekele, 2019). In 2017, a process began which would enable Afan Oromo to also function as a working language, in addition to Amharic, in the federally administered City Administration of Addis Ababa (the capital city). The implementation of this change has been slow, but it signals a change to the linguistic landscape on the federal level and a greater recognition of the diversity of languages in the country.

The ethno-linguistic grouping with which one is affiliated influences the choices of day-to-day life such as whom to marry (and not marry) and where one chooses to live (or not live), as well as components of life that might not often be associated with ethnicity or religion, such as which bank one uses and where one chooses to shop (or not shop). These choices are purposeful and made at an individual level. Some of these choices are displays of power, such as when federal government personnel speak *Tigrinya* to each other in government offices (not the federal language) and similarly when the regional Oromia government personnel only speak Afan Oromo (Amharic: *Orominya*) in Oromia regional state offices, even when Amharic is known and the service-seeker is not a speaker of Afan Oromo.

Religion plays a significant and divisive role in Ethiopian society. In many cases, religion is perceived to be a part of ethnicity. While this

---

7   "Ethnic federalism" was formalized with the change of government in 1991. Theo-
     retically, this aligns administrative borders with ethno-linguistic groups. In reality,
     this division is much more complicated (see Vaughan, 2003).

is not always the case, Ethiopians make and reinforce relationships of this kind: Amhara are Orthodox, Somalis are Muslim, Wolaitans are Protestant, Hararis are Muslim, Gumuz practice a traditional faith, Agaw are Orthodox, Afaris are Muslim, and so forth. These are generalizations that do not reflect the full realities of the country nor these ethnic groups. Nonetheless, in the view of many, socio-religious and ethnic identities overlap, and their impact on personal choices and societal engagement reflect this, thus establishing a religious-linguistic-ethnic nexus.

Developmental Context & Challenges

For more than a decade, Ethiopia has experienced rapid economic development, ranging between 8% and 13% annual gross domestic product (GDP) growth (World Bank, 2020). This made Ethiopia consistently one of the world's fastest growing economies. In 2018, for example, Ethiopia was Africa's fastest growing economy (Gray, 2018). Despite its economic advances, however, Ethiopia continues to have one of world's lowest gross per capita national incomes. In 2018, the per capita GDP was US$770 (World Bank, 2018).

During this period of growth (2006-present), school enrolment has risen rapidly, reaching 95%. But while children throughout the country are gaining access to education, the national literacy rate is 47%, and is significantly lower for women at 38% and also disproportionately lower in rural areas (CSA, 2012). Life expectancy has increased to 64 years, higher than the average for sub-Saharan Africa and for low-income countries worldwide (World Bank, 2016). Poverty has declined from 45.5% in 1995 to 29.6%, an achievement that has occurred amidst significant population growth (World Bank, 2016). However, it ought to be noted that the declines in poverty that are often touted by the government have been challenged as being inaccurate, or at best as only part of the story. Dereveux and Sharp (2006) find problems with the government's methodology, cite studies showing the opposite trend and highlight the neglect of seasonality (e.g., data collection after harvest seasons or during the lean season). Research by Devereux and Sharp (2006) identify high levels of poverty and that the number of people living in poverty is increasing over time, not decreasing. Part of the challenge is the aggregating and averaging of per capita incomes, because macroeconomic growth does not necessarily translate into improved incomes or livelihood options for the members of society with the least financial resources or access to financial resources. Sundaram (2016) has also shown that there are methodological problems with many of the assessments that suggest rapid declines of poverty around the world. Nonetheless, the government data is used and promoted by international agencies such as the World Bank and USAID (these data are reflected in Figure 2).

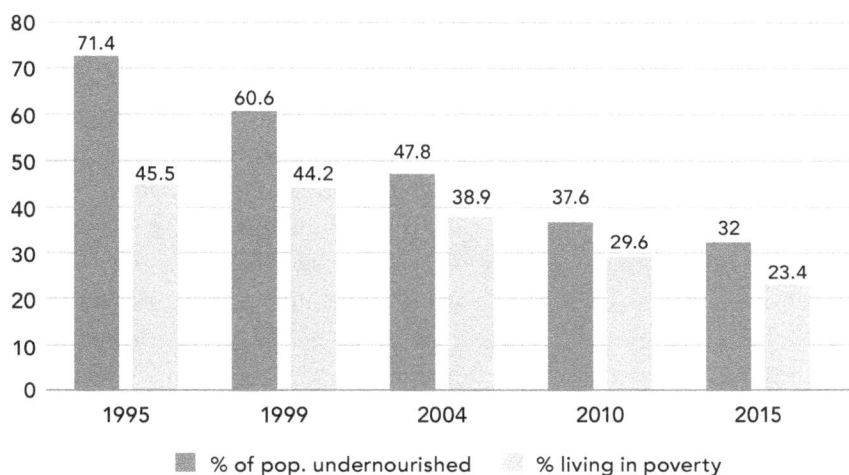

Figure 2. *Falling Rates of Malnourishment and Poverty in Ethiopia (1995-2015)*

Source: World Bank, 2018.
*Percentage of people living in poverty for 2015 is an anticipated figure from NPC (2017).

In addition to improvements in access to education and reductions of poverty, health coverage has risen rapidly since 2006. For example, although providing a complete range of services for HIV and AIDS is complex for health systems—from testing to calibrating diagnostic machines and adjusting treatment regimens—there has not been a single case of treatment interruption during the last decade, and coverage has reached 80%, rising from less than 10% in 2006 (Taddesse, Jamieson and Cochrane, 2015). Yet, significant challenges remain. Although progress has been made in expanding healthcare coverage and providing services, one in every 15 children dies before the age of five; the majority of all births are not attended by a skilled care provider; 60% of children aged 12-23 months have not received basic vaccinations; only 7% of infants and young children (6-59 months) are fed according to the WHO Infant and Young

Child Feeding practices; and maternal deaths account for 25% of all deaths of women aged 15-49 (DHS, 2016). These health impacts are compounded by limited access to clean water and sanitation services. National-level statistics indicate that almost half of all rural households do not have access to an improved source of drinking water, only 4% of rural households have an improved toilet facility, and only 8% of rural households have access to electricity (DHS, 2016).

Based upon health and education indicators, residents of the so-called "emerging" regions of Ethiopia face significantly greater challenges than their fellow citizens—this category is used by the Government of Ethiopia (e.g., MFA, UNCDF and UNDP, 2007), and is defined as faring poorly compared to other regions on the basis of measures of poverty, basic services and availability of basic infrastructure. The "emerging" regions include Afar, Benishangul Gumuz, Gambella and Somali regional states (highlighted in Figure 3), however there are no specified criteria for the classification of these regions as "emerging" and not others. These regions are not populated primarily by minority ethnicities per se (e.g., Somali is one of the larger ethnic groups). While the "emerging" regions are not core members of the EPRDF political coalition (which includes the main parties from Amhara, Oromia, SNNP and Tigray), the marginalization and under-investment in the "emerging" regions has a deep history, one to which all governments have contributed.

These "emerging" regions have been largely excluded from nation-building; colonialism is a better fit for the experiences of many of the residents of these regions. Weber's description of the processes occurring in rural France in the 1800s resonates strongly with Ethiopian government efforts in recent decades: "the unassimilated rural masses had to be integrated into the dominant culture as they had been integrated into an administrative entity. What happened was akin to colonization and may be easier to understand if one bears that in mind" (1976: 486). In the Ethiopian context this includes the administrative description of residents of these areas as backward, as well as residents themselves resentfully describing the federal language as a "slave" language and its use a constant reminder of the dominance of northern highland peoples over the rest of the country.[8] Despite these regions having being brought into the

---

8   On one occasion in eastern Ethiopia some people refused to speak with me be-
    cause I speak the "slave language" and not a local language. This is not just a linguis-

nation-state administratively, measures for health and education here are significantly lower than national averages, primarily because investment in infrastructure and service provision has been much lower than elsewhere, and thus far less coverage and opportunity exists for people in these regions (Cochrane and Rao, 2019).

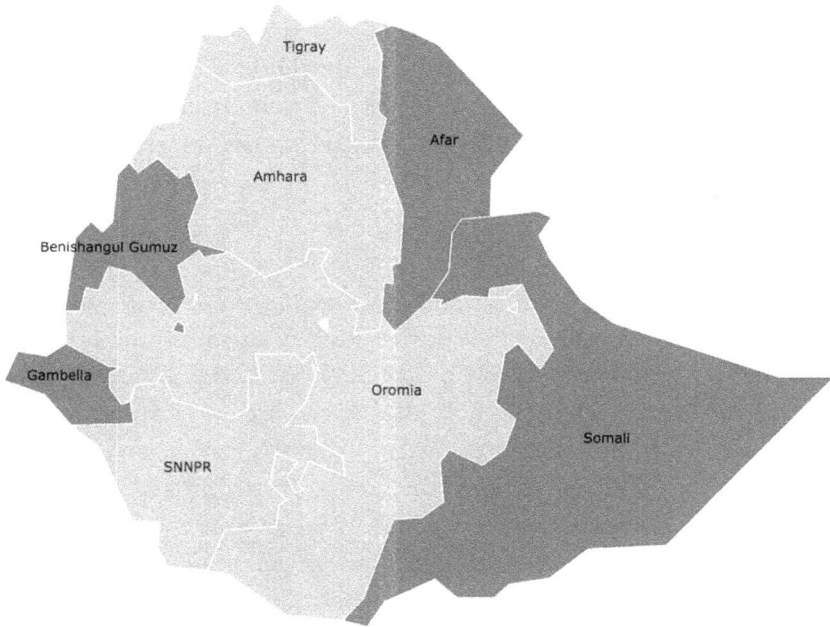

Figure 3. *Emerging Regions of Ethiopia (dark gray being the "emerging" regions)*

---

tic issue but also historical and cultural; many regions pass on detailed histories of the atrocities they endured as their people were brought under the control of the Ethiopian state (for many this occurred in the late 1800s, but for some it continues). The stories of oppression and injustice are reinforced in a variety of ways. One example of this comes from eastern Ethiopia where the interior of a certain part of every house is painted red, representing the blood of their young men killed by the government. The 2015 election provided many examples of ethnic-based rhetoric and the perception of colonization, whereby people were encouraged to vote for someone from "their people" so that the invading northerners could be ousted from their lands and their properties confiscated. These examples show how many people still view Amharic, or "highland" people more generally, as colonizers who treat others with disdain, hence the continued reference to Amharic as a "slave" language (not literally meant, however).

Because of the country's heavy dependency upon agriculture, climate change is considered to be a significant threat to national development. In terms of vulnerability to climate change, Ethiopia has been ranked as the 10th most vulnerable in a ranking of 230 countries (ACCRA, 2011; CGD, 2014). The changes in rainfall, temperature and weather variability have already begun to negatively affect lives and livelihoods in parts of Ethiopia, and the projected changes are expected to continue and worsen in impact due to the country's limited capacity to adapt (Di Falco et al., 2011; Kassie et al., 2015; ND-GAIN, 2016; Wheeler and von Braun, 2013). Finding options to adapt to these changing conditions is a key priority for Ethiopia and its economy.

Agricultural Sector

Ethiopia is primarily an agricultural economy built upon smallholder agriculture (Box 2). Almost half of the GDP is agriculturally based, and smallholder farmers cultivate more than 90% of the agricultural land (Taffesse, Dorosh and Gemessa, 2012). Exports are primarily agricultural, including coffee, khat, oil seeds, fresh cut flowers, cereals and vegetables (Cochrane and O'Regan, 2016; NBE, 2014). Nearly 85% of employment is within the agricultural sector, which is an area of the economy that continues to grow in importance with time (Loening, Durevall and Birru, 2009). The foundation of this sector, individual smallholder farmers, faces vulnerabilities due to unpredictable rainfall and a lack of irrigation (Cochrane and Gecho, 2016).

In Ethiopia, "smallholder farmers" are defined as those who cultivate less than 25.2 hectares of land and largely produce for their own consumption with the surplus for market sale (Taffesse, Dorosh and Gemessa, 2012). In practice, holdings by farmers in Ethiopia are much smaller: 60% of smallholder farmers cultivate less than 0.9 hectares of land and 40% less than 0.52 hectares (Taffesse, Dorosh and Gemessa, 2012). In the highland areas, average household landholdings have dropped from 0.5 hectares in the 1960s to 0.2 hectares as of 2008 (Spielman, Mekonnen and Alemu, 2012). Smallholder farming is almost entirely rain-fed (CSA, 2009), and due to declining landholding size as a result of population growth, productivity per household and average yields per capita are declining (ACCRA, 2011). Yet, yields on the national level have tended to increase as the smaller plots are more efficient and intensively used (Central Statistics Agency, 2004;

2005; 2006; 2007; 2008; 2009; 2010; 2011; 2012; 2013; 2014; 2015). While comparable nationally representative data sets are not available, there are reasons to question these trends (e.g., Cochrane and Bekele, 2018a).

Box 2. Terminology

It is worth pausing and making a note on terminology. I use the terminology "smallholder farmer" throughout this book as the term references the individuals and their livelihood practices as opposed to other terms, such as peasants, which primarily focus on the relationship individuals have with the government. In the global context, "smallholder" tends to refer to landholders with 2 hectares or less; in Ethiopia they are defined as those with less than 25.2 hectares of land. I have placed "traditional" in quotes because the term can have negative connotations and is suggestive of a static state, neither of which should be applied to the practices of farmers that differ from technology-intensive forms of "modern" agriculture. While the quotes are somewhat cumbersome, the continued use throughout is a reminder for readers to reflect critically on the meaning of this term and what it might imply.

For decades, the Government of Ethiopia has encouraged the use of inputs (fertilizer and pesticide) and improved seed varieties (see detailed discussion on this in Chapter 6). The government provides inputs to smallholder farmers, however uptake of improved varieties has been mixed; 71% of the area planted with wheat was with improved varieties (Lantican et al., 2005) but only 20% of the cultivated maize area, and adoption of improved varieties of other crops is lower still (Spielman, Mekonnen and Alemu, 2012). Studies suggest that about a third of all smallholder farmers use fertilizers (the CSA reported 39% and the ERSS 32%), largely for teff, wheat and maize production (Spielman, Mekonnen and Alemu, 2012). Credit barriers and low and inconsistent levels of input supply are among the reasons that prevent greater uptake. Agricultural practices advocated by agricultural extension workers, such as crop and seed types, experience mixed uptake, with a discontinuation rate potentially as high as a third (Bonger, Ayele and Kuma, 2004; EEA/EEPRI, 2006).

Based upon many of the newly developed agricultural policies, strategies, plans and agencies of the Government of Ethiopia, it might be assumed that the push for increased inputs in the agricultural sector is relatively new and initiated by the current EPRDF government. It is not. Inputs have been distributed in rural parts of Ethiopia since the early 1970s (Rahmato, 2007). In fact, limited forms of agricultural extension have been offered since the 1930s (Belay, 2003). Despite long-term advocacy by the government for farmers to utilize fertilizer, amongst other inputs (e.g., pesticides and improved seeds), uptake has been moderate. Amongst the range of innovations provided to farmers, including the agricultural inputs mentioned above as well as new planting methods and credit services, fertilizer uptake is arguably the greatest success (Taffesse, Dorosh and Gemessa, 2012). However, according to national data only 32% to 39% of smallholder farmers use fertilizers (Spielman, Mekonnen and Alemu, 2012). To varying degrees, all of these services have been promoted for decades (Rahmato, 2007) and international research projects seeking to understand poor levels of adoption have been conducted since at least the 1980s (Kebede, Gunjal and Coffin, 1990). Given almost fifty years of advocacy, this is a dismal failure.

One of the reasons farmers are reluctant to take up these innovations is that they worry about becoming dependent upon the providers of these inputs and about the new risks related to inconsistent, poor quality or delayed supply. Consider a new seed type: if farmers adopt a new seed variety distributed by the government extension system for several years in a row, they progressively lose the seed they traditionally saved and used. When seed is no longer distributed, not sufficiently distributed, or distributed too late, farmers have few alternative options. Thus their livelihood becomes vulnerable to a new set of variables. Some studies indicate that the percentage of households receiving full packages of fertilizer and seed can be as low as 22% (Tadesse, 2014). Some have suggested that this low figure is not a result of non-adoption, but about low levels of availability and access, which is supported by data on fertilizer distribution in Wolaita Zone starting in the 1970s through to the present (Rahmato, 2007: 15; Cochrane, 2017c).

Smallholder agriculture is the primary livelihood practice for the vast majority of Ethiopian families who experience food insecurity, malnutrition and micronutrient deficiencies. Paradoxically, it is also these smallholder farmers who are the foundation of the national economy and who are the main source of Ethiopia's exports (Loening, Durecall and Birru, 2009); agricultural products account for 55% of all exports (OEC, 2014). It is smallholder farmers, as opposed to commercial operations, who farm more than 90% of all cultivated land (Taffesse, Dorosh and Gemessa, 2012).

Commercial farms, held by the state or by the private sector, are defined as being larger than 25.2 hectares. Research by Taffesse, Dorosh and Gemessa (2012) shows that the average commercial holding is 323 hectares in size, the products of which are limited in quantity, making up about 4% of national production but accounting for large shares of specific crops such as coffee (19.1%), fruit (19.4%), vegetables (23.7%), sugarcane (78.1%) and sesame (42.6%). Commercial farms more commonly utilize mechanization, irrigation and external inputs, whereas these technologies are utilized less often on smallholder farms. Yields per hectare can be as much as three times higher as a result (Taffesse, Dorosh and Gemessa, 2012).

Over the last decade, the Central Statistical Agency of Ethiopia has reported that steady and significant gains have been made in average yield per hectare in teff and maize on the national, regional and zonal levels (see Cochrane and Bekele, 2018a). However, that data is questionable and highly politicized. This type of data should be viewed as a component of a government narrative of growth and progression toward the government-mandated targets as much as they are reflections of actual agricultural output. Development narratives from the Government of Ethiopia, like all narratives, are shaped by the inclusion and exclusion of information, the selection of metrics and the interpretation of the data. Research on the quality of statistical data in Africa suggests data quality issues are common in national statistical agencies (Carletto, Jolliffe and Banerjee, 2015; Jerven, 2013; Sandefur and Glassman, 2015), and examples of the problematic nature of data in Ethiopia are discussed throughout this book.

Examples of the difficulties of using government data for agricultural production include data on sweet potato, enset and taro. The CSA data on sweet potato for the Southern Nations, Nationalities and Peoples regional state (SNNPR) from 2007 to 2011 are stable, but during this time sweet potato virus disease infection is known to have been extremely high and was affecting roots, weight and cuttings (Tefera, Handoro and Gemu, 2013). During the 2007/08 season a higher yielding variety of taro was introduced and was widely adopted, yet no increase was recorded in the government statistics in the years that followed. In the 2012/13 planting season, the yields per hectare of taro and sweet potato, two crops of primary importance in southern Ethiopia, tripled according to government data. For example, in Wolaita Zone taro production rose from 86 *quintal* (100 kg units) per hectare to 327, and sweet potato rose from 106 *quintal* (100 kg units) to 241 and then to 364 in the two following seasons. According to the Head of Agricultural Statistics at the Central Statistical Agency of Ethiopia, the reported improvements were the result of changes in methods for calculating yields in the annual surveys and not necessarily actual changes in yields (Personal Communication 3 April 2016).

Even if we accept these increases in yield as being accurate, the reported figures are averages. In describing how states utilize data and the ways they diverge from lived experiences, Scott explains that an individual "farmer rarely experiences an average crop, an average rainfall, or an average price for his crops" (1998: 46). This is also the case for Ethiopia. Average yield per hectare does not highlight localized crop failures due, for example, to unpredictable rainfall or disease. Nor do increased average yields result in improved or equitable access. For example, Sen (1981) found that in the 1973/74 Ethiopian famine there were few shortages of food but significant shortages of purchasing power. Similarly, during the 1982-1984 famine period, average national yields were stable, with regional spikes of prices (de Waal, 1997, 2018). In his study of famine in Ethiopia, Wolde Mariam (1986) highlights timely access to information and accessibility as key issues in mitigating famine, as it was not the case that the country as a whole lacked food supplies but only specific areas. Furthermore, average agricultural yields of smallholder farmers can increase while food security remains chronic due to poverty, declining landholding size and increasing inequality. Increased average yields, in reality, often equate to significant positive change for the relatively better off smallholder farmers who have larger holdings and who are able to sell to the market, whereas smaller landholders struggle to produce a sufficient amount to provide for the needs of their own household. Amidst improved productivity, therefore, there can be increased vulnerability, poverty and food insecurity. The decades of attention Ethiopian food insecurity has received leads us to question what development means and who benefits from development activity. This is the subject of the next chapter.

CHAPTER THREE

ENCOUNTERING

Having critically analyzed the concept of food security in Chapter 1, and then situated it in the Ethiopian context in Chapter 2, this chapter widens the scope and examines concepts often associated with attempts to address food insecurity: aid and development. Broadly speaking, humanitarian aid focuses on shorter-term responses to emergency situations, while developmental activity seeks to address long-term goals of building strong service systems (e.g., education, health, agricultural extension). These supportive services are often provided by governments for their own citizens, with the support of external partners and alongside NGOs. The first part of this chapter considers the fraught history of the concepts of aid and development, and critically analyzes them drawing upon Ethiopian experiences. The second part of this chapter integrates power and politics into the discussion of aid and development, which acts as an introduction to some of the specific challenges that are experienced in attempts to strengthen food security in rural Ethiopia.

What of the decades of public sector investment and activity by the Government of Ethiopia, aid given by donors and work done by non-governmental organizations? Ethiopia began receiving aid, first from the UK and then the US, after World War II. One estimate suggests that between 1950 and 1970 Ethiopia received US$600 million in aid (Keller, 1991). The donor landscape shifted in the 1970s and 1980s, when Ethiopia received aid from the Soviet Union (as discussed below, smaller flows of aid, including food aid, were given by other nations during these years). Significant amounts of aid began to flow in the 1990s after the change in government and the adoption of a structural adjustment program in 1992/93 (Alemu, 2009). There was a drop in international aid during the late 1990s when Ethiopia fought a war with Eritrea, but it again rose in 2000 and remained high thereafter. Net disbursements of official development assistance from states reporting to the OECD (largely being OECD member states) to Ethiopia rose from a 2000/01 average of US$1.3 billion to more than US$4 billion in 2016 (see Figure 4; OECD, 2018).[9]

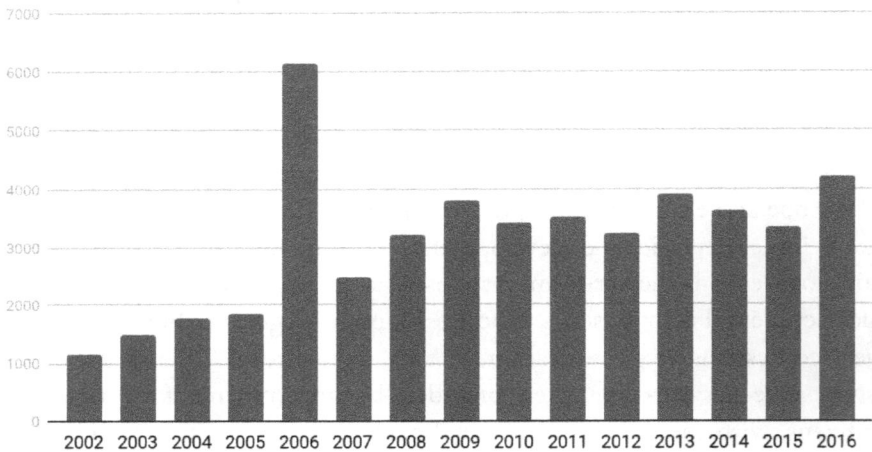

Figure 4. *Trends of Aid to Ethiopia (all donors, all types, US$), 2002-2016*
Source: OECD, 2018

How can there still be poverty and hunger in Ethiopia when US$4 billion was given in aid in 2016 alone? We need macro-context to understand these seemingly immense figures. I currently live in Ottawa, Canada. The city is the nation's capital, home to about a million people. There are several general and specialized hospitals in the city. In 2018, plans for a new hospital were announced, and the estimated cost was CDN$2 billion (approximately US$1.5 billion). That is just to build the structure, not to operate it. If Ethiopia were to spend its entire aid budget on building hospitals, which it critically needs, it would get just over two and a half if we use the Ottawa hospital as a model. An extension to the light rail transit system in Ottawa cost over CDN$2 billion (approximately US$1.5 billion). Billions add up quickly when you are building infrastructure for a nation.

---

9   US$ at 2015 prices and exchange rates (OECD, 2018).

These are also not the best examples. Labor costs are not the same; building codes differ; the type of machinery used would differ; the quality of the final product would probably not be as high. For example, Ethiopia built a light rail system in Addis Ababa for less than US$0.5 billion, one-third the cost of a short extension of light rail in Ottawa (which was plagued with issues once finished). Furthermore, Ethiopia does not really get to decide what is done with funds given in aid. This is all hypothetical. Aid is given conditionally, to specific sectors with set purposes, or to non-governmental organizations. Furthermore, not all needs are equal. Sometimes priorities result in short-term activities being selected over long-term investments. In 2018, the Ethiopian Humanitarian and Disaster Relief Plan outlined a need for US$1.6 billion to provide emergency food and health support that was immediately required (UN OCHA, 2018). Demands such as these make building infrastructure difficult to do.

Presenting figures such as those above provide insights into the difficulty of development. The Government of Ethiopia has clearly stated that it does not have enough resources, financing or capacity to meet the needs and developmental objectives of the nation (NPC, 2017). The government is left with very difficult decisions. Understanding food security, therefore, brings us to bigger questions regarding development. These questions are not specific to aid. The Government of Ethiopia funds, or obtains financing for, the majority of its expenditures. Aid plays a role in development, but the question of development is much bigger.

Ethiopians have experienced some improvements in their lives and livelihoods. Services have improved and infrastructure is expanding. These improvements are relative. Ethiopia remains one of the poorest nations in the world, on a per capita basis. The methods to assess national-level financial advancement are useful but also leave out much important information. Typically, one looks at GDP, which is a measure of all economic activity of a country, and divides that by the population to get a per person figure. Without taking into account inequality, this average figure has limited usefulness. However, for what it is worth, according to the World Bank (2018) Ethiopia has a per person GDP around US$770, putting it amongst the world's lowest (exact rankings of all countries are difficult as some countries do not have up-to-date data). GDP per capita in the US is just under US$60,000 and in Canada it is slightly more than US$45,000.

It might be assumed that assessments of poverty are more useful for our purposes. However, the methods by which poverty is assessed, and therefore the results, vary greatly (Box 3). In most instances, national poverty levels are used, making cross-country comparisons challenging. The Oxford Poverty and Human Development Initiative, using 2011 data, finds that 71.1% of Ethiopians live in severe poverty (OPHI, 2017). The United Nations Human Development Report suggests 67% live in "severe" multidimensional poverty, which includes metrics beyond income such as factors related to health, safety and livelihood (UNDP, 2017). The World Bank and the Government of Ethiopia find the percentage living in poverty is roughly half that amount (NCP, 2017; World Bank, 2018). Within each of the respective frameworks, the percentage of people living in poverty in Ethiopia is amongst the highest in the world. Almost all of the data used by international organizations (e.g., World Health Organization, USAID, UNICEF, World Bank) are primarily drawn from Ethiopia's Central Statistical Agency. The World Bank and the United Nations, however, use a higher population figure than the Government of Ethiopia. Ethiopia is by no means the only country accused of underreporting population, but the reasons for doing so include inflating per capita growth to support the image of a nation worthy of investment and to demonstrate GDP growth objectives are being met. This discrepancy of figures has implications for poverty measures assessed on a per capita basis.

Box 3. Encounters

As a researcher, some experiences force me to confront severe inequalities and injustice. I echo a reflection offered by Uvin (2009: 2) in his study in Burundi: "the lives of most of the people we interviewed… are an affront to human dignity and totally deny any notion that there is an international community that stands for any values of equity or justice… They die from easily preventable or curable diseases—tetanus, malaria—at scandalous rates… The poverty of Burundi, and the stinginess of the international community when dealing with it, is revolting in our world of over-consumption." In my own field work, in a single focus group discussion three of eleven men were suffering from severe cases of elephantiasis, a parasitic infection that causes swelling. While preventative measures are well known, currently available treatment only stalls the spread of the disease and does not cure it. In interviews I engaged with individuals struggling with extreme hardship. For example, an elderly woman caring for a blind grandchild was removed from the safety net program for not selling her land to the community chairman, reducing her to begging and living in a state of constant concern for what would happen to her grandchild upon her death; an elderly couple, both of whom were practically blind and without relatives, described their severe and consistent lack of food; a gentleman who had lost all his fingers and toes and was disfigured by a battle with leprosy sat surrounded by his children and described how he was unable to move, save sliding around within a small radius of his house. While many may have heard such stories, I lack the ability to convey what these experiences feel like, sitting face to face with individuals experiencing such difficulties in remote areas where there is little expectation for any positive change to their lives. The "experience of suffering, it's often noted, is not effectively conveyed by statistics or graphs" (Farmer, 2005: 31).

Encountering

The idea of "encountering" draws upon two books, each offering significantly different perspectives on development as a concept and as a practice. The first is *Encountering Development* (Escobar, 1994) and the second is *Encountering Poverty* (Roy et al., 2016). The former takes a strong oppositional position against "development" as a failed concept and practice. Escobar argues that development has caused underdevelopment, famine, poverty, malnutrition and violence, and that development is a tool of control akin to colonialism (Escobar, 1994: 4). This position is echoed by other critical scholars such as Dambisa Moyo (2010) who has argued for the ending of so-called aid. Disengagement is also echoed by researchers of development, such as Tania Murray Li (2007: 3), who suggest their approach to research is "antithetical to the position of an expert." On the other end of the spectrum, there are promoters of aid, who suggest the problem is not too much but too little aid (Sachs, 2005). Arguments that promote aid focus on the positive changes that have been supported or enabled (Kenny, 2011). Between these two opposing positions, Roy and colleagues argue that one must position oneself within the development discourse, academically or as a practitioner, "to be engaged in the battle of ideas. Instead of positioning critics as those situated outside of development, we seek to explore how those within the system can participate in such struggles" (2016: 46). One might suggest that on a spectrum of framing development positively or negatively, Roy et al. (2016) offer a middle ground of critical engagement. These positions regarding aid and the perspectives of scholars on various points of the spectrum will be returned to throughout this chapter.

The nuances of these authors' various definitions of "development" are often lost when we focus on where they line up on this spectrum While Escobar (1994) is an advocate of civil society action for reframing development based on local realities and priorities, he also refers to the common metrics used by Kenny (2011), such as income, health, food security, stability and peace. Roy et al. similarly draw upon these metrics but add "dignity, voice and power" (2016: 31), not as measures per se, but as ways to assess development activity. The diverse means of conceptualizing and assessing development are part of the reason such divergent opinions exist. More problematic, however, is that "development" is often not explicitly defined, and thus the nuances may not be immediately obvious (Andrews, 2009; Bellu, 2011; Sumner and Tribe, 2008).

The framing and dynamics of the development discourse change over time as new ideas emerge. For some, development as a concept and practice emerged in the pre-WWII period as a colonial enterprise (Riddell, 2007). As Eyben (2014) notes, the transition from colonialism into something recognizably different was a slow process. Indeed, many processes are still in this transformation. As countries gained independence, international development efforts largely focused upon macro-economic growth (e.g., Lewis, 1955; Millikan and Rostow, 1957; Rostow, 1960). This continued throughout the "Development Decade" of the 1960s. Framing development as macro-economic growth continues to be common, such as in the works and projects of Sachs (2005).

Although neither income distribution nor inequality were on the agenda in the immediate post-WWII period, the 1948 Universal Declaration of Human Rights set the groundwork for new directions that would emerge in the following decades. It was in the 1970s that poverty alleviation became focal, but it was limited to raising income per capita and employment (Riddell, 2007). It was not until the 1980s that development encompassed health, education and living standards, largely based on the work of Sen (1981; 1983; 1985). It was Sen (1999) again, in the 1990s, who was the driving force behind another shift: incorporating opportunities and capabilities in conceptualizing poverty and the emergence of the annual United Nations Human Development Reports, which institutionalized a broader definition of poverty which included Sen's elements. Many of the resulting metrics would be used in developing the Millennium Development Goals (2000-2015). The Millennium Development Goals period, however, was influenced by increasing ties between development initiatives and military action in the War on Terror (e.g., Heinrich et al., 2017; Spear, 2016), akin to the politicization and securitization of development and humanitarian activity during the Cold War. The 2030 Agenda and the Sustainable Development Goals offer some new directions: a global focus, rather than just upon specific countries in the Global South; an interconnected approach, as opposed to singular metric objectives; aims of inclusion with the objective of "leaving no one behind," as opposed to target reductions (e.g., "no poverty" as opposed to reduce poverty by a set percentage); a new focus on the most vulnerable, in "starting with those most behind"; among others (UN, 2016).

It is not just the type of activity but the impact and sustainability of the change it produces that some view as more important when evaluating development initiatives. For Soubbotina (2000) and Barder (2012), the definition of development must encompass lasting change and should not be limited to a measurement in one moment of time. The focus on the durability of change emphasizes the important role of permanent actors, notably government institutions and civil society, and the ways in which economic, political and social systems contribute to, or negate, sustained development (Acemoglu and Robinson, 2006; 2012). Thus, the most effective and/or appropriate implementing body for development varies based on what objectives are prioritized. With these additional layers of complexity emerging, development activity is increasingly difficult to define. As a response, Chambers (1995) opted to refer simply to "good change".

How development is understood is, therefore, not only the product of one's theoretical approach, but also the time period within which it is written about and the objectives sought. In reflecting upon the idea of "good change" proposed by Chambers (1995) it appears that the critiques waged by Escobar (1988; 1994) and the enthusiasm offered by Kenny (2011) can be brought together wherein nuanced analyses may assess the complex impacts of development initiatives (e.g., for whom good change occurs and in what forms; for whom negative impacts result and in what forms; the timing of impacts and their duration; and who decides what activities occur when and where). Such an assessment would need to take into account the complex ways that development activity can result in both positive and negative change for individuals and communities. Development activity can result in good change, but the benefits of any change are rarely distributed equally or experienced in the same way by all that are affected. "Good change" also has the potential to result in negative change, often affecting those already marginalized.

Since the 1930s, the Government of Ethiopia and its partners have positioned agriculture as a key area to focus activity under the banner of "development" (Belay, 2003), a history of which is covered in Chapter 6. The objectives of the programs and policies it has implemented reflect the various ways development has been defined by the government and its partners. However, interventions made in the name of development within the agricultural sector do not necessarily aim to enhance the food security of all people equally, including those most vulnerable to food insecurity.

In some instances, such as with the agricultural extension program, the primary focus has been on high-potential agricultural areas and export crops, excluding the more marginal areas and those whose livelihoods are not geared toward export markets. Government-supported cooperatives tend to benefit certain segments of society, specifically those with more land and assets. Microcredit services are only accessed by a small minority of Ethiopians, often those with enough assets to ensure repayment regardless of rainfall. Other programs that are designed to support the most food insecure, such as the Productive Safety Net Program, have dual purposes of entrenching elite control and disempowering citizens in their implementation (as explored in Chapters 6 and 7).

The foundation of our understanding of development ought to be that there are diverse, and at times divergent, meanings of development being employed. With this foundation, it is insufficient to simply explore the relationship between food insecurity and land size. Examinations must also assess who is gaining access to government supported services and who is not. For example, my research (Cochrane, 2017c) shows that in southern Ethiopia those who had not been trained by an agricultural extension worker had smaller average land size than those who had; those gaining access to fertilizer had significantly larger average landholdings than those who did not have access; those who gained access to government-supported and distributed improved seed had larger average landholdings than those who did not. Effectively, those with least assets were being excluded. The explicit drivers of these biases are that the government has, for decades, prioritized the higher-potential areas. The result is that those with little or no land are not included in these rural initiatives, despite their higher level of vulnerability to food insecurity and need for support services. As explored in Chapters 5 and 6, some forms of services, such as microcredit, are only accessible to those with greater assets. Other services, such as planting fruit trees, are only available to those who are able to invest in longer-term returns with short-term costs. Due to the gendered nature of agricultural extension (the workforce, participation in, design of), women have largely been excluded, as have, until relatively recently, forms of livelihoods that fell outside of cereal production, such as pastoralist livelihoods and root crop-based cultivation. Globally, these biases were identified as problematic at least since the 1970s (e.g., Huntington, 1975). In Ethiopia, Percy (2000) wrote about a two-year FAO project started in 1994 that identified the issue. Yet, as the decades pass, no structural changes have occurred in the Ethiopian agricultural extension services to address these biases.

As Tefera (2015) has explained, the impact of agricultural extension has been the marginalization of the most vulnerable rural households, despite these programs being created with the stated intention to do otherwise. Unfortunately, this conclusion is not new. For the donor-supported agricultural development projects of the 1960s and 1970s, the "main beneficiaries were the more prosperous peasants and those with secure tenure... [while] the poor and a majority of the tenantry benefited the least" (Rahmato, 2008: 57). It comes as no surprise that 45% of farmers said they were dissatisfied with this freely provided service (Elias et al., 2015). How is it that these services, which are supposed to be offered equally and in the name of development, disproportionately benefit those with more assets and exclude those who most need them? Clearly, the benefits of development are not shared equally and some people are being left behind. Knowing who is being left behind, and why, requires grappling with power and politics.

Power and politics

When the Tigrayan Peoples' Liberation Front (TPLF) fought to overthrow the Derg government, foreign agencies acted as "the relief wings of the rebel movements, and no realistic distinction could be made between food that fed guerrillas and food that fed civilians" (Gill, 2010: 68). This clandestine humanitarian assistance was given without conditions to enable the rebel movement to advance its goals (Prendergast and Duffield, 1999). The United States violated the sovereignty of the Ethiopian government by offering food aid via Sudan to the rebel-controlled territory because the rebels were actively fighting against the Soviet-influenced Derg government. As this example suggests, the political interests of powerful actors can influence how and why humanitarian and development activity occurs. Political neutrality is an ideal many adopt, but it is complicated in practice (Carothers and de Gramont, 2013; Donini, 2012). Zinn (2002) argues that action and non-action speak volumes about political positions and priorities, in other words there is no such thing as neutrality.

It ought to be added that these political priorities are not new, nor are they only politicized by external actors. The history of King Tewodros II (1818-1868), one of Ethiopia's great reformers, is outlined by Rubenson

(1966). His research suggests that King Tewodros II sought foreign support in establishing his rule, and specifically sought support from the British toward the end of his reign. When the desired technical assistance did not materialize, Tewodros II held members of the British mission captive. In response, the British sent a battalion to attack Tewodros II, and rather than die at their hands, the Ethiopian leader is said to have taken his own life. After defeating Tewodros II, the British looted the country, and many of the stolen items remain on display in European museums. Another historian, Bahru Zewde (1991), documents that when King Yohannes IV (1837-1889) rose to power three years after the death of Tewodros II, he fought against the Italian colonial expansion in the Horn of Africa, viewing it as a threat to Ethiopia. Following attacks on Italian forces and significant losses of Italian troops surrounding the Battle of Dogali in 1887, the Italians increased their support to Menelik II, who had been supported by the Italians since 1876 as an ally and mutual opponent of King Yohannes IV. The Italians crafted agreements with Menelik II so that he could acquire weaponry from Europe. Later, when Menelik II became King, the friendship ended. It was King Menelik II who led the Ethiopian army to victory against the Italians in their colonial pursuit of Ethiopia at the Battle of Adwa in 1896 (Rubenson, 1964; Bahru, 1991). However, the role of external actors ought not to be viewed as deterministic, nor should the role of external actors be overstated. As Rubenson (1966) notes, the factors leading to the rise of Tewodros II were not primarily foreign, nor were the factors leading to the rise of the TPLF. External actors played important roles, but the major actors were domestic. Overemphasizing external roles in these historical processes in Ethiopia perpetuates a Eurocentric view of the importance of foreign actors, granting little or no agency to Ethiopians and their leaders. In the examples of Tewodros II, Menelik II and the TPLF, the paths these actors were on were well established and leadership changes were ongoing, driven by their respective leadership abilities and domestic support. Foreign actors merely hastened the change.

The influence of political objectives upon development is not limited to the way in which international agencies and/or states interact with one another; the politics of power also influences action within the state, including the overthrow of governments (Abraham, 1994). During the Derg government, relocation was used as a tool to control the eastern regions of Ethiopia and, in the case of government-promoted resettlement in the famine-hit north, food aid was withheld due to a lack of "volunteers" for the program (Terry, 2002). Although in different forms, these influences continued in the governments that followed.

The motivations that drive the Government of Ethiopia may be purposefully hidden behind the stated objectives. For example, policies might be designed to appease international donors, with little intention to see them through (Andrews, 2013). Programs may be well designed but implemented to meet unstated objectives (Berhanu and Poulton, 2014; Cochrane and Tamiru, 2016; Planel, 2014; Pausewang, 2002). According to the late Prime Minister of Ethiopia, Meles Zenawi, who led the country for two decades, the circumstances of Ethiopia required that a "developmental state" (strong, stable central government) exist in order for democracy to emerge. Zenawi writes: "One can therefore conclude that the prospects of a stable democracy in a poor country are intimately related to the establishment of a developmental state and achieving accelerated development" (Zenawi, undated: 14). Yet, when contradictions emerged between democracy and the developmental state, as was the case in the 2005 election, Meles Zenawi opted for the developmental state (Abbink, 2006; Kebede, 2013; Tronvoll, 2010). Zenawi's vision of development and democracy is reflected in the ways programs and policies have been waged in the name of development, which have prioritized centralized plans and macro-economic growth over democratic processes and thereby inhibited the transition to inclusive institutions.

The expression of power in order to maintain political control can also take the form of physical force. Under the leadership of Meles Zenawi, the EPRDF government adopted a developmental state approach to governing, which emphasizes the importance of long-term stability of rule as a means to achieve developmental objectives. In order to maintain this stability, the government frequently utilized force. For example, it is estimated that as many as 500 protests occurred in response to a federal proposal to expand Addis Ababa city administration planning (federal jurisdiction) into Oromia Regional State (regional jurisdiction) between November 2015 and March 2016. The government responded with lethal force and mass arrests, resulting in up to 400 protesters being killed (HWR, 2016). In July and August of 2016 there were large-scale protests about the rezoning of districts, resulting in 97 protesters dying (Amnesty International, 2016). Between 2011 and 2014 regular protests occurred in response to the government seeking to mandate individuals for religious leadership positions. In response to these protests, the government conducted mass arrests with reports of mistreatment of those detained (HRW, 2012b). Prominent leaders of the Muslim community were detained without charge in 2012 and held until convicted under anti-terrorism legislation in 2015 with sentences ranging from seven to 22 years (Fasil, 2015). The common narrative adopted during these years was that stability was critical to development, and alongside foresighted planning, had enabled the high levels of economic growth experienced.

The expression of power and control can also be ideological (Gramsci, 1971). Expressed in this form, power can be normalized within mundane, regular activities and practices (Foucault, 1977). The concept of governmentality was proposed and developed by Foucault (1979) to assess how power is expressed and control established. Foucault describes governmentality as the "ensemble formed by the institutions, procedures, analyses and reflections, the calculations and tactics, that allow the exercise of this very specific albeit complex form of power" (1979: 20). Drawing upon governmentality as a framework for assessing power, the (non)actions, policies, programs and statements of a government can be evaluated as a means to shape individuals within society to align with the government's objectives. Governing can therefore be viewed as an assertion of power and an exercise of control.

The ways in which programs have been used to strengthen government control and elite power have been well documented in the development literature (Bayart, 1989; de Waal, 2015; Ferguson, 1990; Li, 2007; Scott, 1985). However, these studies have tended to be anthropological in nature, and limited progress has been made with regard to integrating these perspectives and findings into development practice or in confronting development practice itself (Carothers and de Gramont, 2013). A number of researchers have reflected on how development actors have been unable or unwilling to engage with the politics of power (Autessere, 2010; Ferguson, 1990; Starn, 1991; Uvin, 1999). This exploration of food security approaches the questions of vulnerability to food insecurity and the low adoption rates of government-provided services with a recognition of the ways in which development is politicized, acting with dual purposes of achieving a particular development outcome as well as an expression of power and establishment of control (a point that is returned to when exploring the

Ethiopian programs and services in Chapter 6). This study is informed by the fact that development has been used as a means to centralize control and that much activity done in the name of development has been done to achieve alternative objectives (Uvin, 1999).

Even if the politicization of policies and programs becomes normalized and routine, in the long-term it can foster opposition, and have negative impacts on the wealth generation that the elites are attempting to capture. In focusing on the history and role of institutions, Acemoglu and Robinson argue that politicization and patronage of this nature can create a negative cycle:

> When extractive institutions create huge inequalities in society and great wealth and unchecked power for those in control, there will be many wishing to fight to take control of the state and institutions. Extractive institutions then not only pave the way for the next regime, which will be even more extractive, but they will also engender continuous infighting and civil wars. These civil wars then cause more human suffering and also destroy even what little state centralization these societies have achieved. This also often starts a process of descent into lawlessness, state failure, and political chaos, crushing all hopes of economic prosperity (2012: 366-367).

Although the above prediction is a bit too deterministic, the historical study conducted by Acemoglu and Robinson (2012) demonstrates that this cycle has often repeated. Although it has taken decades of research and advocacy, even actors such as the World Bank are beginning to advocate for citizen power to "select and sanction leaders who have the political will and legitimacy to deliver public goods needed for development" as opposed to the traditional development assistance, which "can contribute to the persistence of government failures" (Devarajan and Khemani, 2016: 1). While changing policy and practice has yet to be seen, the about face from the structural adjustment programs of the past to the 2017 flagship World Bank report highlighting the need for greater reflexivity on power within state-citizen relations and those mirrored or reinforced by development activity offer a glimmer of hope that institutions may slowly be changing.

Viewing political action from a perspective that is attentive to power in Ethiopia assists in answering the above-raised question: how and why is it that the services designed to support all people, or the most vulnerable, disproportionately benefit the relatively better off? One explanation is that the programs and services are politicized, expressing power and asserting control. Within Ethiopia, Berhanu and Poulton (2014), Planel (2014) and Pausewang (2002) have found this to be the case in the implementation of the agricultural extension program. Chinigo (2013) has also found it in rural land reform. Cochrane and Tamiru (2016) have identified it within the Productive Safety Net Program. de Waal (2015) notes that the politicization of access to services and the provision of goods has been commonplace in rural Ethiopia for decades. In fact, the roots can be traced back to the Imperial period, as noted by Acemoglu and Robinson (2012: 358, 361), highlighting the broader historical context within which these practices, and cycles of practices, exist. This broader contextualization of qualitative and historical knowledge was emphasized by Mintz (1985), and, to the greatest extent possible, has been integrated in this book. The reasons why politicization occur are often rooted in the maintenance of power and control, which may also be highly profitable but are not always so (such as the dictatorial ways in which community leaders govern in some parts of rural Ethiopia). The current Prime Minister, Abiy Ahmed, has argued that these forms of governing are valorized in Ethiopian tradition and folklore, thus partially explaining their continuity across places and scales of governance (Ahmed, 2017).

Understanding the ways in which power and control are embedded within development activity is not only a matter of improving implementation or enhancing effectiveness, as Acemoglu and Robinson (2012) point out. Vulnerability to food insecurity is reduced, managed or increased by development activity as much as political action and power relations (Watts, 1983). Neglecting these components may blind us to the factors that contribute to food insecurity, the barriers to change, and the processes that marginalize certain groups of people. Neglecting to understand power relations and politics, which is common in studies of food security, effectively makes invisible some of the most important processes that enable some people to be food secure while others remain vulnerable to food insecurity or face chronic food insecurity. Thus, questioning the ways food security is assessed is important. The next chapter reflects on the questions asked, the methods used and the metrics employed in seeking to understand food security as well as respective implications of each of these aspects of analysis.

CHAPTER FOUR

HOW WE KNOW

Methods, metrics and measures

Information influences action. If we believe that food insecurity is largely a problem of insufficient production, as we did in the 1970s, we will measure production and strive to increase it. No matter how precise the data and how regular the reporting, programming done to strengthen food security that is based solely on the assumption that production is the problem will have limited impact. We now know that food insecurity is only partly a problem of production. In this chapter, we will explore if it is in fact the case that sometimes incorrect assumptions are made, the wrong questions are asked, and metrics that are not appropriate are used when seeking to understand food security. Additionally, we will explore if, in the design, collection and analysis of data, consideration is given to which voices are included or excluded. This exploration will consider a wide range of manifestations of social differentiation and inequality (e.g., ethnicity, religion, language, livelihood, gender, age, ability, health-status, location, class or economic status, socio-cultural status, marital status, political affiliation). The latter of these considerations is explicitly one of power.

There is a range of potential ways to understand food security and the lack thereof in Ethiopia. A household survey could be developed and the data analyzed. The Government of Ethiopia, along with its partners, engages in these sorts of activities, such as the annual agricultural survey. The International Food Policy Research Institute (IFPRI) also conducts studies of this sort in Ethiopia. Alternatively, one could conduct a detailed ethnographic study and gain a wealth of qualitative information regarding the perceptions and processes of food insecurity on a local scale. This approach has been undertaken by anthropologists over the past few decades and has provided insightful answers. However, these anthropological and ethnographic works are often presented in a form that is difficult for decision-makers to readily use to inform the design, implementation and evaluation of programs and services. The first section of this chapter explores the commonly used scales and metrics in analyzing food security. This is followed by a discussion of the metrics employed within research and assessments. Having outlined these tools and the respective strengths each offers, I outline a knowledge co-production research approach that I have used to better enable a contextualized understanding of food security and improve assessments of programs and services supporting smallholder farmers.

Scales and metrics

Food security can be measured on difference scales (e.g., global, national, sub-national, community) and with different metrics (e.g., production, diet diversity, nutritional content, number of meals per day). Each scale and metric both highlights and obscures aspects of food security. No single metric or scale is sufficient. Not all metrics and scales can be used at all times. Understanding what each scale and metric offers and how this evidence can be applied in decision-making, enables a better understanding of what questions we ought to ask and how we ought to ask them.

From a national perspective, food security often focuses upon domestic food self-reliance, or self-sufficiency, so that all citizens have access to food at all times (Africa Leadership Forum, 1989). Domestic self-sufficiency is a goal few nations are able to meet. In fact, the majority of nations, 131 countries, are net food importers and are reliant upon trade to meet their domestic needs (Bailey and Willoughby, 2013; Ng and Aksoy, 2008). Assessments of food security conducted at the national scale tend to focus on aggregate demands and availability (Alamgir and Arora, 1991). This does not take into account the complex barriers to availability throughout the nation and to accessibility by everyone in specific locations.

In analyzing sub-national food security, regional assessments can support the identification of geospatial trends, such as regional food deficits and rural-urban differences, as well as socio-cultural and political factors, such as disproportionate exclusion from emergency food aid (Barraclough and Utting, 1987; Stamoulis and Zezza, 2003). The FAO (2013b) advocates analyzing food security using this sub-national approach. However, sub-national scales of food security do not shed light on the detailed dynamics of food distribution within communities and households, and thus may not capture the reasons that certain groups of people in society, such as minorities, castes, classes and genders, face food insecurity while the sub-national region is food secure. To address this, household-level approaches to food security are used. These approaches assess whether all members of the household have sufficient, safe and nutritious food at all times. These methods, however, also tend to aggregate demand and availability (Alamgir and Arora, 1991). They also share the shortcomings of the sub-national assessments at the micro-level because they fail to examine the way food is distributed within households based on a range of demographic factors like age, ability, health status and gender. New manifestations of household surveys have attempted to take these dynamics into account (USDA, 2008).

In response to the limitations of household-level assessments, individual-level food security assessments have been employed. In some instances, this simply involves conducting the household survey with multiple members of the household independently. Foundational to this shift in focus is an effort to ensure all people have their needs and rights met. The results of such assessments can highlight micro-level discrimination, marginalization and exclusion. In turn, these results can support the creation of specific policies and programs, such as school-based food programs or conditional cash transfer programs and policies to eliminate gender bias. Taking a rights-based approach to ensuring food security is a political endeavor and may result in nations considering state regulation of markets. In these cases, national interest may conflict with international conventions and agreements.

Community-level food security approaches attempt to better integrate issues of justice in their assessments, addressing some of the concerns raised by the food sovereignty movement. One of the shifts in prioritization in many community-level assessments of food security is a focus on the broader economic, environmental and social components of the food system (Hamm and Bellows, 2003). As a result, a much greater emphasis is explicitly laid upon issues of justice and sustainability. Community-level analyses of this nature are less common, often due to the specificity and cost of the studies, but emerging ideas in the field of food security studies suggest that future investigations will place far greater emphasis on "system thinking that incorporates a diversity of disciplinary perspectives" (Westengen and Banik, 2016:15-16). The insights gleaned from community-level analyses have the potential to alter the ways in which food security studies are done at all scales, focusing upon the dynamics of food systems (which may include aspects of seasonality, dietary transitions, unhealthy diets, etc.), in addition to the specific measures of a system.

In household- and individual-level studies, the most common metric of assessment is caloric intake. This aggregate assessment is useful, but it does not identify the composition of diets. For example, surveys may ask how many meals and how much food was consumed. What is excluded from these measures is the quality of diets, and thus some surveys have begun to focus on dietary diversity, whereby consumed foods are categorized by type so that macro- and micro-nutrient consumption assessments can be integrated. The challenge with this approach, however, is that a relatively straightforward set of two or three questions may balloon into pages of food groups, some with hundreds of food items, which are complicated by language and classifications, as well as by limitations of what is and is not included. Nonetheless, studies of dietary diversity can provide significant insight into the quality of diets, the differences of dietary composition within the household, and the impact of seasonality on diets (Hirvonen, Taffesse and Worku, 2015).

One food security scale does not fit all purposes. Each of the scales of assessment contribute unique information and advance our understanding of food security in different ways. Furthermore, different scales of information are used by different decision-makers in determining how resources are allocated—this may be globally, nationally, sub-nationally, within a community or within a household. As a result, the selection of a scale, or the analysis of the results, ought to take into account the objectives, needs and stakeholders of the research, while outlining its respective limitations. For example, while community-level studies can significantly advance knowledge about systems, individual-level analyses present unique data on intra-household distribution, and global studies highlight the trends between nations. Each of the scales, therefore, is important. The deconstruction of food security approaches by scale highlights what the different foci emphasize. Doing so supports the prioritization of scale within research so that the expected results align with the informational gaps and the requirements of decision-makers. This deconstruction emphasizes the limitations of each scale, enabling a more nuanced critique of food security studies.

Measuring

Challenges of definitions and scale are only the tip of the iceberg. How food security is measured is even more diverse. The concept of availability, for example, may encompass a wide array of factors including quality, quantity, production, distribution, exchange, storage, processing, transportation, packaging, crop type, ownership, management and harvesting. Security and stability might require analyses of precipitation, water, seasonal variation, market vulnerability and volatility, export bans, input and fuel costs, conflict and gender. Understanding sufficiency, safety, nutrition and appropriateness poses similar challenges.

Access to food, for example, might be affected by a range of factors: financial, geographic, ethnic, gender, religious, health-status, socio-cultural, ability and age. Even more problematic is the unavailability of seasonal data, as the timing of data collection significantly impacts the results. For instance, a study in Ethiopia shows an almost 10% difference based simply on the timing of data collection (Chirwa, Dorward and Vignen, 2012; Dereveux, Sabates-Wheeler and Longhurst, 2012). As both Gibson (2012) and Barrett (2010) note, when researchers do not have an adequate direct measure to assess food security, they often utilize proxy measures. Yet, these proxies have a series of limitations and pose a number of challenges, even when attempts are made at using different sources to validate a finding—the "laudable aims" Gibson explains "are racked with disunity and inconsistency" (2012: 16). The diverse proxies researchers employ significantly influence the way in which results translate into policies and programs, and therefore impact their effectiveness. "Each measure," Barrett explains, "captures and neglects different phenomena intrinsic to the concept of food security thereby subtly influencing prioritization among food security interventions" (2010: 826). Later in this chapter, three sets of metrics are analyzed to further elaborate on this phenomenon.

A common proxy metric for understanding food insecurity is stages of malnutrition. This metric is commonly utilized in emergency contexts, which is reported on in the Famine Early Warning Systems Network, and by health-oriented actors such as the World Health Organization. Acute food insecurity is defined as insecurity over limited time period for which one requires short-term assistance to cope with a temporary or unusual condition. Acute food insecurity can also be protracted, resulting in malnutrition (a deficiency or imbalance in the diet essential to good health). Chronic malnutrition occurs when dietary deficiencies or imbalances occur over a long period of time, and can eventually result in starvation when prolonged or severe.[10] Famine occurs when there is a widespread and persistent lack of food and is often characterized by an unusually high number of deaths due to chronic hunger, malnutrition and starvation (Butterly and Shepherd, 2010). These technical, often medically diagnosable, terms provide one means of measurement. However, as pointed out by Sen (Edkins, 2007; Sen and Dreze, 1999), food security cannot be analyzed as a biological or environmental phenomenon; it must be analyzed as an embedded political, economic and socio-cultural outcome.

In the case of Ethiopia, droughts occurred in 1999-00 and 2002-03, the latter of which resulted in over 14 million people being in need of emergency food aid. In the 2002-03 drought, the significant international response was made possible by the United States serendipitously sending a large amount of food to the Gulf of Aden in anticipation of humanitarian food needs in Iraq (Gill, 2010: 102). This highlights some of the extra-national factors affecting countries with limited capacity and ability to respond to events of severe food insecurity. Although drought has played a significant role in the history of Ethiopian famines, so too have intra-national politics and socio-economic factors. Both of the recent famines took place in areas populated primarily by minority ethnic groups, suggesting that mechanisms of political inclusion and/or democratic processes are not functioning well (Lautze and Maxwell, 2007).

The measurement of food security varies greatly. To demonstrate this, consider the differences between the metrics outlined in two FAO data collection tools: (1) Common Food Security Indicators and Possible Data Sources, and (2) the Food Insecurity Experience Scale.[11] In presenting these examples, the objective is to explore the ways in which indicators

---

10   The "double burden" of under- as well as over-nutrition, combined with dietary transitions and dietary diversity are changing definitions and approaches to understanding malnutrition.

11   These tools were shared by the FAO on December 30th, 2015, including translations into three Ethiopian languages (Amharic, Oromiffa and Tigrinya). In addition, reference was made to work by Ballard, Kepple and Cafiero (2013). A range of other tools exist (e.g., McArthur, 2016; WFP, 2009). In the comparison made here, FAO tools have been used because of they are widely applied. This analysis is not meant to exclude other approaches but to summarize the challenges of metrics and measurement.

can significantly vary, not to analyze each indicator in depth. The first of the tools, Common Food Security Indicators and Possible Data Sources, has five categories of indicators, reflecting the "four pillars" of accessibility, availability, stability and utilization, to which the FAO has added measures of malnutrition (see Table 1). The FAO provides twelve indicators for accessibility, half of which are proxy measures drawn from national data such as GNP and GDP per capita and percentages of the population below the national and international poverty lines. The survey data focuses on individual expenditure such as share of income spent on food, share of own production in household food supply and number of people in need of food transfers/assistance. Measures of availability, of which there are nine, are all derived from agricultural and trade data, such as agricultural production growth, share of food imports, and daily per capita supply of calories, protein and fat. The FAO proposes seven indicators for stability, which also focus on agricultural and trade data (e.g., variation in grain yields, variation of food imports), and include survey questions about seasonal variation of food supplies. The proxy indicators for utilization are health oriented, while the final category of measures for malnutrition are medical in nature, such as the percentage of undernourished, underweight, stunted, and wasted individuals in society.

Table 1. *Common Food Security Indicators and Possible Data Sources (FAO, 2009a)*

Access to Food Measures	Data Sources
GNP per capita (US$/annual growth rate)	Statistics
GDP per capita in PPP (purchasing power parity) US$	Statistics
Population below national poverty line (%)	Statistics, Surveys
Population below poverty line of US$1 PPP/day (%)	Statistics, Surveys
Poverty gap at US$1 PPP/day (%)	Statistics, Surveys
Income distribution (Gini coefficient)	Statistics
Food expenditures by different income groups	Surveys
Share of household income spent on food (average %)	Surveys
Share of own production in household food supplies	Surveys
Household Food Insecurity Access Scale (HFIAS)	Surveys
Household Dietary Diversity Score (HDDS)	Surveys
Number of people in need of transfers/food assistance	Surveys

Food Availability Measures	Data Sources
Food production index	Agricultural statistics
Agricultural production growth per annum/capita	Agricultural statistics
Average yield food grain production (kg/ha)	Agricultural statistics
Share of food aid in annual food grain supplies (%)	Trade, food aid statistics
Daily per capita supply of calories (kcal)	Food balance
Food calorie availability as percentage of requirements	Food balance
Daily per capita supply of protein (g)	Food balance
Daily per capita supply of fat (g)	Food balance
Stability of Food Supplies Measures	**Data Sources**
Annual variation of food grain production (metric tons, %)	Agricultural statistics
Variation of grain yields (metric tons, %)	Agricultural statistics
Annual variation of food imports/exports (metric tons, %)	Agricultural, trade statistics
Annual variation of food supplies (metric tons, %)	Surveys
Volume/variation of (public, commercial, household) food stocks	Surveys
Variation in food aid deliveries	Records
Food Utilization Measures	**Data Sources**
Population (number, %) without access to safe water, health services, sanitation	Statistics, surveys
Prevalence of water borne diseases	Medical statistics
Malnutrition Measures	**Data Sources**
Undernourished population (number, %)	Statistics, surveys
Underweight children under 5 (number, %)	Nutrition surveys
Stunted children under 5 (number, %)	Nutrition surveys
Wasted children under 5 (number, %)	Nutrition surveys
Low birth weight (< 2,500g) (number, %)	Medical surveys
Pregnant women with anemia (%)	Medical surveys
Prevalence of diseases related to malnutrition	Nutrition, medical surveys

The 37 proposed indicators are largely proxy measures of food security and rely almost entirely on national census data and basic household survey data. As explored in the measures of scale, this survey would typically be employed for global, national and sub-national assessments. The results would provide high-level detail about the extent and trends of food security and allow decision-makers to determine where and when additional resources are required. Although not captured in this FAO list, recent studies have sought to add measures related to governance and policy, covering issues such as political commitment and the existence and quality of national nutrition policies (te Lintelo et al., 2016).

The Food Insecurity Experience Scale, on the other hand, which was also developed by the FAO, offers detailed individual-level insight, including perceptions of food security and thus entering into the realm of subjectivity and relative food security. With this set of metrics, the FAO is seeking to assess the severity of food insecurity based upon people's experiences of it and thus offering a very different picture than the results of the first data collection tool examined above. While the first data set explores macro-level outcomes that aggregate varied types of food insecurity, this data collection tool offers insight into the severity of food insecurity. For example, the survey includes metrics that ask the following:

In the last 12 months:

- **(Y/N)** You were worried you would run out of food because of a lack of money or other resources
- **(Y/N)** You were unable to eat healthy and nutritious food because of a lack of money or other resources
- **(Y/N)** You had to skip a meal because there was not enough money or other resources?
- **(Y/N)** You ate less than you thought you should because of a lack of money or other resources
- **(Y/N)** You went without eating for a whole day because of a lack of money or other resources

The survey process could include men and women, different ethnic and religious groups, and respondents of all ages. The results could provide a detailed picture about the distribution of food insecurity within a country (if done nationally) as well as at the community and household levels. As outlined by Ballard, Kepple and Cafiero (2013), the findings can support the creation of targeted programs and support processes by which needs of various communities are prioritized.

In some of my own research, the process of designing the data collection tool resulted in an unintended natural experiment about such tools. During the ethics application process at the University of British Columbia in Canada, the reviewers understood that the survey would be co-created with community members during the research phase, but they wanted a sample survey to review the expected types of questions. As a result, the questions and metrics I developed in the preliminary survey could be compared to the final outcome (Table 2). I was not new to food security studies in Ethiopia, having worked with a number of non-governmental organizations on related subjects. With several organizations, I have been involved in household surveys. The preliminary survey that I had developed as a sample had 34 questions, only eleven of which (32%) were unchanged in the final co-created version, and four of those questions were set questions based on changes over time; thus only a fifth of the questions (21%) that were subject to discussion were left unchanged. Examples of this include basic questions, such as the number of people living in the household and the availability of assets (metal roof, mobile phone, radio). During the collaborative community-based process of creating a household survey, almost a third of the questions I had initially proposed were not considered as important for inclusion in the co-produced version, resulting in eleven of the initial questions not being asked at all (32%). For twelve other questions, the metrics were changed (35%). Important to the co-production process was that fourteen new questions were added, including questions about migration, methods of plowing, the number of fruit and cash crop trees, time spent collecting water and firewood, number of malaria cases and the presence of a vegetable garden (Table 2). Based on these significant changes, it is clear that local knowledge and experiences of food security offer significant insight and are sources of information that tend to be excluded in the design phase. The FAO Food Insecurity Experience Scale, for example, used focus groups to test the questions and assess the language of translations, but not to determine the questions or the metrics. The comparison of my own preliminary survey and the one I co-created with communities demonstrates how varied the questions and metrics can be. The participatory, co-produced approach to creating data tools enabled typically unasked questions to be explored and appropriate measurements to be applied.

Table 2. *Adapting Data Collection Tools through Knowledge Coproduction (examples)*

Original	Revised
Number of people living in household?	Number of people living in household? Number capable to work? Number dependent?
How often (per month) do you interact with an agricultural extension worker?	How many times per year do you interact with the agricultural extension worker?
On average, how many days of the month do you not have sufficient food to meet the basic needs of the family?	How many months of this year did you have insufficient food?
Do you use fertilizer? If yes: How much (by 50 kg bag) per hectare?	Do you use fertilizer? If yes: Do you buy with cash or credit?
Is any family member employed off the farm? If yes: How many?	Have any household members migrated outside of the community for work? If yes: How many for skilled work? How many for unskilled work?
Not included	Number of trees (avocado, mango, banana, coffee, enset)?
Not included	Do you plow with oxen or by hand?
Not included	Do you save your own seed?
Not included	Time spent collecting water per day (hours)?
Not included	Time spent collecting firewood per day (hours)?
Not included	Average number of malaria cases per year
Languages spoken by members of household?	*Removed*
Distance to market from house?	*Removed*
Distance to cooperative from house?	*Removed*
Distance to road from house?	*Removed*

The results obtained using the revised survey are explored in greater detail in the next chapter. What is worth noting here is that while the researcher had identified some uncommonly used proxy indicators (e.g., household debt and borrowing practices), the community introduced others (e.g., migration and type of migration). Other indicators were introduced (e.g., method of plowing, time spent collecting water and firewood, number of trees and type) while factors that could be averaged for the community were removed (e.g., distance from market, cooperative, road), thereby reducing the number of questions asked. The resulting new tool had more appropriately framed questions, provided insight into household characteristics, and reduced the burden on participants by removing questions that community members felt were unnecessary.

Maxwell, Vaitla and Coates (2014) undertook a similar process, but rather than focusing on the questions and metrics, they examined how the results differ when determining severity levels of food insecurity. In two districts of Tigray Regional State they compared the results of seven tools, which resulted in significantly different prevalence rates of food insecurity. The first difference they outline is one explored above, the use of different questions and metrics. However, they also posit that certain tools may be more appropriate for certain severity levels of food insecurity and that the determination of what is and is not indicative of food insecurity is not uniform. Importantly, they conclude that food security "has no accepted gold standard," and "it is difficult to say which indicator performs 'best' in correctly and reliably identifying food insecure households" (Maxwell, Vaitla and Coates, 2014: 107). It is, therefore, worth emphasizing that like other approaches, the co-production process I have undertaken has strengths and limitations, and it is not presented as a model that is best suited for all places and purposes (Cochrane, 2017a).

Knowledge co-production

There is a significant amount of information available about food security worldwide. For example, the FAO, along with national governments, conduct regular food security surveys, and the Famine Early Warning Systems Network (FEWS NET) publishes regular reports on indicators and projections to support the prevention of famine. This data has provided a wealth of information about the trends and extent of food security in Ethiopia. I have presented data from these sources throughout this book. In conducting national or regional surveys, which require a degree of consistency in metrics for aggregation, information essential for understanding the complex causes of food insecurity may be lost (Chambers, 2008). In addition, the selection of metrics, such as how many meals are eaten in a day, shapes the type of findings that emerge, which may result in the exclusion of crucial information, such as the composition of the meals, and cause unintended outcomes, such as entrenching intra-household disparity by not understanding the distribution of food between family members. The existing methods and metrics are valuable, despite their respective challenges, and have all contributed to the understanding of the scale, trends and extent of food security.

To integrate knowledge coproduction into the broader research process, I developed the Stages of Food Security methodology, which was adapted from Krishna's Stages of Progress methodology (2004; 2005; 2010). This new methodology was not needed because of a lack of data on food insecurity. The methodology complements existing data by providing an approach to identify effective and appropriate means to understand vulnerability and strengthen food security. I believe that it contributes new insight, provides a means to ask different questions, asks old questions in new ways, and enables new ways of measuring food security. It provides a way in which contextualized, locally specific qualitative and quantitative information can be integrated with existing data, with a specific aim of enhancing policies and programs that strengthen food security. In developing this methodology, I emphasize the experiences, ideas and priorities of community members in understanding vulnerability to food insecurity. This methodology is founded upon a participatory approach whereby community members co-create quantitative surveys with researchers, with the objective of identifying opportunities, strengths and challenges that may not be sufficiently addressed in the existing data.

In order to enhance and expand existing knowledge on vulnerability to food insecurity the Stages of Food Security methodology seeks new perspectives and approaches to understanding what makes smallholder agricultural households vulnerable to food insecurity. While the question is not new, the process of answering it presents new ways of obtaining information, offers different perspectives, and generates unique insights for changing programs and services. Typical surveys conducted on food security, including those used in Ethiopia, draw upon data collection tools, household survey questions, and metrics based on assumptions about vulnerability that are not embedded within, or reflective of, the lived experiences of those encountering food insecurity. Because they use broad metrics, national surveys miss relative differences within and between communities, and the questions used in these surveys often prioritize export crops, which may not be relevant for smallholder livelihoods or their food security. As a result, the data emerging from the large-scale surveys can render important aspects of food security invisible. Importantly, the resulting recommendations may therefore not be appropriate for all people, and in particular may not meet the needs of the most vulnerable. Thus, there is a need for new approaches that complement (and sometimes challenge) existing knowledge. Using knowledge co-production approaches helps researchers and study participants to determine which questions are most relevant and which metrics most appropriate.

As discussed in Chapter 2, Ethiopia's smallholder farmers have been offered extension services and agricultural inputs for at least half a century, but the uptake and adoption of these services remains low (Bonger, Ayele and Kuma, 2004; EEA/EEPRI, 2006; Gebrehiwot and van der Veen, 2014; Spielman, Mekonnen and Alemu, 2012; Taffesse, Dorosh and Gemessa, 2012; see Box 4 for a discussion of "adoption"). The Stages of Food Security methodology draws upon the work done by the Government of Ethiopia, the FAO and FEWS NET, and uses a participatory, co-production approach to analyze policies and programs, with a view to explore opportunities for improving them or for proposing new ones. As Burns and Worsley (2015: 51) point out, the "data upon which policies are based is often aggregated to give synthesized statements that indicate how many people are affected, but gives little sense of why these symptoms occur." The Stages of Food Security methodology provides insight into symptoms so that programs and policies can be tailored, targeted and made more effective.

Box 4. Terminology

Before proceeding to the details of the methodology, it is worth reflecting on the concept of "adoption," (the utilization or integration of a new input or practice) which I frequently use in the discussion of the Stages of Food Security methodology. Adoption in its use in this book most commonly refers to farmers adding a new input that has been advocated by extension services, such as the "adoption of a new seed variety". I am in agreement with Glover, Sumberg and Andersson (2016) that "adoption" can imply an assumption of superior knowledge, reminiscent of colonial attitudes. It is also a concept that if taken alone can be "too linear in both spatial and temporal terms, too binary, too focused on individual decisions, and blind to many important aspects of technological change" (Glover, Sumberg and Andersson, 2016: 4). As the discussions throughout this book demonstrate, I do not assume that new inputs or practices advocated by governmental agricultural extension services are necessarily the most effective or appropriate. Rather, we need new approaches that will inform policy, programs and services so that supports align with the needs and priorities of those involved, in this case smallholder farmers. The concept "adoption" can also be used to challenge assumptions, for example in showing that farmers adopt components of packages or reject services entirely. Glover, Sumberg and Andersson (2016) argue that there is a need for a new concept, to replace adoption; I Agree. Until we have a better term, I use this term but attempt to regularly contest the assumptions that might be implied with its use. My experiences in Ethiopia show that much can be learned from the practices of farmers themselves. Paying attention to their practices offers different insights than merely assessing the use or non-use of the technologies and packages they are offered. This does not address all concerns raised by the "adoption concept" but it recognizes its contested nature and reframes the term.

The Stages of Food Security methodology builds upon the academic work of Krishna (2004, 2005, 2010) as well as my personal experience working with communities in Ethiopia over the last decade. Krishna, a professor at Duke University and former development practitioner, developed the

Stages of Progress methodology to understand the dynamics of poverty, and specifically to assess the extent to which individuals overcome or fall into poverty as well as identify the causes of these changes. As development studies expanded its investigation into the dynamics of poverty, the Stages of Progress methodology reiterated that those experiencing poverty are not a static group. Rather, Krishna's (2010) work helps to highlight that those experiencing poverty are a more dynamic group wherein significant numbers of people overcome poverty, while almost as many fall into it (Krishna, 2010). The methodology has been applied on four continents, in an array of diverse countries and settings. In this methodology, "stages" are not assumed as linear pathways through which all must pass (be it nations, as suggested by the modernization school, or, by analogy, individuals). Rather, these are conceptualizations developed by community members to help categorize the different experiences and vulnerabilities within their community. As noted in Table 2, the metrics range widely from livestock and tree holdings to borrowing practices and indebtedness as well as migration.

In the Stages of Progress methodology, the "stages" were defined by community members in a participatory process. Embedded in the household survey data collection tools were retrospective comparisons of personal situations and, if change took place, the causes of that. Individual interviews were utilized to explore the wide range of experiences within the resulting stages. The findings were used to recommend policy that would provide the supports necessary so individuals would not fall into (or back into) poverty and provide greater access to the opportunities that helped individuals overcome poverty. However, Krishna also found a glass ceiling. While many were able to overcome poverty, there were significant limits on the potential for economic advancement, indicating that structural and systemic inequalities have to be addressed in order for socio-economic transformation to occur.

In comparison to Participatory Rural Appraisal approaches, such as that done by Tsegaye and Struik (2002) in southern Ethiopia, the Stages of Progress methodology places a greater emphasis on community participation in the research process and the codification of the steps. While the research of Tsegaye and Struik (2002) used participatory wealth ranking, sought input on indicators and conducted relative wealth ranking, it provided limited detail about the processes involved, such as who was included in the process and the representativeness of the categories used in the study. Krishna specifies how the Stages of Progress methodology takes place, in what ways diverse experiences are included and how verification occurs. In some regards, one might consider both the Stages of Progress and Stages of Food Security as expanded and more developed Participatory Rural Appraisal methodologies, which place an explicit focus on participation and co-production.

Key to Krishna's methodology is the localization of how poverty is categorized. Community members themselves determine the factors that ought to comprise a "stage" from relative poverty to relative wealth. The contextualization of the metrics in this fashion enables the analyses to reflect dynamics relevant and appropriate to that specific place and time. In contrast, national surveys conducted by governments use metrics that apply to a much broader array of livelihoods, economic situations and agroecologies, resulting in metrics that can be applied generally, and therefore may exclude essential nuance. For example, relative to the country as a whole, the majority of the population of a sub-national region may experience chronic poverty [note: definitions of poverty can vary significantly, such as by using different thresholds (e.g., at or below US$1.25, US$1.90 or US$2.50 per day using purchasing power parity[12]) or by using national definitions as opposed to these international measures]. Within that population, however, there are significant relative differences. The localization of poverty can capture these differences, based upon community-determined metrics that are relevant and appropriate to their lives. In addition to identifying relative differences, the participatory process may identify factors and metrics that are not commonly included in other studies, providing new insights into the complexities of poverty and the means to assess it.

In addition to the work of Krishna, my experiences in Ethiopia have shaped the ways in which I have developed the Stages of Food Security methodology. One of the ways this methodology is distinct from Krishna's Stages of Progress is a geospatial component, which recognizes that differences may be significant within a region based on accessibility

---

12 Purchasing Power Parity (PPP) is an assessment of commodity prices in different countries based on their currencies in order to compare how purchasing power compares. A PPP adjusted figure takes into account the differences in purchasing power for a set of commodities.

of services, infrastructure and markets. Data that incorporates location enables place-based comparative studies in order to analyze the impact of location. Building on Krishna's work, this model expands the types of research questions being posed and enables community members to co-create the questions and the metrics. It also creates opportunities to correct errors, provide greater context and highlight interconnections that may have otherwise been missed.

"Participation" is a fraught term with a wide range of uses. Some equate participation with agreement or consent (as the Government of Ethiopia has done), while others position participation as being involved in decision making and having the power to change decisions. Although Krishna employs the term, to avoid a lack of clarity about what is being referred to, the methodology used in this study is framed as knowledge co-production, meaning that researchers and community members are partners in arriving at research questions, creating research tools, analyzing data and arriving at research findings. Burns and Worsley (2015: 46) argue that involvement is a "prerequisite for change in complex social systems." As partners in the process, community members contribute their knowledge about the dynamics of food security and the broader systems within which it exists. The knowledge, ideas and priorities of community members also provide insight for identifying areas where action would be appropriate and effective. However, participation is not just about a better research process. People "have a right to be heard and a right to engage in the issues that affect their lives; and when people feel that they have a personal investment in a process, this leads through networks of social relationships to strong community ownership" (Burns and Worsley, 2015: 46). At the same time, I am cognizant of the "global web of unequal relations" that shape the interactions between researcher and participants and do not posit that a co-produced, participatory approach results in the erasure of power imbalances (Farmer, 1999: 6). Nonetheless, for effective action to be sustained, and for that action to increase in scale, participation "can be seen as a foundation stone" when working in complex social environments (Burns and Worsley, 2015: 46).

Qualitative studies provide a wealth of contextualized and locally specific information, yet they are often not used to inform policy and programs because they tend not to speak the "language" of decision makers. The Stages of Food Security methodology, which explicitly seeks to inform policy and programs, addresses this challenge by using a mixed-methods approach that draws upon qualitative and quantitative processes. Akin to what has been advocated by Chambers (1983), the methodology utilizes co-production so that the ideas, experiences and priorities of community members can shape the research questions and the ways in which measurements are made. In order for the co-production process to be productive, the researcher needs to be well versed in the socio-cultural, economic, historical and political context within which the research takes place. Having researchers who are fluent in the lived realities of the individuals within the communities where the research is conducted enables the co-production process to be a two-way learning process rather than a one-way extraction of information or simple facilitation.

There are six key steps within the Stages of Food Security methodology, including: (1) contextualization, (2) community perception and survey development, (3) household survey, (4) verification, (5) replication and (6) engagement (see Figure 5). The objective of this section of the chapter is to explore alternative pathways of understanding food security and to focus on one way this can be done. A brief overview of the processes of the Stages of Food Security methodology follows. The details are summarized here, however to better understand how the methodology has been implemented, readers are encouraged to consult my earlier research (see Cochrane 2017a, 2017c). This methodology was also utilized in the case study presented in the following chapter.

Community 1   **Community 2**   **Community 3**

```
┌─────────────────┐
│ Initial Individual │
│   Interviews      │
└─────────────────┘
         │
         ▼
┌─────────────────┐   ┌─────────────────┐   ┌─────────────────┐
│ Conduct focus groups │ Conduct focus groups │ Conduct focus groups │
│  in first community  │  in second community │  in third community  │
└─────────────────┘   └─────────────────┘   └─────────────────┘
         │                     │                     │
         ▼                     ▼                     ▼
┌─────────────────┐   ┌─────────────────┐   ┌─────────────────┐
│   Survey first    │   │  Survey second   │   │   Survey third   │
│   community       │   │  community       │   │   community      │
└─────────────────┘   └─────────────────┘   └─────────────────┘
         │                     │                     │
         ▼                     ▼                     ▼
┌─────────────────┐   ┌─────────────────┐   ┌─────────────────┐
│ Plot geospatial   │   │ Plot geospatial  │   │ Plot geospatial  │
│ distribution of   │   │ distribution of  │   │ distribution of  │
│ first community   │   │ second community │   │ third community  │
└─────────────────┘   └─────────────────┘   └─────────────────┘
         │                     │                     │
         ▼                     ▼                     ▼
┌─────────────────┐   ┌─────────────────┐   ┌─────────────────┐
│ Conduct in-depth  │   │ Conduct in-depth │   │ Conduct in-depth │
│ household interviews│  │household interviews│ │household interviews│
│ in first community │   │ in second community│ │ in third community │
└─────────────────┘   └─────────────────┘   └─────────────────┘
                                                       │
                                                       ▼
                                              ┌─────────────────┐
                                              │  Compare and     │
                                              │ contrast findings │
                                              └─────────────────┘
                                                       │
                                                       ▼
                                              ┌─────────────────┐
                                              │ Analyze research │
                                              │ findings with all │
                                              │  communities     │
                                              └─────────────────┘
```

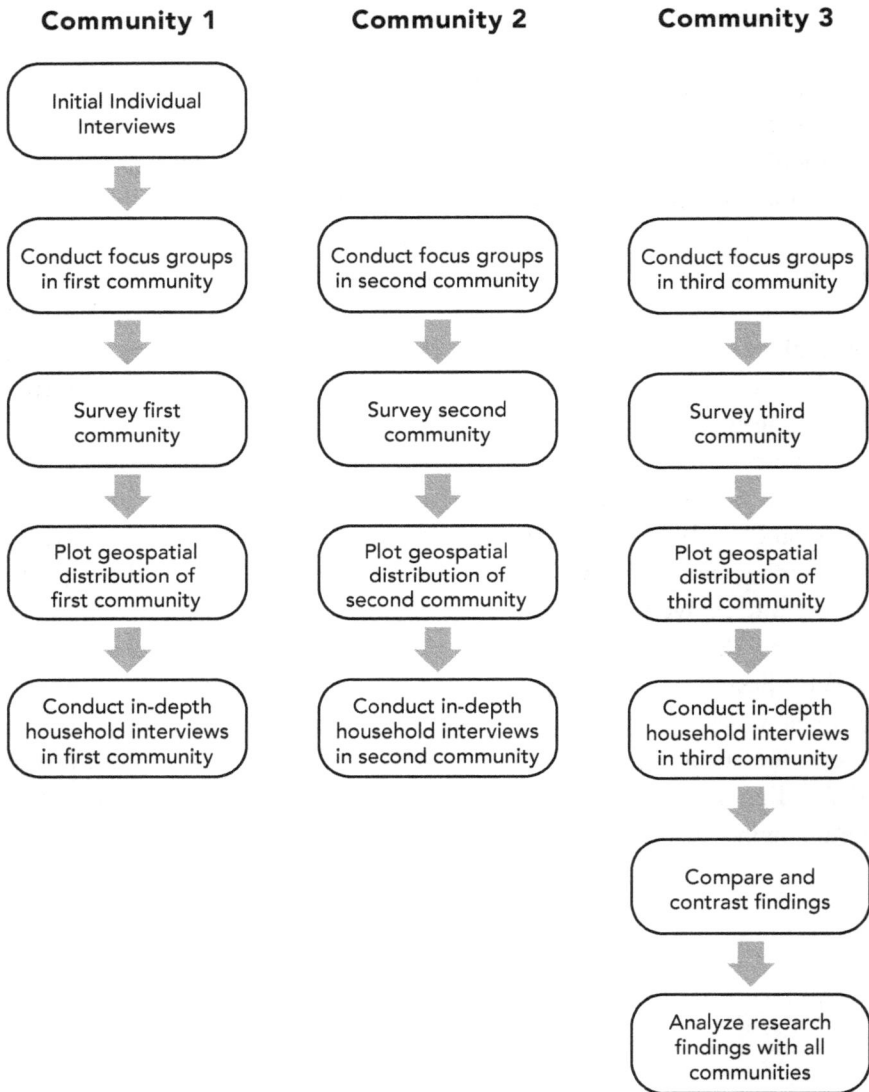

Figure 5. *Stages of Food Security Methodology*

Step 1: Contextualization

In Step 1, a series of semi-structured interviews is conducted in order to gain initial insight into vulnerability to food insecurity, the varied ways in which food security has been strengthened and the opportunities that exist for policy and programs moving forward. Interviews are conducted with government employees at the respective government levels as well as with NGOs, academics and (semi-)private entities. Within communities, individual smallholder farmers are interviewed as well as agricultural extension workers. The interviews focus on the level at which the individual operates, such as community-level program implementation or national policy making. These interviews are conducted in order to contextualize the research area, research questions and experiences regarding food security in rural areas. The number of interviews is arbitrary, and although some research outlines a level of "knowledge saturation" (Bowen, 2008; Glaser and Strauss; 1967; Guest, Bunce and Johnson, 2006), I believe that researchers will never reach a point wherein no new insight is obtainable; rather one should seek sufficient confidence of knowledge to speak fluently about the issues at hand.

Step 2: Community perspectives and survey development

Following the approach developed by Krishna, the Stages of Food Security methodology attempts to have the priorities, experiences and ideas of community members shape the research questions, process and results. The co-production components of the methodology begin in this second stage, in which community members co-create the household survey, including the questions as well as the metrics.

A series of focus group sessions seek to identify discrete stages of food security, which are defined by specific metrics proposed by community members. One of the challenges in discussions about food security is that there tends to be a focus on a few limited factors, often those emphasized in national surveys, such as land size and livestock holdings. However, the co-production approach taken in Step 2 supports conversations that arrive at more nuanced and detailed conclusions. In many instances, this occurs as the researcher poses open-ended questions for discussion. Some of these questions, as outlined in Cochrane (2017a), can include:

- What is the most appropriate measure of food insecurity (by days, month, type)?
- How is gender related to food insecurity? (also age, ability, ethnicity)
- Which crops are grown by different groups? Do they serve different purposes?
- Are there specific crops that require additional attention (fruit trees, cash crops)?

- Does access to improved seeds and fertilizer differ for people in the community? Why?
- Is there a difference in the access households have to extension services/training?
- Are there differences in amount sold to the market and consumed by the household?
- What about other assets (improved housing, radio, mobile phone, electricity)?
- What about household-level context (number of dependents and capable of work)?
- Does the level of education obtained in the household affect food security?
- Are indirect measures related (ability to pay for healthcare and education)?
- Are there programs serving the most vulnerable people? How are they selected?
- Is migration (skilled or unskilled) linked to the food security situation?
- What are common non-agricultural livelihood activities, and do they differ by stage?
- Does access to credit and level of debt differ? Who receives remittances?

While the above questions are not listed as prescriptions for anyone implementing the Stages of Food Security methodology, they are examples of how the researcher can encourage more contextualized and diverse discussions. At the same time, community members raise their own issues, priorities and questions, resulting in a two-way learning process.

As the factors affecting food security are proposed, some metrics can be drawn directly from emerging ideas, such as land size or number of livestock; others require discussion about what an appropriate metric would be. An example of the latter is migration: How should we differentiate between types of migrants and between different forms of migration? Another important discussion is why differentiation exists between factors. For example, why is it that some communities have more unskilled migrants than others? This line of discussion moves the conversation away from the specifics of individual households to the broader systemic issues that affect food security. The conclusions of these discussions provide unique insight into the enablers and barriers for change, which then transition into a conversation about how vulnerabilities could be reduced and opportunities strengthened.

The Stages of Food Security methodology is not entirely participatory or co-created. As the first two steps outline and as I will detail below, some components are co-produced while others are not. I have opted not to include participatory, co-produced processes for all components of the methodology, but rather to use co-production purposefully in respecting the time of community members. I have taken this approach based on the literature about participatory approaches, which can misplace burdens onto community members (Cooke and Kothari, 2001). I agree with Hurlbert and Gupta (2015) that participation should be viewed in light of the questions being posed and the tasks required, rather than as a process that ought to be applied in all places, at all times, for all purposes. As such, the approach includes both participatory, co-produced processes and non-participatory processes.

For example, the focus group discussions utilize participatory approaches to co-produce the household survey, while the implementation of the survey is not done in a participatory fashion, meaning that community members were not expected to participate in conducting the survey. In recognizing that community members have busy agricultural livelihoods and respecting their time as valuable and limited, I did not burden them with conducting a household survey. In the focus group settings, participatory and co-production approaches enable collective learning, a process wherein community members may become newly aware of the extent of some issues, which were previously less clear or not discussed in public forums. Debt is an example of community learning. Everyone knew that borrowing was common, but it was not an issue that was commonly discussed as a community. In addition, the purposeful use of participation allows the opinions, ideas and priorities of community members to determine the direction of the research. The result is that the strengths, opportunities, challenges and barriers as understood and experienced by community members, are explored in the data collection process. The questions and metrics are localized and contextualized using participatory approaches, a process that can highlight unknown, unseen or undervalued aspects of lives and livelihoods (Chambers, 2008). For some advocates and researchers, participation has become a mantra. This approach seeks to add nuance to the conversation about participatory approaches by highlighting how, when, and why participation was used, and not used.

Co-production was used intentionally, as opposed to community-driven or community-led approaches that position all activities as being done by community members. Based on my past experiences conducting similar processes in rural Ethiopia, I have found that community members may be hesitant to explore issues that are socio-culturally or politically sensitive. This might include gendered labor burdens and gendered distribution of resources or who has access to irrigation and why. Community members might also refrain from discussing issues that are typically considered personal matters such as borrowing and debt. However, it is not only potentially sensitive issues that community members avoid discussing. For example, some aspects of people's livelihoods that are normalized or routine for a particular community but are specific to that region may be taken as a given, such as the role of specific crops during times of food insecurity. While I was implementing this methodology in southern Ethiopia, one of the key crops for food security (the root crop enset) was absent from the initial listing of crops in focus group discussions by community members. This may have been because the crop is not harvested as others are (it is perennial and most surveys focus on the annual cereal and root crops) or it may be because other research efforts do not consider it (it is not included in some data collection surveys as it is a crop only grown in some parts of the country). As with other roots crops (e.g., taro, sweet potato), there has been limited attention given to enset by researchers and the government, the latter having more interest in export-oriented crops. Co-production allows the researcher and community members to engage as fellow participants, each contributing their thoughts and reflections. It was my contribution that brought enset up for consideration in the conversations. After raising the issue, we delved into a detailed conversation about its role and uses.

Researchers can also contribute insights from other contexts and evidence from other scholars. For example, community members may not be aware that programs, policies and services differ across their country. Exploring these differences can allow for an assessment of new possibilities. While the researcher's knowledge has biases and limitations, dialogue between the community members and researchers can address a wider range of issues and in more complex ways. During the co-production process, two-way learning is facilitated, and thus space for transformative learning is created.

Step 3: Household survey

Using the survey that is co-created and refined in focus group sessions, individual or household surveying can begin. Following data collection, a random sample of surveys are verified to ensure data accuracy. The verification process is important as it can identify key errors. For example, a verification process I did found that one surveyor was collecting data in hectares while the others were using a local measurement of land (one quarter the size of a hectare); despite instruction and training these types of errors do occur. Had this verification not been done, the data would have been inaccurate. In my use of verification in the past, this process has also helped to identify poor program implementation. For example, a household experiencing food shortages in every month of the year was not included in the Safety Net, to which the local government staff responded that "there were some intake issues." This form of verification seeks out additional context for outlier data.

Verification can also identify much more problematic issues such as the politicization of data and data collection. In one instance, a surveyor assumed that validation would not occur (unfortunately, this is common) and falsely entered positive data regarding questions that reflected the work of the agricultural extension staff. The surveyor said that he was pressured to do so by the lead development worker in the community. After identifying these issues, the entire data subset had to be redone using a different surveyor. This experience not only emphasizes the importance of data verification, it also highlights the ways in which data can be influenced. It is common that surveys in Ethiopia are conducted by government agricultural extension staff, as it is argued they have detailed local knowledge and that using these community-based staff offers a low-cost route for large-scale household surveying. However, this instance highlights the fact that extension staff are cognizant that some questions consider their own performance, and the data can be altered. Since this experience, I have had lengthy discussions with multiple organizations about the inaccuracy and biases that can emerge as a result of using government personnel for household surveys.

The hiring and training of data collectors, location selection and sampling methodologies should all be informed by the context and objectives of the study.[13] Including geospatial data is encouraged, where possible. In some rural and remote areas it may not be possible to use low-cost global positioning system (GPS)-based options due to a lack of internet- or cellular-based coverage. The alternative is satellite-based GPS. However, providing these tools to all the data collectors can present a significant cost. In the case that GPS data is not obtainable, participatory maps could be created as an alternative.

Step 4: Replication

The replication step is a repetition of Steps 2 and 3 in additional communities. The number of additional sites will depend on the research questions posed. Step 1 may need to be repeated if the communities are in a different socio-cultural or agroecological setting. The replication process enables researchers to compare and contrast differences that exist between communities, which in turn allows for an assessment of the impact of geospatial differences, and specifically to assess differences in access to services and infrastructure.

Step 5: Co-analysis

Upon completion of the household survey, the findings are discussed in focus groups with the same communities that created the survey. In some instances, participants may disagree with the results, while in others fruitful discussions can explore the findings in greater detail. As a participant in these conversations, I have found that the disagreements did not necessarily imply that the data was false. Instead, these conversations opened avenues for new explanations, which supported the development of additional unplanned research activities. While important for providing supplementary qualitative data to support the household survey, these sessions also act as a quality check mechanism to verify that the findings align with the experiences of community members. Having multiple co-analysis sessions within and across communities also provides a means of triangulation.

The process of co-analysis is an important stage of the learning process. For example, some people may not fully know the extent to

---

13   See Cochrane (2017a, 2017c) for a host of challenges that might be encountered. See Sana, Stecklov and Weinreb (2012) on the selection of local or outsider data collectors.

which inequality exists within their communities. In my experience, many participants were surprised not by the averages of assets but by the difference between the poorest and most affluent in their community, such as the number of livestock and fruit trees, size of landholdings and credit access. For some individuals, this information was not only surprising but also raised concerns about how goods and services were being distributed in a way that fostered increasing inequalities.

The analysis step also includes conducting follow-up interviews with the interviewees from Step 1. These follow-up interviews have two purposes: verification and information sharing. As with the focus group discussions, the preliminary results are presented to interviewees for their feedback. What is sought from these interviewees, particularly government employees and NGO staff, are their reflections on potential avenues for policy and programming to strengthen food security, often based on decades of experience.

Step 6: Engagement

The concluding activities of the research process revolve around engagement within and beyond the communities. Researchers often assume that decision makers, government workers and non-governmental personnel read academic publications. In a country like Ethiopia this is rarely the case because no one has access to the academic journals in which research is published. Even if there was access, it is unrealistic to expect all these actors will be able to keep up with the evidence (and do their day jobs). As such, researchers need to reflect on appropriate mechanisms to share information with those decision makers. In addition to one-on-one meetings, this might include translating, summarizing, synthesizing and engaging in forums for dissemination.

Putting knowledge into action and ensuring research is used is a complicated task, the limitations of which are particularly challenging when the issues are highly politicized, and in many instances implemented for political purposes, resulting in layers of disincentives for change. Other barriers relate to capacity: in the ideal scenario, all people would have access to irrigation infrastructure, but, unfortunately, the Government of Ethiopia does not currently have the capacity to do this. Recommendations must also, therefore, be actionable, lest they be viewed as irrelevant.

Using knowledge co-production in research is time intensive in comparison to typical household surveying (where a survey might be created from afar or utilize existing survey guides). However, the process can highlight important details that would have been otherwise missed. Many surveys ask if farmers use improved seeds or pesticides, yet farmers do not make the same decision for all crops at all times. Knowledge co-production can assess why these decisions are made and what influences them. In addition to adding depth, knowledge co-production may identify new research directions. In my own case, the implementation of the Stages of Food Security methodology and its findings has resulted in unexpected research directions, such as conducting a survey specific to borrowing and debt, an exploration of the experience of climate change (specifically rainfall changes), qualitative research on the gendered experience of youth migration, community mapping to understand land fragmentation over time, and research on the safety net.

CHAPTER FIVE

VULNERABILITY

The reasons people in Ethiopia experience food insecurity or are vulnerable to it are diverse. The causes in urban areas are different than rural ones. Pastoralists' experiences differ from those of agriculturalists, and wage earners' experiences differ from both. The vulnerabilities of root crop-based agricultural livelihoods differ from cereal-based and swidden practices. Cash-crop practices, typically non-food ones such as khat, coffee and biofuels, differ from food crops grown primarily for household consumption. High elevations differ from low ones. Arid regions in the east differ from the rainforests in the south. A single chapter cannot summarize the complexity of vulnerabilities to food insecurity in Ethiopia, nor could a book for that matter. In fact, there is much we still do not fully understand about the vulnerabilities that lead to food insecurity.

This chapter presents a case study from some of my research in southern Ethiopia. It is not representative of the country and it ought not be generalized. However, using a case study allows us to grapple with a more manageable task, and it allows us to gain insights into the vulnerabilities that are related to food insecurity. The information presented in this chapter summarizes a series of more detailed publications.[14] This chapter does not focus on the details of particular vulnerabilities, but the generalities. Readers interested in the specifics may refer to the other publications. The objective of this chapter is to reveal key insights on what

---

14 This includes Cochrane 2017a, 2017b, 2017c; Cochrane and Adam, 2017; Cochrane and Cafer, 2018; Cochrane and Gecho, 2016; Cochrane and O'Regan, 2016; Cochrane and Skjerdal, 2015; Cochrane and Tamiru, 2016; Cochrane and Thornton, 2017, 2018; Cochrane and Vercillo, 2018.

makes smallholder farmers vulnerable to food insecurity. After presenting
some details about the research areas, thematic subjects are analyzed
(food insufficiency, seasonality and rainfall, land size, population growth,
location, infrastructure, inequality, poverty and debt,and diversification).
Each of these sub-sections present details about lives and livelihoods that
inform why the food security situation is the way it is. The chapter concludes
with reflections on why particular ways of conducting research may unveil
or obscure types of evidence about food security.

Case Study Context

This case study draws upon research conducted in the Southern
Nations, Nationalities and Peoples' Region (SNNPR) of southern Ethiopia
since 2015. The reason SNNPR was selected was the convergence of two
unique factors, both of which play a significant role for food insecurity.
The first factor is that SNNPR has the highest rural population densities
in the country (CSA, 2007), and in many ways what is happening in parts
of SNNPR now may be indicative of what will happen elsewhere as the
population continues to increase.

The second factor that makes SNNPR unique, or at least the central
part of SNNPR, is rainfall. Central SNNPR is neither rain secure,[15] as the
highlands tend to be, nor does it consistently lack rainfall as is common
in the arid Somali and Afar regions. Rainfall is particularly important
in SNNPR as the vast majority of smallholder farmers practice rain-fed
agriculture. Year-to-year variability provides insight into the dynamics
of inequality, population, land size, seasonality, rainfall, climate change
and the impact of interventions designed to strengthen food security. In
years when rainfall is too little, too late or at the wrong time, the impact
can be devastating. For example, consecutive seasons of low agricultural
production resulted in emergency situations in 2011 and 2012 (FEWS
NET, 2012b); in the latter year 55% of the districts in SNNPR were
chronically food insecure (FEWS NET, 2012b).[16] Difficult rainfall years,

15 This is not a technical term. It refers to the highlands that experience relatively
regular and sufficient rainfall.
16 The use of chronic food insecurity refers to the dimension of time. As opposed
to a short-term, transitory or emergency period of insufficient food, chronic food
insecurity refers to a long-term or persistent inability to meet minimum food requirements.

such as 2012, result in multifaceted, negative impacts that include the loss of assets and significant increases of child malnutrition. In other years, such as 2013 and 2014, the region experienced relatively higher levels of food security and relatively low levels of child malnutrition (Cochrane and Gecho, 2016). Even in years when harvests are strong and food security increases for SNNPR, a significant minority of the population remain chronically food insecure. Thus, unique environmental and demographic factors make SNNPR a particularly challenging context.

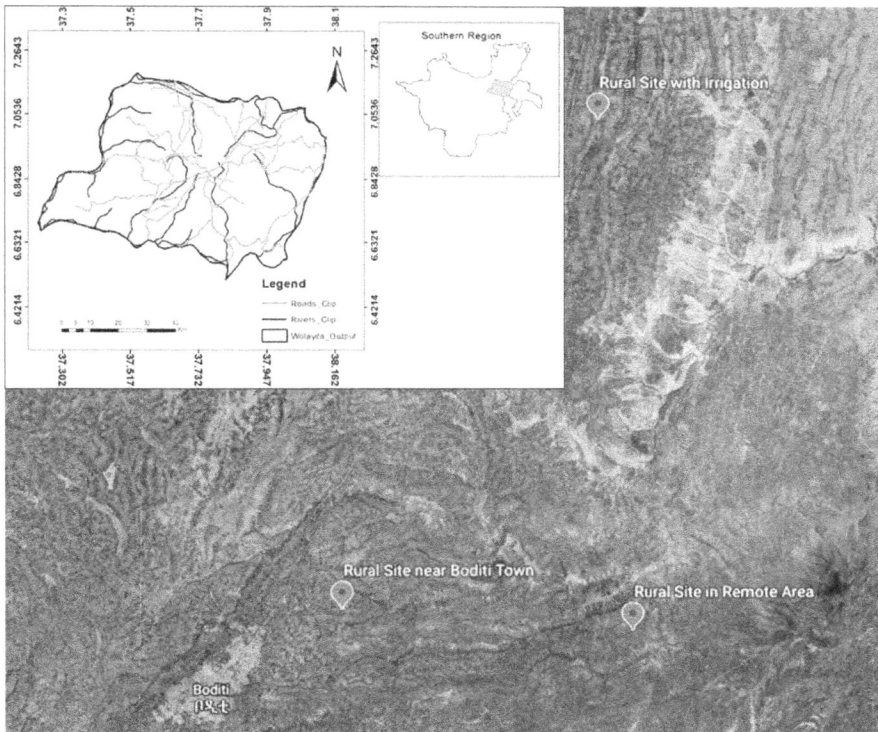

Figure 6. *Map of Study Areas*
Source: Google Earth

For the majority of this chapter, I focus on data that was collected from three sub-districts (*kebeles*) within Wolaita Zone (see Figure 6; also see discussion on ethics in Box 5). These areas were selected for the factors mentioned above (high population density and variable rainfall) as well as high levels of chronic food insecurity. The three locations were determined based on their respective differences within a similar agroecological setting: one rural and remote, another rural but near to a market town, and the third rural with irrigation infrastructure. The root crop-based agricultural system is practiced by the majority of farmers in Wolaita Zone, which includes crops like enset, taro and sweet potato. The selection of these three districts for study was in response to the complex and overlapping layers of vulnerability experienced within them (Husmann, 2016; Rahmato, 2007). While there are local particularities, the vulnerabilities people experience in Wolaita are an expression of national, regional and local influences, which affect the opportunities, limitations and barriers farmers navigate in their lives and livelihoods.

Box 5. Ethics

In conducting research in Ethiopia, I have obtained approvals from federal government agencies, regional government agencies and national universities. Many social science research projects conducted in Ethiopia do not obtain ethics approval from Ethiopian authorities. Instead, international researchers and projects rely upon approval from their home university or host organization. The exceptions are those who collect biological samples or conduct medical tests on humans during their research, because the government is understandably stricter about regulating research of this nature. Most social scientists, nationals and foreigners, were astonished when I explained the ethics approval options and process from Ethiopian authorities. Many stated that they had not heard of others obtaining any such approval. One argument is that the main reason why ethics clearance is not obtained is that the regulations, application and approval processes are not well known and are difficult to navigate when they are know. In addition, throughout much of the country, social science research projects tend not to raise the alarm of ethics concern, so long as the research is not seen as political in nature. Another perspective views foreign researchers' neglect of Ethiopian ethics approval processes as a continuation of colonial attitudes. Given the pervasive nature of ethics review requirements in the Global North, the latter seems more compelling.

My obtaining of ethics approval from Ethiopian authorities was greatly facilitated by formal and informal connections within Ethiopia, without which the time required to obtain clearance may have been greatly increased. There are different approaches to obtaining ethics approval: (1) at the Federal level from the respective federal agency, such as the Ethiopian Public Health Institute, (2) at the regional level, from the respective regional agency, such as the Regional Health Bureau, and (3) via an Ethiopian university.

Completing these processes have been important because I have experienced how the Government of Ethiopia is trying to institute a system of quality control regarding the research that is conducted within the country. The main motivation to describe this process here is to inform other researchers of the challenges of obtaining ethics approval in countries such as Ethiopia where these systems are in an emerging stage of development. It is also to emphasize the importance of doing so. This should be standard minimum practice for all foreign researchers. Firstly, not doing so replicates colonial attitudes that outsiders can decide what is, and is not, ethical for another country. Secondly, it is important to contextualize risk and benefits, specifically so that national authorities can ensure the country benefits from the research that is undertaken. In my own work, this has included being required to involve Ethiopian graduate students and to ensure that the results are shared with relevant authorities and made available more generally in Ethiopia. These requirements ensure research done in Ethiopia benefits Ethiopia and its people. Thirdly, this establishes a mechanism to enforce accountability.

While there are unique aspects to each of these districts, the institutions and systems that operate within SNNPR are common in nearly all parts of Ethiopia, and thus this research offers broad insights into the nature of food security in Ethiopia and the vulnerabilities that people encounter. There are findings and recommendations that are specific to Wolaita and even the districts within Wolaita wherein the study took place, and these ought not be overgeneralized. While the findings presented here are specific to Wolaita, I also draw out broader lessons. At the same time, the research provides new knowledge on broader questions within the food security discourse that are applicable for audiences in Ethiopia, East Africa and beyond. In particular, the Stages of Food Security methodology provides new avenues for assessing and understanding food security.

The ethnicity of the zone where the case study was conducted is almost entirely Wolaita; according to the 2007 census the figure was over 96%. Ethnic homogeneity is a product of the political restructuring along ethnic lines that took place in 2000, thus general linguistic, cultural and ethnic homogeneity is expected. The SNNPR region, however, is home to a diversity of 56 ethnicities. While Christianity is the dominant religion in Wolaita, there are two major sects, which can result in significant tension: 55% are Protestant, 40% Ethiopian Orthodox. The remaining 5% are Muslim (CSA, 2007). These dynamics differ significantly from national religious affiliation: 43.5% Ethiopian Orthodox, 33.9% Muslim, 18.6% Protestant, 2.6% "traditional," 0.7% Catholic and 0.6% "others" (CSA, 2007). As is common in Ethiopia, religious adherence is important in daily life in Wolaita, and it influences with whom one interacts, and how.

Historical population data on Wolaita Zone is unavailable until the 1960s, around which time the Zonal administration began to consider the high population density as a problem (Rahmato, 2007). At the time, the population was estimated to be 600,000 people (CSO, 1966; cited in Rahmato, 2007). By the 1994 national census, the population had almost doubled to 1.13 million (CSA, 1996). In the 2007 census it had risen to 1.5 million (CSA, 2007), and by 2014 it had risen to 1.9 million.[17] The population is almost entirely rural and not experiencing urbanization at the same rate as other parts of the country. In 2005, only 8% of the population was urban; this figure has only risen 1% since 1994. By contrast, the national urban population was 14% in 1994 and 16% in 2005 (CSA, 2011; Rahmato, 2007). In the Imperial times of the 1960s, when population pressure was identified as a problem by government officials, the proposed solution was resettlement, including to low elevation areas within Wolaita Zone. This resettlement approach was enacted at the time (Rahmato, 2007) and was advocated by both the Derg and EPRDF governments in the decades that would follow.

In the "traditional" Wolaitan system, when a sufficient amount of land was available, households divided their land into sections: (1) enset around the home, (2) the *darkua* area with mixed root crops and non-root

---

17   Based upon data from the Zonal Administration Office, provided on May 14th, 2015.

crops, (3) the *shoqa* field for cereals, and occasionally (4) an *outa* for trees and grass (Rahmato, 2007). The utilization of space as designed in the "traditional" Wolaita system is remarkably similar to the models advocated in contemporary research about permaculture, which takes into account the distribution of organic material as well as required labor (e.g., Altieri, 1995; Holmgren, 2002; Mollison, 1991). However, this "traditional" system was disrupted by declining land size per capita as well as advocacy by the government to shift to cereal crops, which are primarily for market sale and export (Eyasu, 2000, 2002). Rahmato writes that the "strategy of changing the cropping system pursued by WADU [Wolaita Agricultural Development Unit] by encouraging a shift from emphasis on root crop cultivation to cereal cultivation was, under the prevailing circumstances, ill advised" (2007: 33).

While the shift of land use and crop choice negatively affected "traditional" agricultural systems, arguably the greatest change was that the required size of landholdings to implement this system no longer existed. Rahmato has described Wolaita as "a land of micro-holdings" wherein "holdings have always been small relative to other parts of the country" but have "been growing smaller through the decades" (2007:3). Rahmato's differentiation between "smallholder" and "microholder" is based on land size less than 0.5 of a hectare, a plot size he argues can no longer sustain those who farm it and which experiences "collapse under even minimum pressure" (Rahmato, 2007: 10). The majority of smallholder farmers in Wolaita farm micro-plots, and this is the result of decades of high population growth and land fragmentation. In parts of Wolaita the average landholding has fallen to as low as 0.25 of a hectare (Cochrane, 2017c). Rahmato's research indicates that root crop-based agriculture can provide sufficient yields for household consumption with plots ranging from 0.1 to 0.8 of a hectare (Rahmato, 1995). However, the potential for self-sufficiency using root crops must be considered in light of the decline of cattle holdings, which is an essential contributor of the manure fertilizer required by root crops. It must also be considered in light of the low protein, carbohydrate-based diets that result from the consumption primarily of root crops, which can result in nutritional deficiencies.

In addition to the challenges of fragmentation into micro-plots, smallholder farmers are vulnerable to unpredictable rainfall—too much, too little, too early or too late. Only 0.4% of the land in Wolaita is irrigated

(Rahmato, 2007). The result is greater demand from smaller plots, which has pushed farmers away from the "sound and sustainable" practices of land use and crop choice to those that provide the greatest benefit in the short term (Rahmato, 2007: 9). Rahmato concludes that agriculture in Wolaita "has exhausted its potential and is becoming increasingly unviable for the great majority" (2007: 17). The percentage of the population reliant upon food aid reflects these changes. Based on available district-level data, the percentage of the population enrolled in the Productive Safety Net Program, which serves rural food-insecure households, ranges from 14% to 31% (Cochrane and Vercillo, 2018).[18]

Rahmato (2007) appropriately draws attention to a segment of society in an even more difficult situation than those farming micro-plots of land: the landless. For this segment of the population, Rahmato states that almost no data is available, but he suggests that the landless make up as much as 15% of the population. The livelihood of the landless revolves around the work they do as farm laborers or as sharecroppers—engaging in migration by necessity (Cochrane and Vercillo, 2018). The landless commonly engage in a range of off-farm and non-farm activities: trading of small goods, unskilled wage labor, handicraft production, collection and sale of wood, charcoal or grass, as well as individual service provision, such as care work.

Throughout all three communities where this research took place, food insecurity was chronic, with average food shortages lasting for several months each year. Significant percentages of households reported not being able to afford to send their children to the tuition-free public school due to associated costs of travel, books, uniforms and lost labor as well as accessibility barriers due to distance. Household assets differed, but the majority had a metal roof and did not have a radio or a mobile phone. Regardless of location, at least a quarter of households did not have a member with a fourth-grade education or higher. In a significant number of households (a third to a half depending on location) someone had migrated from the household for skilled or unskilled work. A small minority received domestic remittances, and very few received international remittances.

---

18   Food aid, in the past and present, refers to food distributions in response to specific emergency needs. The PSNP provides regular, multi-year transfers to households for six-months of the year. In most regional states, the transfer is made in the form of cash payments, for which labor contributions are required (see Cochrane and Tamiru, 2016).

The three communities, despite being located in the same district, were quite distinct from one another. Before exploring the insights offered by comparative findings, it is noteworthy to highlight where similarities exist. For example, total population per community was different, but the structure of households was remarkably similar. According to the household surveys, 60% of household members contributed to the household as primary workers, or had the potential to do so, whereas 40% were dependent, most being children or elderly members. The stages that were coproduced in the research process to assess food security, despite the differences between the communities, point to the trends that unite them, such as the factors and metrics for the household survey developed in the focus group sessions. Across the three communities, the themes, questions and metrics were remarkably consistent.

Community members recognized factors that support the strengthening and weakening of food security. Declines in food security may be caused by environmental changes, including drought, disease, frost, fire and irregular rainfall, as well as human activities that result in erosion and soil fertility loss. Greater numbers of dependent household members negatively affected food security, while more working members increased yields and opportunities. In years of difficulty, when government support was available, these resources were highlighted as being a key mechanism to support families to meet basic needs and avoid asset depletion. Smallholder farmers also recognized opportunities to take action to strengthen their own situation by improving land management to reduce erosion, such as by creating bunds, or by adopting new methods and utilizing new inputs. A selection of these factors and actions are explored in the sections that follow. However, at the outset it should be emphasized that these themes are best understood as interacting and intersecting in overlapping and dynamic ways. The thematic presentation of them is for the ease of readability.

Food insufficiency

Assessing food shortages requires some context. In my research I have used a self-assessment tool to determine the months of the year wherein households did not have sufficient food. This approach results in approximations of trends. It does not assess the severity of shortages or the extent of deficiencies in variety and amount. As a result, the metric lacks specificity, but it is one with which smallholder farmers are familiar.

Most household members explain that food shortages began in a certain month and ended in another and count the time period by the number of months. Food shortages typically occur in specific "hunger seasons" of the year, and therefore spot checks of meals and foods consumed in the most recent week also pose limitations (unless regular surveys are conducted to incorporate the seasonality of food shortages). While this period of time was relatively uniform in the study area due to common agroecology and crops, this season varies considerably throughout Ethiopia. For example, some highland areas have two rainy seasons while other highland areas have one; the pastoralist cycles in the east of the country differ from the west. These variations demonstrate the importance of detailed contextualization and the highly localized factors affecting food security.

Between a third and a half of all households experienced food insufficiencies during five or more months of the year. Food insecurity in these households is chronic. Although these figures are high, they align with other studies of Wolaita Zone, which have found that upwards of 50% of households are food insecure (Eneyew and Bekele, 2012; Gebeyehu, Regasa and Tebeje, 2015; Gecho, 2014) and that these rates are similar to levels of food insecurity and poverty found throughout Ethiopia (Abdulla, 2015; Hill and Porter, 2015; Muche, Endalew and Koricho, 2014; Thome et al., 2016). Within Wolaita, food insufficiency was greatest in the remote community selected for this research. This is counter intuitive because landholdings in the remote community were twice as large as those living near to the town. The difference in food insufficiency is related to opportunities available to those living near a town such as waged work and a market to sell handicrafts and agricultural goods. Those who lived near the town were better able to obtain daily paid labor to purchase food and smooth consumption during the lean seasons of the year. Whereas, those who lived in more remote areas could not walk to work on a daily basis. To work in the town on a regular basis would require relocating, which would involve significant costs.

Seasonality and rainfall

A primary cause of food insecurity is too much, too little or unpredictable rainfall. While seasonality has gained some traction in the literature (e.g., Dercon and Krishnan, 2000; Deverux, Sabates-Wheeler and Longhurst, 2012), the role that this factor plays is often underappreciated due to the ways in which rainfall data is commonly presented, which tends to be in the form of seasonal or annual averages. Figure 7 outlines the two rainy seasons experienced in Wolaita based on averaged rainfall per month over a 10-year period. Farmers, however, do not experience averaged rainfall. They encounter significant variability from season to season and from year to year, which only appears consistent when presented as averages. Watts (1983: 14) calls "normal" rainfall a "statistical fiction."

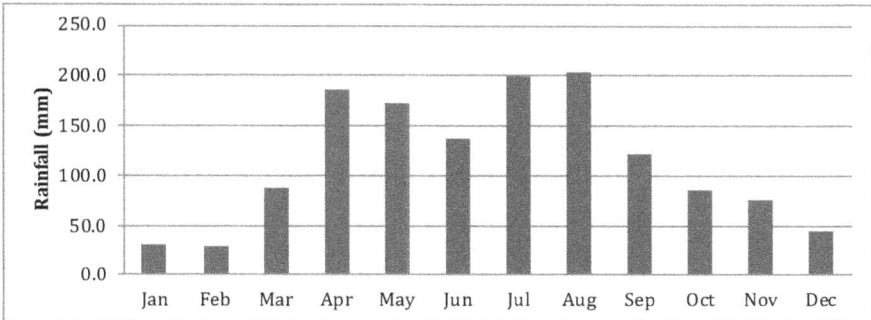

Figure 7. *Average Rainfall in Wolaita Sodo (2003-2013)*
Source: Data provided by the Ethiopian National Meteorological Agency in 2015.

To demonstrate the lived realities of farmers and the impact of rainfall variability, compare the same 10-year period (2003-2013) shown in Figure 7 to that in Figure 8. Whereas the former aggregates data by month, the latter provides a range of years by month. In some years one or both of the rains fail entirely, while in others they are excessive, late or early as compared to the expected norm. For farmers, rainfall variability can be disastrous. Sweet potato, an important root crop that is relied upon to overcome food shortages, is sensitive to moisture changes and the crop can be lost entirely in situations of rainfall variability. In 2015, the rains failed, something that was unexpected for farmers, who planted maize as they normally would; their crops withered halfway through the typical growing season. Wolaita Zone was one of the many parts of Ethiopia that experienced an emergency food insecurity situation in 2015 and 2016, which was the worst experienced in decades. Over 10 million people required emergency food aid and almost half a million children required treatment for severe acute malnutrition (ReliefWeb, 2016).

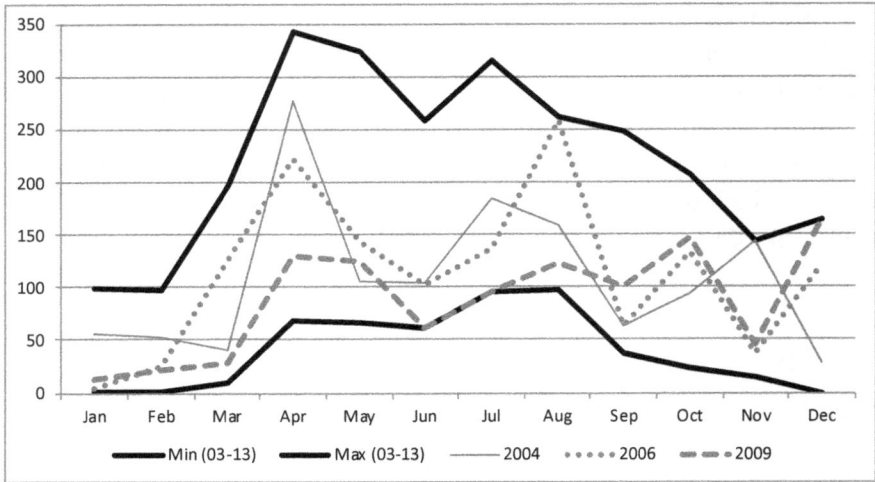

Figure 8. *Rainfall Variability in Wolaita Sodo (2003-2013), selected years (in mms)*

Source: Ethiopian National Meteorological Agency

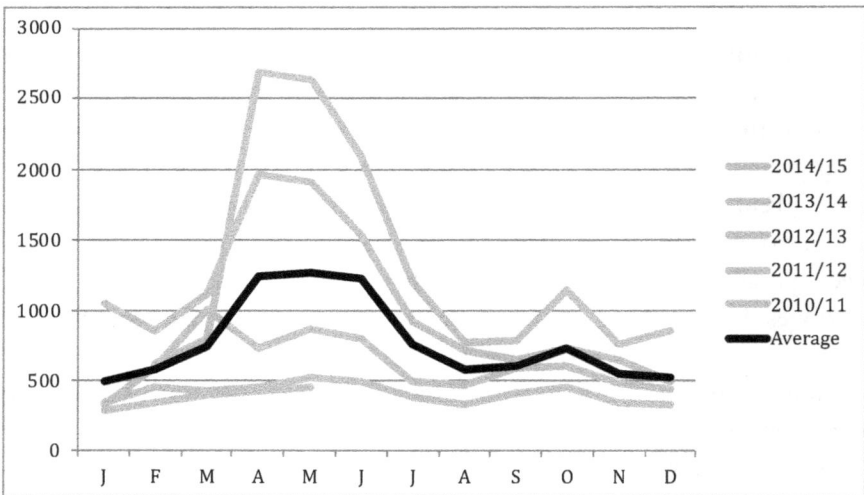

Figure 9. *Seasonal Malnutrition in Wolaita Zone, 2010-2015 (New Intake of Out-Patient Child Malnutrition Cases)*

Source: Wolaita Zone Health Office

Community-level data on malnutrition cases is not available, but data from the Zonal Health Authority identify how seasonality impacts the experience of food insecurity. Cases of diagnosed child malnutrition spiked during the "hunger season" (March to June) every year—the only difference was the extent (see Figure 9; Cochrane and Gecho, 2016).

There are two ways this information about rainfall variability and seasonality could encourage actions improve farmers' situations: (1) improving access to meteorological information and drawing upon existing information dissemination for rural smallholder farmers, such as the experience of the Ethiopian Commodity Exchange (detailed in the following chapter), and (2) conducting research that integrates "traditional" knowledge with meteorological data to arrive at innovative and more accurate prediction approaches, as has been done in other East African countries (Chang'a, Yanda and Ngana, 2010; Guthiga and Newsham, 2011; Kalanda-Joshua et al., 2011). More broadly, the lack of access to irrigation is a root cause of this vulnerability that can be addressed (climate change being beyond the sphere of control of domestic actors).

Seasonality has many indirect impacts as well. One of these is seasonal dropout from school. However, seasonal dropout does not appear in enrollment statistics because absenteeism is not reported on. As a result, seasonal dropout is invisible to higher authorities. During the agricultural season when more labor is needed or during periods of food shortages when youth migrate out of necessity, children and youth stop their education to work on the farm or to obtain short-term wage labor. Research in southern Ethiopia finds that the frequency of absenteeism is much higher within food insecure households (Tamiru et al., 2016). This is an example of a poverty penalty which disproportionately punishes those who are most vulnerable (e.g., have the least assets available to draw upon in times of shock). Mendoza (2008: 1) describes the "poverty penalty" as "higher costs shouldered by the poor, when compared to the non-poor."

Seasonal migration has been associated with poor early childhood development (Dereveux, Sabates-Wheeler and Longhurst, 2012). However, my research suggests that it is not migration per se that is the cause of negative childhood development outcomes, because some migrants move to permanent, relatively well-paying positions. Rather, it is chronic food insecurity that has caused malnutrition in children, which is a primary cause of unskilled migration in response to vulnerability. This potentially explains the correlation. As the data from Wolaita shows, the majority of migrants were from food-insecure households who were forced to seek unskilled labor positions (Cochrane and Vercillo, 2018). Food insecurity is not related to all forms of migration, but it can be the cause of distress migration that can cause negative impacts on early childhood development.

Land size

The Derg military regime (effectively 1974-1991) nationalized all land and implemented a large-scale land redistribution (detailed in the following chapter). Soon after coming to power the regime confiscated land from large landholders, which were redistributed to those without land. The implementation and effectiveness of this system are discussed in Chapter 6. Supporters of the land redistribution view it as ending a feudal style landlord system and granting rights to the users of the land. Critics view the processes as reducing everyone to equality in poverty and entrenching tenure insecurity. If we assume a degree of equality in land holdings was achieved, that has slowly been undone. In these three communities in Wolaita, 9% of inhabitants are landless, having 0.125 of a hectare or less and 13% could be considered larger landholders, having 0.75 hectares or more (Cochrane, 2017c). As noted earlier, even the largest landholders have very small plots (one or two hectares at most). Despite differences in wealth and landholding size, vulnerability is pervasive, and even those community members who are relatively more affluent are often subject to it. These findings are mirrored elsewhere in Ethiopia; the gap between the landholding assets of the poorest and most affluent Ethiopians has widened since the Derg redistribution due to economic reasons as well as population growth and limited land availability (Tolossa, 2003). The causes of land loss include fragmentation due to inheritance, government appropriation, debt (formal and informal), and an inability to utilize the land due to ill-health or insufficient labor.

Insufficient landholdings were particularly problematic in the community near the town. The average household in this site (which comprised 5.3 people) held only 0.2 ha of land. As a function of these small landholdings and greater pressure on communal lands, those living near the town also had fewer livestock than in the other sites. In the remote community, average landholdings were nearly double this size (0.38 ha, average household size 6) and nearly triple this size in the community with irrigation (0.55 ha, average household 7.5). However, all of these land sizes are very small and make for a challenging agricultural livelihood. Only in the community with irrigation does the average household's land area cross the minimum threshold of 0.5 ha that Rahmato (2007) outlined as required for survival. Yet, obtaining good data on land size using self-reported data is extremely difficult in rural areas (Ege, 2019). If we consider the range of landholding size from the survey data, in all three communities many households effectively held no agricultural land (having only a home and small garden within the compound). The maximum household landholdings were 1 ha (in the site near a town), 2 ha (in the remote site) and 2 ha (held by two households in the irrigation site).

Not all communities have equal access to acquire goods from the market. Remote communities are much less able to attend marketplaces, and this reduces their ability to sell as well as acquire goods that would enable new opportunities such as growing fruit trees. It is tempting to assume that distance from markets is the key factor, however there are intra-community factors, such as land size, that affect how individuals are able to take advantage of such opportunities. When looking at land size, which is key for fruit trees as they take a significant amount of land out of annual crop production, the intra-community differences are just as important.

A factor that may be less obvious to non-farmers are costs related to land size such as the form of plowing utilized. There is an inverse relationship between land size and the ability to cultivate by hand using a hoe as labor-intensive hand-cultivation is not viable on larger plots. For the households that do not have the two oxen required for plowing, they must borrow or rent these animals. When oxen are acquired in this way, the timing of plowing is less ideal as ox owners prioritize the plowing of their own fields, forcing those without sufficient draft to wait until the animals are available. The result is that the most vulnerable landholders face an "uncounted" cost, or a non-formal and indirect poverty penalty, that takes the form of decreased yields due to less than ideal plowing and planting periods. Typically, the poverty penalty concept is applied to service provision such as access to credit, healthcare, water or electricity. However, there are also indirect poverty penalties faced by the poor in non-market settings such as the lower yields and decreased livelihood options that result because of a lack of assets.

The data on landholdings within the three communities examined in this study provides insight into how food insecurity data differs from that of traditional poverty assessments. Land size would typically be taken as a primary measure of wealth, which it is, but it does not necessarily correlate with the level of food security. The community with the highest level of food security is not the one in which the greatest percentage of households have more than 0.5 hectares of land. Rather, this research shows that the opposite holds true in this case: the remote community had the greatest number of households holding more than 0.5 ha of land but it was also the most food insecure.[19] Just as land size and food security did not necessarily correlate at the community level, neither did correlations between land size and number of working age people in the household, as per the idea that the use of land intensifies as plot sizes decrease and household size increase.

In addition, on the individual level, these correlations are less direct than might be assumed. For example, in reviewing household surveys I identified a household for verification based on my own assumption. It held a large plot of land, but the survey indicated it was chronically food insecure. Through the verification process we found that the death of the male household head and the lack of available labor resulted in the household opting for sharecropping, which meant the household received only a portion of the harvest. By contrast, the survey showed that another household with almost no land was food secure. In verifying the survey data we learned that the household was supported by international remittances. These were not anomalies. In fact, households such as these provide insights into the realities of rural dynamics that are typically lost in averages. While land size is an important factor, broader assessments need to take into account the diverse causes of vulnerability (and strength).

Population growth

Land fragmentation due to inheritance consistently arises as a grave concern throughout rural Ethiopia. Evidence indicates even as smallholder farmers intensify their agricultural practices and supplement their crops with inputs, land constraints caused by fragmentation are a primary cause

---

19   Note that averages were previously used to describe landholdings in the three communities, whereas in this instance the percentage of community members is used. The result is a different ordering of the communities. This highlights the importance of critically assessing metrics and analyzing data from different perspectives.

of rural poverty and food insecurity (Headey, Dereje and Taffesse, 2014). The land size per capita in Wolaita is amongst the smallest in Ethiopia, and fragmentation due to inheritance continues to place immense pressure on household food security. Even with yield per hectare increases and the introduction of greater yielding varieties, the amount of harvest per household is declining due to decreasing average land size.

As the population has grown from about a million to two million over two decades (1994-2014), the number of households farming less than 0.5 of a hectare has risen steadily, from approximately 45% in 1989 to 57% in 2013 (Rahmato 1992, 2007; CSA 2013; and information provided by the Damot Gale Agricultural Office). These are the households cultivating "micro plots," which Rahmato argues are insufficient to meet needs and "collapse under even minimum pressure" (2007: 10). As the population continues to grow, and because off-farm options are limited, it is expected that land fragmentation will continue, resulting in more households crossing the <0.5 ha threshold throughout Wolaita.

The two trends of population growth and land fragmentation are not new concerns. Local government officials recognized them as key challenges for Wolaita in the 1960s (Rahmato, 2007). Over the decades, resettlement has been proposed as a potential solution, including resettlement to lowland areas. However, these programs have struggled due to the presence of animal diseases that are not found in the middle and high altitudes (e.g., trypanosomiasis), and higher levels of malaria (climate change is expanding the area of malaria occurrence into higher altitude areas as temperatures rise) (Siraj et al., 2014). Efforts to control disease in recent decades have facilitated new flows of migration and resettlement (Rahmato, 2007). Resettlement and villagization are large-scale controversial programs, which will not be explored in detail here (see Berry and Ofcansky, 2004; Cohen and Isaksson, 1987; de Waal, 1991; Rahmato, Pankhurst and van Uffelen, 2013; Tareke, 2009; Woldmeskel, 1989).

Rising population poses serious challenges. However, I am cautious in focusing too much attention on it. The primary reason for my caution is because population discourses tend to place responsibility on individuals without sufficient attention to government. This is often justified as individual choices are problematized and often result in recommendations that restrict agency (e.g., population control initiatives). All people should have access to family planning information and options, and this is something that Ethiopia needs to make greater progress on (there are large gaps between demand and accessibility of family planning options). At times, the conversation on population faults individuals, essentially blaming the victim. Within that conversation, we cannot allow the responsibilities of the state to be neglected. Instead, I have opted to focus on how the programs and services offered to smallholder farmers are not meeting their needs.

Location

A primary factor for determining where food security exists in Ethiopia is location, and specifically the location of the community (as opposed to the place of an individual household within a community). This largely depends on the infrastructure and services that are available as a result of where one lives. Levels of food security vary accordingly, with access to irrigation infrastructure having the largest positive impact. For instance, households with access to irrigation on average experience food insecurity for shorter durations than those without access (3.5 months of the year in the community with irrigation versus 4 and 4.3 months in those without). Conversely, communities without irrigation where almost twice as likely to be enrolled in the safety net than those without irrigation (21% and 22% versus 12%). Communities with irrigation were also more likely to feel they are able to afford to send all their children to school (61% in the community with irrigation versus 38% and 47% in communities lacking irrigation).

The most remote of the three communities requires a full day to walk to and from the nearest town, making these trips infrequent. This community is not very remote by Ethiopian standards; many parts of the country are located in areas where access to the nearest town is more than 10 hours away on foot (CSA, EDRI and IFPRI, 2006). For people living in such remote communities the distance is such that they are largely unable to access the services in towns such as secondary schooling, improved healthcare services and microfinance. The inaccessibility of a market is reflected in low levels of cash crop utilization (e.g., coffee plants and mango trees), despite relatively greater land availability. This is also a reflection of accessibility to saplings as well as the market for sale of goods.

Farmers in the remote community also received less training by government extension workers. Robert Chambers (2006) has called this the roadside bias, whereby individuals and communities nearer to roads receive greater attention by government and non-governmental development activity simply because it is easier to access such individuals and households, and because of that ease of access also appear as more 'cost-effective' as such activities try to reach as many people as they can on limited budgets. The roadside bias effect also occurs at the micro-level within communities. For instance, those households nearest to the Farmer Training Center are better able to access the services than those located several kilometers away.

Infrastructure

The irrigation scheme that exists in one of the communities had significant positive impacts. The direct impact was the reduction of risks of rainfall variability. An emphasis on infrastructure is important because when presented with irrigation proposals, NGO and government actors commonly state that they are too costly. In this community with irrigation, a donor government worked in collaboration with the regional state of SNNPR to construct a gravity-fed system that requires no motors or electricity and was almost entirely constructed out of locally sourced materials. It was completed around 2006 and uses the contours of the valleys to collect the rainfall of the two rainy seasons and fill a moderate size reservoir for use throughout the year. The medium-size dam was almost entirely built out of blocks of broken rock, with machinery being brought in to deepen the collection reservoir and cement used with large stone blocks for the primary irrigation canals. Each morning a valve is opened for one hour, bringing water to 240 households throughout the year. The households who receive this water went from having irregular harvests, usually one or two, to consistently having three or four harvests annually. This allowed them to diversify their crops, most notably adding vegetables—tomato, cabbage, peppers and carrot—which are produced throughout the year.

At the time of construction, the cost was ETB 5,000,000 (US$550,000 in 2006). If one considers the activity and budget proposals submitted to the local Wolaita Zone authority for approval, this irrigation system equates to 2%. In other words, there are large budgets that could integrate such irrigation activities. Yet, not a single NGO listed irrigation as one of its proposed activities in 2013 and 2014 (the relevant authority only provided the complete data for these years). The experience in Wolaita shows that small- and medium-scale dams that are built with local materials and managed by community members are relatively low cost and sustainable. Recall the light rail system in Addis Ababa mentioned in Chapter 3, which cost US$0.5 billion. Without delving into a comparative impact assessment of users and long-term benefits, that same amount could potentially fund the construction of irrigation systems for more than 800 communities in rural Ethiopia.

As one community member explained, infrastructure is beyond the capacity of the community to construct, but it is necessary to strengthen their livelihoods:

> For food security, for us with the changing weather, we need irrigation. We have rivers. If the government facilitates irrigation it will help us immensely. It is beyond our capacity to build these canals, but we are willing to extend our hands [contribute time and labor] to have irrigation (Community Member).

Irrigation facilitates increased yields, multiple harvests and the production of diversified high-value crops leading to better nutrition and income. However, the impact of irrigation extends beyond these benefits. In the community I researched, irrigation has also contributed to changed social relations, including an expansion of social capital. Since so many more families sell their yields on the market, they have formed numerous groups for collectively selling their farm products (a type of informal cooperative). The networks and income enabled new businesses to emerge such as investing in hybrid chickens for egg sale and working on high-value handicrafts, such as woodwork items.

There are also indications that the irrigation system has changed citizen-government relations. For example, while many residents could afford to purchase water from a nearby town, at 5 ETB (US$0.23) per 50 liters, they viewed their water situation as particularly poor. Residents (almost always women) typically walk an hour to purchase the water, which is hand transported in a locally made cart. "We are raising the issue with the district government," a group of women in Wolaita explained. Even if no response has materialized, the other two communities studied as part of this research have not actively engaged with their governments to request improved provision of goods and services. Although the linkages are indirect, it appears that the new forms of social capital made possible by irrigation and its benefits are enabling new forms of citizen-government interactions. While irrigation does not alone explain changes to citizen-government relationships, there are, nonetheless, indications that it has contributed to changes well beyond agricultural output. It is also the case that extreme vulnerability restricts opportunities to interact directly with government, often because communities in dire need are dependent upon authorities.

Infrastructure includes much more than irrigation. Roads, markets, schools, health centers, agricultural training centers, electricity grids and telecommunications networks all enable new options and opportunities. With the rare exception of those living near a road, most people in these communities did not have access to electricity or piped water to their homes. Community members prioritized challenges related to water and fuel in particular. In the community with irrigation, the average walking time to obtain water was 1 to 1.5 hours daily. Firewood was emphasized because the community lacked access to electricity, and collecting firewood is a laborious and time-consuming task. As a result of increased demand for firewood, forests are also being unsustainably depleted of resources. Considering that obtaining water and firewood are regular, often daily, activities, these community-level inequalities consume large amounts of girls' and women's time. This is time that could be used in other activities; one study in Ethiopia found that a reduction of time spent in obtaining water resulted in an increase in food consumption (Aklilu, 2013).

Inequality

Within communities, various forms of inequality results in some segments of society experiencing greater vulnerability to food insecurity than others. Challenges and opportunities vary according to a wide range of factors like gender, age, education and so forth, and thus communities should be conceptualized as a complex dynamic system wherein households experience food security in diverse ways and for diverse reasons. Although the communities researched in this study are largely homogenous with regard to livelihoods, ethnicity, religion and language, in other parts of the country these factors are aspects of social differentiation that impact food security in a range of ways. For example, people who practice certain livelihoods (e.g., pottery, metalwork) continue to experience exclusion and marginalization; sharing food with these people is considered shameful (Lyons and Freeman, 2009). Women have been largely excluded by an agricultural extension system designed for and implemented by men. Marginalized ethnic groups remain excluded from safety net programs, despite facing chronic food insecurity (e.g., as in Gambella and Somali regions). Historically, in parts of the highlands Muslims were not allowed to own land (Ahmad, 2000), resulting in economic divisions based on religion. Linguistic minorities continue to be excluded from many programs and services because the providers do not speak their local language (e.g., Amharic-speaking agricultural extension workers in communities in Benishangul Gumuz that speak the Gumuz language). As a result, these forms of social differentiation (including others such as gender, age, ability, health status, location, economic status, socio-cultural status, marital status and political affiliation) have direct impacts on land and assets, and thereby opportunities and food security.

In the most general terms, rural life in Wolaita is highly gendered. Men are primarily occupied with farming and livestock-related activities, while women acquire water and wood, prepare meals, care for children and maintain the household. However, when we look closer at people's daily lives we see that gender norms are more fluid than a general picture suggests and vary according to individual households. For example, women contribute to agricultural practices, and in focus group discussions both genders mentioned going to the market for trading purposes.

The burden that water and firewood collection places on girls and women highlights how the inequalities that exist between communities result in gendered impacts. Where water and firewood are available, men's responsibilities and activities remain relatively constant. This example highlights the importance of considering the gendered impacts of interventions seeking to facilitate positive change. For instance, improving access to water will improve the overall health of the community but also reduce burdens girls and women face. Similarly, improving access to electricity will reduce deforestation and at the same time reduce burdens on girls and women as the necessity of gathering firewood diminishes and the time required for preparing meals decreases. Conversely, interventions that improve cattle sales though regional markets tend to benefit men while dairy-related income generation activities support women but also place a greater burden on them as they are responsible for milking dairy cattle and preparing butter. Ensuring that women have the opportunity to engage in new income-generating activities will require a reduction in their daily burdens, such as by improving access to water and electricity.

Inequality in access to education has long-term impacts on livelihood options. These consequences can be viewed in experiences of migration, those able to migrate for permanent skilled positions and those migrating due to vulnerability and distress to precarious and low-paid daily work. This inequality is apparent when we compare the communities with irrigation, who were the most food secure, and those without it. Elders in the community with irrigation commented that "we see most of the youth leave from the non-irrigated land, and this is because of their poverty and difficult situation." The household and land size are similar, the elders pointed out, but "cannot meet the needs of the household." In contrast, youth from "households with irrigation tend not to leave, except for university." The opportunities that come with greater and consistent yields translate into higher levels of education and therefore skilled migration. In contrast, the non-irrigated land is subject to variability and thus increased vulnerability which in turn leads to distress migration in search of unskilled labor work. This then has a negative impact on migrants' educational opportunities. Community analyses of the survey results explained that high levels of migration, and specifically of unskilled workers, was linked to a lack of accessible employment (i.e., impossibility of commuting as a day laborer) and relative poverty and food insecurity. Using 10 years of panel data from Ethiopia, Bezu and Barett (2010) identified a gendered dimension to these opportunities, in that women have lower off-farm participation than men, and when they do participate in paid labor work it tended to be unskilled, reflecting gendered socio-cultural barriers as well as skill and resource limitations faced by women.

The nature of unskilled migration in these communities was linked to an inability to afford or access education. Many people in such households were not able to obtain education beyond Grade 4 or 8. As was stated emphatically by one community member, "no one who had obtained a university education stayed" in the rural areas where they lived and worked. However, education is not the sole determinant in out migration. In communities where farming livelihoods were more viable, due to factors such as land size or irrigation, fewer unskilled youth left as migrants, thus indicating that vulnerability plays a key role as a push factor in unskilled migration. Cochrane and Vercillo (2018) call this migration by necessity; others have termed it distress migration (Loevinsohn, 2012) or migration as a forced response (Turin and Valdivia, 2012). These short-term, often seasonally influenced, relocations are also impacted by long-term trends of land fragmentation which have resulted in few options for viable rural livelihoods. As a result, youth often seek alternative livelihoods (Bezu and Holden, 2014). Kubik and Maurel (2016), drawing upon research conducted in Tanzania, link climate change and weather-related shocks to agricultural production and migration. Specifically, they find that a 1% reduction in agricultural income as a result of climatic and weather-related events increases the probability of migration by 13% for the year following that loss.

The gendered nature of youth migration also tells an important story of gender inequality (as outlined in Cochrane and Vercillo, 2018). Much of the literature on youth migration highlights the flow of young men from rural areas to towns and cities (Quisumbing et al., 2014; Shipton, 1990), whereas in Wolaita many young women are also migrating. Both young men and women are pushed out by poverty and food insecurity, and the precarious work they obtain in towns and cities often fails to meet their basic daily needs. Yet, young women who had migrated to the nearest town explained that they were pushed to migrate because of gender discrimination. One study found that despite laws about equality in inheritance, only 6% of head of households were even considering granting land to their daughters (Bezu and Holden, 2014). While all migrants, regardless of gender, cited factors related to land shortages in their decision to migrate, young women experienced disproportionate exclusion (such as from future land holdings) and expressed that there were no opportunities for them in rural areas. Female community members also faced additional barriers to educational attainment, which then reduced the availability of non-farm work opportunities (Bezu and Barrett, 2010).

Skilled migration, by contrast, occurs when people purposely choose to seek economic opportunities elsewhere, and this decision is often made possible through education, which is enabled by greater and longer-term food security, assets and relative wealth. Community members felt that migration was important to include in the household survey and suggested that metrics explore the nuances of migration, specifically between skilled and unskilled migration. The results tell an important story about inequality between these communities: while the community with irrigation has a similar number of households with migrants, they are two to three times more likely to be skilled migrants, obtaining permanent jobs that are relatively well paid. Those migrating for skilled labor do so because they are attracted by new opportunities, whereas the majority of those migrating for unskilled labor do so out of necessity.

This finding relating to skilled and unskilled migration was another example of how the co-production of questions and metrics can highlight key differences and important factors related to inequalities that tend not to be included in surveys assessing food security. The division of skilled and unskilled migration categories that was proposed by community members for this study has been utilized by other researchers working in Ethiopia. For example, Bezu and Barrett (2010) analyzed long-term data using similar categories and found similar trends in migration, although these researchers gave less emphasis to the ways in which some non-farm paid work options are expressions of vulnerability or maladaptation. The mixed-methods co-production approach utilized in our study enabled these details to emerge.

This section analyzed a selection of intra- and inter-community inequalities in order to highlight how food security is increased or decreased by various forms of relative inequality. Between communities, this includes differential access to clean water and the impact of migration due to unequal educational and work opportunities. Within communities, inequalities of land, labor and assets impact what resources a family can draw upon to strengthen its food security. Within households, gender is a key factor of social differentiation and cause of inequalities. In addition to exploring the existence of inequalities, the section highlighted how interventions must be considered in light of inequalities, as their impact will differ between and within communities, as well as within households. Yet, these are only some of the many ways in which such inequalities are manifested. They also exist in gendered educational opportunities (Rose and al-Samarrai, 2001), nutritional outcomes (Decron and Singh, 2011), access to markets (Aklilu et al., 2007; Geleta, 2016), access to programs and services (Peterman, Behrman and Quisumbing, 2010; Ragasa et al., 2013), access to healthcare (Cochrane and Rao, 2019), intrahousehold vulnerabilities (Holmes and Jones, 2010; Uraguchi, 2010; Turin and Valdivia, 2012), amongst others.

Poverty and debt

"Poverty," Gibson notes (2012: 492), "is perhaps the single biggest obstacle to achieving food security." The definitions, metrics and framings of poverty will not be delved into here. Rather, the focus will be on what community members felt were proxies for both food insecurity and poverty. As noted in Chapter 4, these proxies took the form of physical assets (e.g., land, ownership of items), experiences (e.g., months of insufficient food in the year) and processes (e.g., youth migration). The community did not set a minimum number for any metric but instead looked at the overall household context when assessing which category a family should be categorized as. In this regard, it is worth noting that "community-based selection" processes are commonly used in rural Ethiopia, whereby community members themselves select who is best suited for the programs. This is done for the safety net program as well as other initiatives. In this regard, the idea of analyzing the overall situation of a household is not a new practice. Based on the metrics community members proposed, chronic poverty is pervasive throughout the three communities. Even those households with higher economic standing have few assets and very little income. In agricultural settings such as these, income is not the best measure of poverty, since many farmers are practicing a subsistence livelihood with only limited engagement with markets.

Poverty in these communities tends to have knock-on effects, compounding the impacts. For example, in difficult years, relatively impoverished farmers do not have savings they can draw on to buy food supplies, and thus they are forced to sell assets. This diminishes their future capacity to adapt as many of the assets that are sold are value-producing ones, such as cattle or goats. When community members do not have assets to sell, they seek loans in what I call "vulnerability borrowing". My research in Wolaita found that every single surveyed household had borrowed money at least once within the past five years. Community members explained that "if you include credit for fertilizer and seed, almost everyone had debt" and that "no one is free from debt."

The majority of loans are taken due to an inability to meet basic needs. As in other contexts (e.g., Watts, 1983), distress- and vulnerability-induced borrowing occurs seasonally. One indication of vulnerability borrowing is a strong relationship between a higher number of loans taken within the five-year period and a higher number of instances of households being unable to repay the loan (Cochrane and Thornton, 2017). This indicates that borrowing in these instances is not a process of securing upfront capital to obtain higher returns (due to agricultural cycles), but rather a sign that people are borrowing as a desperate way of paying for necessities in the short term. For many households, the cycle of borrowing can result in a (semi-)permanent status of being in debt.

Poverty also reduces opportunities in the short and long term. An example of a short-term impact is the inability to access healthcare. One challenge is accessing a facility that offers the kind of care they need. They must also cover costs related to care such as food and medicine. Medical emergencies, which are another cause of borrowing and debt, pose another set of problems. Residents in remote areas face the most difficult situation because their communities do not have cell phone coverage, and therefore they cannot call for help. People in remote areas rely on the few within the community who have donkey-drawn carts or motorcycles and who may charge exorbitant prices for transportation to the hospital. In theory, there is a public ambulance that serves the most remote community in our study, and residents were aware of it, but it was non-functional and thus not an option even if cell phone coverage was extended. While infrequent, these medical emergencies and the costs associated with them can cause lifelong indebtedness and thus chronic poverty.

A long-term impact of poverty is the inability to access education. Like healthcare, primary and secondary education is government-provided, but accessing education is challenging. Very few rural communities have a secondary school, meaning children need to stay with relatives or find boarding options. Many families cannot muster these costs and as a result their children do not gain the skills they need to be able to access better opportunities in the future. Bezu and Barrett (2010) find education to be the most important determinant of non-farm employment in rural Ethiopia. Families recognize the opportunity education offers and will invest in education, when they can afford it, as a long-term mechanism to overcome existing and future challenges (Cochrane and Gecho, 2016).

Conversely, relative wealth confers opportunity. Having a donkey-drawn cart or a motorcycle to transport people and goods creates new income opportunities. Being able to purchase hybrid chicks allows for an increase of egg production and sale. Those with dairy cattle can sell milk and butter, those with oxen can hire them out to plow the fields of households without animals. In contrast, those without such resources rely upon laborious tasks, such as collecting grass and firewood. Following cutting or collection, one must walk to the market to sell what can be carried for very low prices—a full day's labor at this difficult task may result in 15 ETB (approximately US$0.70). Thus, relative wealth confers strength, and those with relative wealth gain disproportionately more than the rest.

Hybrid chickens are a good example of a relatively low-cost investment (compared to a donkey or motorcycle) that only a few households are able to take advantage of due to the risk of failed returns. A single chick costing 70 ETB (US$3.25) offers a recurring source of income from egg production, and after approximately two years when egg production declines is sold for meat. However, in remote communities livestock vaccinations are unavailable and disease can cause significant losses. A project supported by an international non-governmental organization in Benishangul Gumuz Regional State that I conducted an evaluation of provided hybrid chicks as an income-generating business opportunity. However, in one community with that project every single chick was lost due to disease. As with the communities in Benishangul Gumuz, in Wolaita the animal health post within communities had no vaccines. Those who are able to take the risk in starting a poultry business venture have the potential to earn significant new revenues. Thus inequality is potentially exacerbated as those households with the means to invest expand their income and those with limited means miss out on the opportunity.

Diversification

The process of re-allocating investment, time or skills to new and different activities as a means to have diverse sources of income / resources is termed diversification. In the agricultural realm diversification might include introducing new crops or introducing non-farm and off-farm activities, such as starting a small business or obtaining part time labor work. The dominant rationale presented in the scholarly literature is that this is done as a risk reduction measure, in case one form of resource generation fails the others may mitigate risk. Scholars who have focused on livelihoods research have made important contributions regarding diversification such as differentiating between planned (or proactive) and responsive diversification (e.g., Barrett, Reardon and Webb, 2001; Rigg, 2006). Yet, the literature on Ethiopian agricultural and pastoral livelihoods tends to emphasize the value and importance of diversification (e.g., Barth, 1964; Gecho et al., 2014; Headey, Taffesse and You, 2014; Mergersa et al., 2014; Tsegaye, Vedeld and Moe, 2013; Yosef et al., 2013). This is also echoed by governments and their partners, wherein diversification is assumed to be a strength (Cochrane and Cafer, 2018). In order to briefly explore how diversification can be an expression of vulnerability or itself create vulnerabilities, two examples of diversifications in Wolaita will be explored: crops and livelihoods. While some diversification is undoubtedly positive, as a means to reduce risk and take advantage of new opportunities, diversification is not necessarily good or necessarily a sign of improved resilience, risk mitigation or a broadening of opportunities. Diversification can be the result of vulnerability and an expression of individual households and communities facing difficulties. Similarly, a reduction in diversification can result in improved outcomes such as when farmers opt to focus on higher-value crops with stable prices and marketing networks.

Research in rural Ethiopian communities suggests that crop diversification is lowest in communities with the strongest food security, and where risk due to water stress was lowest due to irrigation infrastructure (Cochrane and Gecho, 2016; Cochrane and Cafer, 2018). This, however, is only one part of a complex agricultural response to options and opportunities. In communities that encounter greater vulnerability, and where there is less ability to overcome negative outcomes, diversifications can take the form of long-cycle, higher-yielding crops shifting to short-cycle, lower-yielding crops. Maize might be switched to pulses, for example. These forms of diversification focus on crops with lower yields per hectare, and while successfully compensating for climatic risks, they decrease overall agricultural output. One might view this as turning uncertainty into risk or trading higher return potential for stability. Farmers in Wolaita argue that they would grow long-cycle cereal crops but fear that if the rains fail, the entire yield will be lost. Short-cycle crops also address food shortages in the short-term. The shift from higher-yielding crops to lower-yielding crops due to vulnerability is not a unique finding for Wolaita. In a long-term study in southern Ethiopia, Tsegaye and Struik (2002) found that households with relatively lower to middle levels of resources grew fewer perennial crops, focusing instead on shorter-term seasonal crops. The patterns of crop switching due to higher levels of climate-related risk are also seen outside of Ethiopia (e.g., Burke and Lobell, 2010; Tambo, 2016).

Similarly, in the communities focused upon in this study, the one with irrigation, where average food security is stronger and relative wealth is higher, diversifications were fewer in number and took different forms. Generally, these could be classified as higher-cost options that have the potential to offer increased income, but they also have indirect costs such as multi-year delays to obtain returns on investments. Consider planting an avocado tree. You need to buy the sapling and the land has to be set aside as the tree takes seven years to mature and produce fruit. In diversifications of this type, there are direct (investment capital) and indirect (delay of return) costs. Not all smallholders have the opportunity and ability to do this. Community members in the other communities knew about diversification options of this sort but were unable to overcome the barriers or bear the costs (direct and indirect). Another positive impact of irrigation is that it enables crop diversification, as new crops can be grown (e.g., tomatoes) as well as additional harvests to be reaped (3-4 yields per year instead of 1-2) and more yields to be sold in the market.

Engaging in new and diverse forms of earning one's living, known as livelihood diversification, is also not necessarily a strength. Off-farm and non-farm opportunities are forms of livelihood diversifications and exemplify the diverse meaning that can be drawn from their practice. Some livelihood choices are opportunistic and a sign of strength (e.g., starting a new business of buying and selling goods), while other diversifications are due to vulnerability and a lack of other viable choices (e.g., vulnerability migration to towns to work as a day laborer). The community with irrigation is literally divided by a road: one side has access to irrigation, the other does not. Community members agreed that those on "the other side of the road" were "food insecure" and their "situation is very bad." By contrast, in the irrigated section of the community, only those with limited land or living in specific challenging circumstances faced chronic food insecurity.

Some forms of livelihood diversification can be understood as an expression of vulnerability and food insecurity. For instance, collecting firewood and grass is done as a last resort because these tasks are labor intensive and poorly remunerated: a day or two of this kind of work may result in only 15 ETB (approximately US$0.70). Additionally, these endeavors could be considered maladaptive because the activity is insufficient to meet basic needs and can foster conflict over resource use in communal areas. By contrast, some livelihood diversifications, such as starting a business to make and sell handicrafts like wood products of bedframes and chairs, are high-value. However, these livelihood options require upfront costs (materials, tools) and skills. Selling these products can create a valuable form of income generation outside of the agricultural cycle. Similarly, those with dairy cows, who are amongst the more food secure, enhance their income with the sale of butter and milk. The returns on investment (be that labor or financial) are much greater for these types of livelihood diversification. The contrast between different livelihood diversification types makes clear that governments and their partners (as well as the indicators in the SDGs) need to more critically reflect on the assumption that diversification is a sign of community or household strength/adaptive capacity.

Change over time

Krishna's Stages of Progress methodology emphasizes status change over time, focusing on people falling into and overcoming poverty. In other words, the findings of the methodology have emphasized people who have experienced significant status changes. The Stages of Food Security methodology I employed in this case study was designed with similar expectations. A critical assessment of Krishna's (2010) findings suggests that he may have overemphasized change, as it only applies to a minority of households. While Krishna's work shed light on the movement into and out of poverty, it failed to focus on the stability of the majority of households. As would be expected, households around the world experience some change—life and livelihoods are not static. The data in Wolaita suggests that significant change took place for a minority of households over 10- and 25-year periods and that most experience moderate or minor changes over the long term.

The reasons for positive significant changes in food security status in the three communities in Wolaita varied. For some households, significant positive changes occurred following investments, for example, in a donkey-drawn cart that provided regular income or purchasing fruit trees. Other positive changes included the benefits of long-term investments in education which resulted, for example, in a household member securing local, skilled employment as teachers or healthcare professionals. Access to irrigation was an enabler for significant positive improvements. The direct impacts included more stable crop yields, a reduction of vulnerability and months of food shortages, and increased household income. Other positive changes resulting from access to irrigation included the introduction of new crops and therefore new market sale options; a greater ability to send all children to school and to allow them to complete higher levels of education; and greater investments aimed at increasing income and returns such as new fruit trees, means of transportation and livestock.

The reasons for significant negative changes in Wolaita were similar to Krishna's (2010) findings, including family illness, deaths and burdensome debt. However, a cause more specific to the rural Ethiopian context was due to land being taken by the government (expropriated for the "public good" with minimal compensation and no ability for landholders to contest the expropriation process). These expropriations occur legally as the government owns all the land. The government can, and does, seize land for space to build institutions such as schools, Farmer Training Centers and government buildings. It also expropriates land for infrastructure (e.g., highways and railways) and to lease to investors (discussed in more detail in Chapter 6). In the three communities in Wolaita, government expropriation of land accounted for a fifth of all reported instances of significant negative change of household food security status.

On 10- and 25-year timeframes, our household survey in the Wolaitan communities suggested that the situation for many households had worsened (see Figure 10). The remote community stands out because the situation of more than a third of households significantly worsened. Focus group discussions identified this trend as largely driven by land fragmentation, population growth and a lack of access to services. The negative trends were also related to a lack of market access for sale and purchase of goods, the high costs and barriers in accessing healthcare (particularly emergency care), less access to supportive services (e.g., government activity and NGOs impacted by the tarmac bias; Chambers, 1983) and fewer alternative livelihood opportunities (e.g., day labor in the town or the roadside selling goods) to overcome challenges.

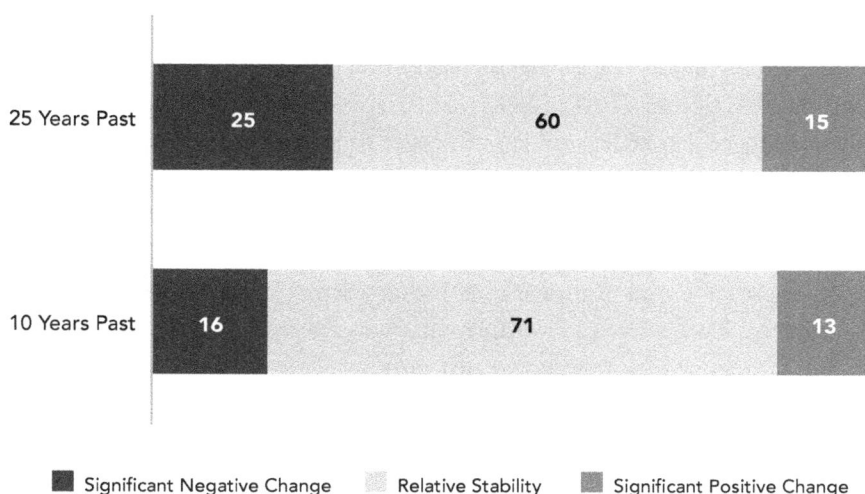

Figure 10. *Aggregated Change (%) of Wolaitan Communities Comparing Present to 10- and 25 -Years Past**

Source: Household surveys, 2015
*Note: Household survey replies of "moderate" and "no change" replies are combined

There are challenges with survey data such as this that relies on self-reported perceptions of change. For instance, data is limited to those who have remained in the community. As well, answers to questions about change depended upon how individuals thought about the past. For example, some who view the past positively recall more stable and regular rainfall, lower costs of goods and more communal land available for livestock grazing. In contrast, those with a more negative view of the past reflect on weak government support, insufficient infrastructure (no roads or irrigation) and fewer opportunities to send children to school. Another potential bias concerns households reporting negative change as a means to secure additional support. As with indicators on generalized input use (see Chapter 6), this critical analysis of metrics and data suggests that greater nuance is required. During this time period in the Wolaitan communities positive change (e.g., introduction of safety net, health posts and school) and negative change (e.g., land fragmentation, climate change, population growth) have occurred at the same time. People experience positive and negative changes in tandem. Yet, in our household survey we inappropriately required respondents to provide one generalized response. Due to these biases and challenges, I suggest that these findings (Figure

10) be taken as trends rather than as authoritative representations of shifts. As with Krishna (2010), I have focused upon the drivers of change, rather than specific figures. This research and Krishna's work highlight the need for more specific metrics and data in order to provide greater specificity.

There is some evidence that supports the general negative trend indicated in Figure 10 (see Mandefro, 2016). As it relates to the case study presented in this book, in 1998-00 Tsegaye and Struik (2002) conducted a Participatory Rural Appraisal in Areka, within Wolaita Zone, wherein community leaders and key informants contributed to the creation of a list of factors used for relative wealth ranking. In comparing the findings, although they are from different parts of Wolaita and were conducted almost 20 years apart, it is notable how similar the distribution of relative statuses is. However, comparing the findings of that older study to our data suggests that asset holdings have generally decreased over the last two decades and that food security has weakened. At the same time, Tsegaye and Struik's approach focused on input from community leaders, which may have affected the definitions of ranking categories, whereas my data came from diverse members of the community.

Strengths

While the sections above highlight various vulnerabilities, numerous strengths and opportunities were discussed as they relate to each factor (e.g., access to markets, irrigation, education, relative wealth). Strengths are also to be found the sociocultural fabric of life in Wolaita. A socio-cultural strength found across these communities was a voluntary, community-based redistribution practice of food gifting. A typical food gift to food insecure households is enset. A mother leading a female-headed household describes the gift givers as having large landholdings, dairy cattle, oxen and donkeys. She says the givers tend to be extended family or households in close proximity, who may send a few kilograms of food once per month. This amount tends to provide for a family with a day or two food. Redistribution is not a fully accurate term, however, as the gifting is not usually done proactively but in response to requests. A recipient of such gifts explained that "no one brings food to poor people's homes; the poor go and ask from them." Nonetheless, having these practices is a socio-cultural strength, where sharing with the most vulnerable is routine and expected.

Families proactively seek to diversify their income sources by investing in the education of their children. While the expectations are not formal, there is an understanding that children who migrate will help their family to the best of their ability. To this end, remittance has gained significant attention in the literature, notably in the recognition that global remittance is three times larger than global aid flows (Provost, 2013) and offers opportunities for poverty reduction (Beyene, 2014; Eversole and Johnson, 2014). Domestic remittances in Wolaita are relatively common, being sent to almost a third of all households. These sums are relatively minor but important nonetheless. And they could be larger if employment opportunities improved via better skills training or general economic development, for example.

Despite enthusiasm in the development studies literature regarding international remittances, the impact in Wolaita, to date, is negligible. The instances when a household in the communities participating in this study did receive international remittances were well known within the community, due to their rarity. This included a priest who was regularly supported by family in Italy, for example. While vast sums of money are flowing globally as remittances, my research indicates that much more research is required to understand where these flows have impact within receiving countries. The experience in Wolaita highlights that it is not the most vulnerable households in rural Ethiopia who receive a share of the large flows of international remittances. It is more likely the case that highly educated urban migrants who relocate internationally are sending remittances to relatively well-off urban residents. There are reasons why this is likely the case. In order to access international remittances, recipients are commonly required to have government-issued identification and access to a bank branch. They also need access to communication technology, which excludes most rural residents. For the majority in rural communities, even these basic requirements pose daunting barriers. However, remittances are a potential strength that has not yet been fully realized in these communities.

Other considerations

Community members felt that malaria was a serious concern that affected their food security status by reducing household labor, causing child mortality and consuming household income. Research by Burlando (2015) indicates that malaria can also have negative impacts on education levels for those living in areas where malaria is endemic. Across all three communities, despite differences in water availability, such as the presence of year-round irrigation, the average annual number of reported malaria cases per household was consistent at 1.8. Malaria was a key concern for residents of the remote community, who highlighted the year-long burden it represented, combined with a consistent lack of medicine at the community health post. Where available, the cost of medicine is 30 ETB (approximately US$1.40) for adults and 15 ETB for children (approximately US$0.70), resulting in many having to decide between food for the day or medical treatment. As noted above, a full day of collecting firewood or grass and carrying it to the town for sale earns the most vulnerable only 10 to 15 ETB. Thus malaria treatment can require up to three days of labor-intensive work.

The government is working to reduce malaria incidence through spraying, including with the use of DDT.[20] This, however, has significant negative impacts on human health, particularly for infants who are being fed foods with high levels of DDT residue. A study by Mekonen et al. (2015) found DDT residue in every single maize sample in southwest Ethiopia, indicating the extent of its use in the region. While this research finds that irrigation has significant positive impacts, it must also be recognized that malaria transmission increases (up to a six-fold incidence increase) around irrigation schemes, requiring agricultural interventions to be integrated with broader concerns and to anticipate as much as possible the impact of unintended consequences (Kibret et al., 2014). Similar unintended consequences, including an increase in the incidence of malaria, have been found with the creation of hydroelectric and irrigation dams elsewhere in Ethiopia (Hathaway, 2008; Yewhalaw et al., 2014).

Reflections on the method and the findings

One of the greatest strengths emerging from the Stages of Food Security methodology is the depth of qualitative insight. The process resulted in a reformulation of questions and metrics, and their co-analysis facilitated the emergence of highly contextualized information about the socio-cultural, economic, political, historical and gendered vulnerabilities to food insecurity. As noted at the outset of this chapter, these findings complement and enrich other approaches and available evidence. The

20   Dichlorodiphenyltrichloroethane

objective of Chapter 4 was to outline what a process using knowledge co-production can look like and why it might be undertaken. This chapter analyzed what these new approaches have contributed in terms of our understanding of food security. The level of detail presented in Chapter 5 was limited, often by way of example and explanation. For the interested reader, detailed papers have been written on the politics of the safety net (Cochrane and Tamiru, 2016), rural borrowing and debt (Cochrane and Thornton, 2017), worldviews embedded within extension systems that diverge from farmer decision-making (Cochrane, 2017b), inequalities related to ethnicity and geography (Cochrane and Rao, 2019), gendered youth migration (Cochrane and Vercillo, 2018), the land certification system (Cochrane and Hadis, 2019), amongst others.

Taking a summative approach, this chapter set out to assess vulnerability to food insecurity using the participatory, co-produced approaches outlined in the previous chapter. The results from the quantitative and qualitative data demonstrated that food security cannot be understood with isolated metrics. Understanding food security requires analyses of interconnected experiences that exist in dynamic and complex systems. This research showed that "common knowledge" for community members may not be considered in typical food security research, such as the role and types of migration or the processes of borrowing and resulting indebtedness. With the quantitative and qualitative insight produced by my field research in hand, along with a deconstruction of assumptions embedded within the metrics and data, the following chapter will seek to explain why, in this context of chronic food insecurity and significant vulnerabilities thereto, the adoption of government support programs and services is low.

CHAPTER SIX

POLICIES, PROGRAMS AND SERVICES

Given the prevalence of food insecurity in Ethiopia, one might wonder why it is that rates of adoption of government programs and services are low. Up to a third of all households discontinue their participation in rural agricultural and livelihoods programs and services before completion (Bonger, Ayele and Kuma, 2004; EEA/EEPRI, 2006; Gebrehiwot and van der Veen, 2014; Spielman, Mekonnen and Alemu, 2012; Taffesse, Dorosh and Gemessa, 2012). Earlier chapters have provided some insight into why this might be the case (e.g., services targeting relative wealthy households are not suitable for the most vulnerable members of society). However, in order to fully understand why low rates of adoption prevail in Ethiopia, we need to look more closely at the rural agricultural policies, programs and services on offer. It should be clear from earlier chapters that households do not experience these offerings in a uniform way. So rather than asking why the adoption of policies, programs and services is uneven, it might be better to ask who is benefiting from the ways in which they are currently implemented and who is not.

The programs and services described in this chapter are, for the most part, federal programs offered throughout most of the country. The services that are analyzed include agricultural extension supports and services via Farmer Training Centers, the land certification system, the social safety net, policies regarding foreign direct investment in agriculture and the initiatives related to the Ethiopian Commodity Exchange. For some findings, the data from the case study of Wolaita Zone ought not be generalized to other regional states. This is due to different socio-cultural, political and historical contexts, and because the programs are implemented in unique ways or have unique impacts in different regions and agroecological settings. However, as Escobar (1994: 109) explains, from "the perspective of institutional ethnography, a local situation is less a case study than an entry point to the study of institutional and discursive forces and how these are related to larger socioeconomic processes." From this perspective, this chapter builds on the case study presented in the last chapter and provides a means to better understand the implementation and impact of programs and services offered to smallholder farmers. It also outlines the role of institutions and the political and power-based drivers of activity.

Rural lives and livelihoods cannot be understood by looking simply at household survey data regarding agricultural practices, and based upon that try to identify the causes for why decisions are taken. The broader, complex environment in which agriculture takes place must also be understood. This book cannot provide a complete picture of this broader context, but it is worth briefly mentioning a small selection of relatively recent changes that have affected rural lives and livelihoods in Ethiopia. Healthcare services and education options have rapidly expanded. Significant infrastructure has been developed and as has broader coverage of telecommunications services. Resettlement and relocation continue to be major causes of positive and negative changes (Berry and Ofcansky, 2004; Cohen and Isaksson, 1987; de Waal, 1991; Rahmato, Pankhurst and van Uffelen, 2013; Tareke, 2009; Woldmeskel, 1989). In parts of Ethiopia the creation of large-scale hydroelectric dams has significantly altered livelihoods and caused displacement (Derbew, 2013; Hurd, 2013; Oakland Institute, 2013). Major changes like these interact with the policies, programs and services discussed in this chapter. We shall focus on the policies, programs and services that have had the most significant impact on food security from a rural livelihoods and agricultural perspective.

Agricultural Extension Service & Farmer Training Centers

Agricultural support services have been offered for the last 85 years in Ethiopia. These types of support services have ranged over time but include activities such as farmer training, the provision of agricultural inputs, the development of demonstration plots, local research centers, the provision of financial credit services and so forth. These services are provided by local government personnel, called "development agents", often several staff having specific areas of focus (e.g., livestock, crops, natural resource management). The durability of these support services is a testament to the primary role that smallholder agriculture plays in the national economy and the fact that it employs a majority of the nation's people (Belay, 2003). In 1931 the government established the first agriculturally focused school, and in 1943 limited agricultural extension services were provided to farmers by the Ministry of Agriculture, while the foundations of modern Ethiopian agricultural extension work were laid in the 1950s (Belay, 2003). In partnership with the United States, the Imperial government established what would become Haramaya University (initially the Imperial Ethiopian College of Agricultural and Mechanical Arts) in 1952, with a mandate to develop a national agricultural extension program and thereafter expanded extension service provision (Rahmato, 2008). A five-year plan in 1957-1961 sought to modernize agriculture, advance physical and social infrastructure and develop industry to meet domestic needs (Bahru, 2014). The following five-year plan (1963-1967) aimed to improve agricultural production and to transform the agricultural economy into an industrial one (Bahru, 2014). However, land given out during the Imperial period was almost exclusively allotted to loyalists, civil servants and soldiers to the exclusion of the rural majority who frequently worked in feudal conditions (Bahru, 1991).

According to Belay (2003), in 1963 the responsibility of the extension program was taken over by the Ministry of Agriculture, at which time there were 77 extension workers employed throughout the country. By 1970, the extension services remained relatively small in scale, having increased its personnel up to 125 regular staff and 75 specialists working in the coffee growing areas of the country (Rahmato, 2008). In 1971, the World Bank began providing funding and support for Agricultural Development Units, which were the beginnings of more substantial, localized support services that included research and piloting of new crops and planting methodologies. Throughout the Imperial period, the government's emphasis, investment and support of agriculture was primarily geared toward large-scale commercial farm operations (Bahru, 1991; Belay, 2003). Notably, however, in 1973, planners of the state argued that smallholder farmers "utilize their cropped areas more intensively and frequently realize higher yield per hectare" than large-scale operations (quoted in Rahmato,

2008: 54). This fact did not lead to policy change; the two subsequent governments continued to prioritize large-scale operations, the Derg opting for large state-run farms while the current EPRDF government has focused on foreign investment in agricultural modernization.

The Agricultural Development Unit in Wolaita was one of the first of such units to be established, in 1971, with support from the World Bank (Belay, 2003; Berhanu and Poulton, 2014; Chinigo, 2015; Rahmato, 2008). A number of services that continue to be offered by extension workers were first offered during the 1960s, including input use, training, field demonstrations, marketing and credit services, promotion of agricultural technologies and support to community-level organizations (Berhanu and Poulton, 2014). Although the coverage of these services was low, and largely limited to roadside communities, there exist seven decades of institutional knowledge and experience about why, how and when extension services are (in)effective, and for whom. For example, as Belay (2003: 56) notes, the government "realized that the comprehensive package projects [in the 1960s and 1970s] failed to serve the very people for whom they were destined," and that instead the main beneficiaries were large landholders and commercial operations. The ability to support rural residents was limited due to the nature of land tenure at that time, with large landholders and tenants operating in a fashion similar to a feudal model (land tenure is discussed in more detail below). Land inequality was one of the first challenges addressed by reforms implemented by the Derg government, which overthrew the Imperial government in 1974 (discussed in more detail below).

Due to the instability that preceded and followed the coup d'etat, agricultural extension work was limited until 1981, when the minimal extension packages introduced by the Imperial government were restarted and expanded to cover more districts, from 280 to 440, out of a total of 580 (Belay, 2003). One of the organizational shifts instituted by the Derg was the division of activities by component (water, crops, livestock), resulting in duplication of limited staff responsibilities and misuse of minimal resources. Extension staff were also tasked with other government activities, such as collecting taxes (Belay, 2003). Notably, the interconnectivity between agricultural supportive services and tax collection continues to be a way that the government extracts resources from rural citizens, which in the current period is done via the land certification system (Cochrane and

Hadis, 2019). Although the government had initially expanded the program coverage, the limitations of staff and resources (as well as a strategy shift, to the Peasant Agriculture Development Extension Program) resulted in it opting to focus on "high potential areas so as to raise their production and productivity by channeling the limited resources and extension services toward them" (Belay, 2003: 60). The number of districts covered by extension activities was reduced to 148 after 1985, thereby disproportionately offering services to those in better agroecological settings and revoking them from those in more precarious and challenging situations. Furthermore, extension activities continued to focus on large, commercial farms, even after the land reform took place. Even with this focus, during the 1981-1985 period, packages continued to be ineffective due to "poor research-extension linkage" (Belay, 2003: 59) and their "inflexible and top-down nature" (Belay, 2003: 61).

Conflict throughout the 1980s disrupted agricultural extension activities. Further disruption took place in the early 1990s, following the instating of the EPRDF government in 1991. The "Agricultural Development-Led Industrialization" plan in 1992 also (re)emphasized the role of modernizing agriculture. Policy and program experimentation occurred throughout the 1990s, with the integration of participatory approaches and demonstration plots and the promotion of improved seed varieties and technology packages, however the extent of 'participation' was questionable or was understood as consenting to decisions made rather than involvement in decision making (Belay, 2003). The focus of activities continued to be in areas of high potential for agricultural production, with a slow expansion over time to include more districts throughout the country. Modernizing agriculture was outlined in the first (GTP I, 2010/11 – 2014/15) and second Growth and Transformation Plans (GTP II, 2015/2016 – 2019-2020). While some of the details have changed, the macro-economic focus on commercial agricultural remained.

However, one notable change was the rapid expansion and geographic scaling of the agricultural extension system. In 1995 there were 2,500 agricultural extension workers (Berhanu, 2012), which rose to more than 14,000 in 2001 (Belay, 2003) and by 2010 there were 45,000, with an aim to reach 66,000 (Berhanu, 2012; GFRAS, 2012). These community-based staff work to support farmers by providing them with knowledge, training and connections to other government services. To train this workforce, the government established 25 Agricultural Training and Vocational Educational and Training colleges, which have graduated tens of thousands of agricultural extension workers. The training offered by extension workers to farmers varies by region, along with crops, soils, rainfall and other agroecological factors, but tends to focus on agronomy (improving crop production, water utilization and management), with lesser attention to supporting community organizations, such as cooperatives (Berhanu, 2012). Farmer Training Centers, which started in 2004, were developed throughout the country as a means to support the agricultural extension workers. The Centers are places where demonstrations and training are held. As of 2012, several thousand of these centers were in operation, with a total of 15,000 planned (Berhanu, 2012).

Berhanu and Poulton (2014: S197) argue that agricultural extension operates with "twin imperatives" of economic growth via improved production and the entrenching of political control. As outlined in this brief history of Ethiopian agricultural extension, non-agricultural political objectives have long been integrated into the activities of this program, such as extension workers collecting taxes (Belay, 2003). This dual purpose may also reflect the government renaming staff from agricultural extension workers to "development agents".[21] Berhanu (2012) suggests one of the primary self-serving political reasons for agricultural extension programming is that the overthrow of both the Imperial and Derg governments were rooted in smallholder support. As noted in Chapter 2, both of their governments fell in relation to severe rural food insecurity events. Rewarding rural supporters, however, is not all that is occurring, according to Berhanu and Poulton (2014). They note that as the program has expanded, so too has rural political control. Rural programs and services, they point out, are monopolized by the government (including the provision of seed, fertilizer and credit) and therefore not politically neutral. Party loyalty is prioritized when staffing decisions are made for agricultural extension posts and the implementation of agricultural extension services is used to reward party supporters. Political patronage in rural service implementation has been pointed out by Cochrane and Tamiru (2016), de Waal (2015), Abegaz (2011), Ketsela

---

21 I have largely used "agricultural extension worker" in this book to ensure clarity, as the new title does not make it immediately clear what this position entails. It appears that the Derg introduced this terminology; I can find no references using it predating 1974.

(2006) and Gudina (2003). Additionally, Berhanu and Poulton (2014) point out that extension workers regularly engage in political activities, including campaigning for the ruling party. Pausewang (2002) writes about how these services, and farmers' reliance on these government-controlled extension services (particularly when indebted due to input purchases), are used to ensure votes for the ruling party.

Conducting research that integrates aspects of power and politics requires intentional design. Quantitative data, such as that obtained through household surveys, may not capture the ways in which agricultural extension services are politicized. Mixed-methods and qualitative data provide opportunities for these contextualizations to emerge. If questions about agricultural extension services are asked with power and politics in mind, as outlined in Chapter 5, new perspectives can be made visible. Consider the data obtained through the utilization of the Stages of Food Security methodology in Wolaita: Table 3 presents quantitative data, which outlines the adoption rates for several major agricultural activities (e.g., adoption of improved seeds, fertilizers and pesticides), as is commonly done in the literature. However, in the focus group discussions the crop- and input-specific nuances were made clear. For example, for farmers it was not a matter of using or not using "improved seed", as many household surveys ask them. Farmers were in agreement that the improved cabbage seed provided by the government was not suited to their agroecology, and therefore they saved their "traditional" cabbage seeds. There was also agreement that the majority of farmers used improved maize seed and the "traditional" seeds were now "lost." Thus, the simple use of improved seed, a common survey question (e.g., Abate et al., 2016; Million, 2014), provides limited insight regarding the knowledge and practices of farmers. A mixed-methods approach, as was used in Wolaita, enabled many additional layers of insight to be drawn out that complemented the household survey data.

Table 3. *Prevalence of Agricultural Practices in Study Sites (by % of households)*

Community	Improved seed	Seed saving	Fertilizer	Pesticide
Rural	58	30	85	82
Remote	80	64	93	64
With irrigation	79	51	94	73

Source: Household Surveys, 2015

Farmers in Wolaita highlight a range of other issues, many of which are not made clear in quantitative survey data. Yet, these are viewed as critical for farmers and their assessment of agricultural extension services. Consider the example of a government-introduced "improved" variety of taro, a widely used root crop, in comparison to cabbage and enset. The new variety of taro came from a regional research center and was widely adopted throughout Wolaita. The popularity of this variety was due to it having a higher yield compared to other varieties and because it was also easier to prepare for consumption. While this taro variety was adopted, the cabbage seed promoted by extension services was not. Farmers explained that this variety of cabbage was not well suited to their soils and did not produce as well as their locally saved seed. Enset is different than taro and cabbage because it has been granted limited attention in agricultural extension services. As a result, farmers themselves cultivate a diversity of enset varieties, using "traditional" methods. Farmers continue to purposefully maintain a range of enset varieties, each with specific traits planted for unique purposes (Tsegaye and Struik, 2002). Enset has a strong socio-cultural connection to ideas of identity and livelihoods. Despite its importance as a crop supporting food security, limited research has been conducted on it. Instead, market and export crops have been given priority, such as avocado and, in the irrigated areas, tomato. These have been newly introduced, with support from the agricultural extension services. When analyzed on a crop-by-crop basis, questions of adoption become more clear. Few farmers in Wolaita adopted the entire "package" advocated by the government extension system, but they did so in very informed ways. Farmers negotiate and navigate the menu of options available to them and determine what they understand as best meeting their needs and priorities.

This is also the case for agricultural inputs, such as fertilizers and pesticides. Farmers explain that pesticides are only used for teff and vegetables, which are both high-value crops sold to the market. While these crops are crucial for annual income, there is an increasing awareness of the negative health impacts of pesticides, which may be another reason why these chemicals are not used on crops typically consumed within smallholder households. It is noteworthy that pesticides are not well regulated in Ethiopia, and there are multiple reports of illness due to exposure (Karunamoorthi, Mohammed and Wasssie, 2012; Nigatu, Bratveit and Moen, 2016).

In theory, assessments of the agricultural extension system would consider adoption as a key measure of its appropriateness and effectiveness. As the above demonstrates, aggregated adoption rates make invisible a wealth of knowledge. A more suitable assessment ought to be conducted on a crop-by-crop, and input-by-input basis. However, answering such a survey would place a heavy burden on farmers. If, for example, one were to ask about the range of inputs used for each primary crop, the survey would balloon in size. For the household survey used in the case study from the last chapter, adding an assessment of the range of inputs used for each primary crop would have added at least 48 questions (twelve key crops for at least four input options). In my experience, focus group discussions were sufficient to provide the detail required, and thus lengthy and burdensome surveys were not used. These purposeful diverse crop- and input-specific practices demonstrate the limited usefulness of survey questions asking for generalizations. Beyond missing nuances (Chambers, 2008), this approach may lead to incorrect findings and therefore contribute to poorly informed design and implementation of programs and policies. At this juncture it is worth reiterating the usefulness of participatory, co-produced research methods, which enabled this richness of information to emerge.

In addition to questions of what seeds and inputs best meet the needs and priorities of farmers, the agricultural system may have low adoption due to limitations in its implementation. Due to poor quality and irregular seed supply, as well as high costs, many farmers continue to save their own seeds. This, however, is not simply a matter of lowering the cost of seeds and improving the supply or selecting for suitability. Many farmers cite issues with later generations of "improved" seed. As expected for hybrid seed, the first generation produces greater yields, but later generations do not retain this performance level. These seeds are not genetically modified (GM) seeds, which remain heavily restricted for food crops in Ethiopia (Abraham, 2013). Instead, they are varieties developed through conventional plant breeding and introduced to farmers via the extension system. Regional agricultural research centers within Ethiopia, which are public enterprises, support seed breeding and replication. Farmers in Wolaita explain that new maize varieties were introduced between 10 and 15 years ago, but it was only in the last three to five years that yields began to drop (this may not only be due to the passing of generations, but also changes to rainfall, temperature and soil quality). Since the varieties performed well when they were first introduced, most stopped saving the seeds they traditionally saved. As a result, farmers in Wolaita explain that the "traditional" seeds "disappeared because the hybrid seeds that were introduced were more productive and all farmers changed their seed." The unintended result may have been a narrowing of the genetic pool, which farmers draw upon to select for different traits other than yield, such as drought tolerance or suitability to different elevations. There are seed bank initiatives in Ethiopia seeking to preserve genetic diversity (Provost, 2014), but they remain few and far between.

Some seeds continue to be saved for suitability, as in the example of cabbage given above (their own variety grows better than the government-distributed one). Seed may also be saved to maintain genetic diversity and unique variety traits. In Wolaita, diverse varieties of enset are intentionally grown; in parts of southern Ethiopia at least 50 varieties of enset are intentionally cultivated (Tsegaye and Struik, 2002). In other parts of the country a great diversity of seed for cereals such as maize and barley are purposely maintained (Beyene, Botha and Myburg, 2005; Samberg et al., 2013). This diversity of options has enabled farmers to adjust to different conditions, such as elevation, soil type and moisture, even if yields are not optimized. Surveys often assess if farmers are adopting all of the advocated practices, crops, varieties and inputs, a "package adoption." However, since very few farmers adopt everything that is advocated, some data suggests that agricultural extension services are a failure. Farmers are not adopting the package of agricultural extension in full. "Failure" here is a relative term; it is a failure for an agricultural extension system that aimed to support farmers and meet their needs. However, agricultural practices as well as data from the Central Statistical Agency of Ethiopia suggests that farmers are making well-informed decisions suited to their environments and are increasing yield per hectare for nearly all crops.

The greatest agricultural extension success is arguably fertilizer. At the household level in all three sites of this study the rates of fertilizer usage are quite high (85-95%). This is reflective of the high levels of national fertilizer use. The finding at the local level is in line with research findings that suggest that higher population density and smaller land size are associated with higher fertilizer use (Josephson, Ricker-Gilbert and Florax, 2014). Population density and land size, however, may not be the only factors worth considering when seeking to understand the adoption of fertilizer.

Some Wolaitan farmers say that they purchase fertilizer on credit because of political pressure, only to later resell it in an attempt to recoup that forced investment. The pressure to purchase fertilizer is serious. In communities in the highlands of Amhara, I was told of farmers being arrested for refusing to take fertilizer on credit. The resale results in a loss. A 50-kilogram bag of fertilizer is purchased for 700 ETB (US$32.50) and might be sold on the market for 600 ETB (US$27.85). This expenditure, and the subsequent loss, may account for a significant portion of poorer households' annual income. For these households, a best-case scenario of laborious collection of grass or firewood along with carrying it for market sale in a single day is 15 ETB (US$0.70); the up-front costs of a fertilizer purchase are thus equivalent to approximately 47 workdays. Community members in Wolaita freely expressed that these inputs were purchased because of political expectations; they "buy it to show the government, and then sell it." Actual input use, therefore, in this case is not a result of farmers' ability to access it or their desire to use it but at least partially related to political pressure.

The apparent successful spread of fertilizer use in smallholder Ethiopian contexts is supported by other research (Taffesse, Dorosh and Gemessa, 2012). In a study of 5,700 rural households, Million (2014) found that households with higher levels of wealth (measured in asset holdings, specifically livestock) were more likely to utilize fertilizer, while those with less wealth were less likely. In addition to having greater wealth, Million's household survey found that the households with better access to training, fertilizer and improved seed had larger landholdings, suggesting a double penalty for the less advantaged. My research has also found this to be the case. As discussed in Chapter 5, there are financial barriers due to having fewer assets, and a lack of assets can result in exclusion from support programs. The programs formally prioritize wealthier farmers because they have higher potentials to produce. Farmers may also informally be prioritized for socio-cultural (e.g., ethnicity and language) and political reasons (e.g., being a member of a political party). All of this is not to suggest that fertilizer is unwanted or unsuccessful, but rather the findings from my research as well as that of other scholars illustrates the complex socio-economic context that limits the use of this input.

While some agricultural extension services have a positive impact (e.g., access to fertilizer in rural and remote communities or access to market information, as discussed below), there are other components of the extension package that perform far less well. Examples of this include agricultural training and the provision of credit. While these are two examples of supports that might be considered as failed components of agricultural extension services, the discontinuation and dismal levels of complete package-adoption do not represent the actual impact of the programs. A much different finding would emerge if the programs and services were provided and assessed based on their individual components. Specific assessments would enable far more specific recommendations to be made, because they would improve understanding about why certain components have worked well while others have not. Yet, ever since agricultural extension began in Ethiopia, packaged approaches have been utilized. After more than half a century, many farmers do not adopt seed and inputs packages in full. In other words, they do not use all the seeds promoted and provided by extension services nor all the inputs, or all the inputs for all the crops they plant. When we look at adoption of seed or input for individual crops rather than complete packages, we find a much more nuanced decision making process; for crops, adoption rates range from 29% to 71%, with significant regional differences (Tefera et al., 2016). As noted, that does not necessarily equate with failure for all components of the package.

The data on credit is challenging to untangle. Farmers in Wolaita perceive the government microfinance institute and the government provision of credit for inputs as a single government entity. While the institutions do technically differ (one being a government microfinance institute and the other a credit service offered via the agricultural extension program), both are government operations intimately connected at the community-level by the same personnel promoting development activities. This makes survey data questionable, and government data on microfinance lending is challenging to obtain. One data set I was given from southern Ethiopia suggests that fewer than 5% of households access credit via the microfinance institute (Cochrane and Thornton, 2017). By contrast, some research suggests there is a positive relationship and even a causal link between access to credit and input use, since fertilizer may actually be obtained through government credit (e.g., Abate et al., 2016).

One of the causes of uptake failure for microfinance is a lack of accessibility; farmers need to come to a microfinance office branch, often located in towns and cities, which is difficult for remote community members, and particularly those with fewer financial resources. An even greater barrier is the inflexible terms of repayment and the very real threat of having assets and/or land taken away as a means of debt collection by the government. Community members explained this was a primary reason why they did not seek such loans. The risk was high. For farmers using credit for agricultural purposes, if rains fail and they are unable to repay, they might lose their entire livelihood, their land, and as a result the potential future livelihoods of their children. Even if the instances of land loss due to loan payment default were few, they are well known. Smallholder farmers do not have control over the most important factor affecting their ability to repay—the rain—and thus the risk is too great. Farmers and policymakers use different rationales in their decision making processes (Cochrane, 2017b). In this instance, policymakers have focused on the potential for higher short-term returns (which are possible) while farmers focus on the risk of default (which is also possible). In this instance the barrier is not only a lack of options or opportunities for investment but also the disincentives for borrowing.

Agricultural training, which is given freely, provides an even more complicated set of results. Based on household survey data, the communities with weaker food security interacted with agricultural extension workers more frequently but received less training (Cochrane, 2017c). Where food security is relatively stronger due to access to irrigation, the number of reported interactions with agricultural extension workers was relatively low but the number of farmers who reported received training was high. Thus, at face value, it would appear that greater interaction with extension staff is correlated with less training and greater food insecurity. The correlation makes no sense if we assume that interactions with extension staff primarily support agricultural livelihoods and offer training. Agricultural extension workers have multiple objectives and tasks, not all of which are related to improving agricultural livelihoods. For example, during election years extension workers often work to pull votes for the ruling party, and this is a time-consuming task. Thus, the higher number of reported interactions with extension workers may actually correlate with areas of greater political insecurity. Viewing the situation from this political perspective, the data becomes more coherent. Food insecurity has been historically related to political discontent, and the most food insecure communities were more actively engaged with by the "development agents" within their communities, who offer both carrots and sticks as incentives and disincentives for securing votes. In one community, an agricultural extension worker threatened to close the safety net program if the ruling party lost the election. As outlined above, political patronage of service and goods provision has long been common in rural Ethiopia and thus little has to be explained explicitly, as the consequences have been normalized.

In some instances, the lack of access to training is because of poor performance of agricultural extension workers. I have come across extension workers in different parts of Ethiopia who do not live in the community they are supposed to serve even though they are expected to do so. Life in rural and remote areas can be difficult, and some personnel instead choose to live in a nearby town. But because they do not have vehicles and are not given a travel stipend, they infrequently visit the community where they are supposed to be offering training. These extension workers rely on local contacts to provide information about the community when reporting to the government. In communities such as these, I found that few people even knew who the extension worker was.

Instituting programs to reduce rural absenteeism in workplaces is a challenge in rural Ethiopia. The Ministry of Health hires and trains community health workers from the area of work and provides housing for staff to ensure they remain within communities perceived as remote or too rural. By contrast, agricultural extension workers are not given housing and are not required to be from the area they serve. When I was working in northwestern Ethiopia, I encountered agricultural extension workers who were hired from different regions and who did not speak local languages.

The situation should not be viewed as dismal or corrupt. There are problems but there are also exemplary people and practices. In southern Ethiopia, I spent time with a group of extension workers at a large, well-functioning and active Farmer Training Center. Numerous crops were being tested and new methods piloted. The Farmer Training Center was selected by the regional government as a "model" for others to learn from. Community members were cognizant of the important role these workers played in actively supporting them and their agricultural livelihoods. However, even in well-functioning Farmer Training Centers like this one, there is only one per community and they serve an extended area. The result is unequal access to training and other forms of support as those living on the periphery of the coverage area have less frequent contact with extension workers and access to services, such as the Farmer Training Center.

Land Certification

Tenure in Ethiopia is often divided into two categories—pre-1975 and post-1975—that is, before and after the Derg government began a land reform program, which included the nationalization of all rural land and that nullified existing tenure agreements (Kebede, 2002). The radical change in tenure introduced by the Derg sought to end a form of property ownership that in most parts of Ethiopia benefited a minority. The Derg sought to redistribute land to the majority through local community organizations, which were also established by the Derg (Rahmato, 2004). The land reforms instituted by the Derg are, to a large extent, the basis of the present land tenure system under the EPRDF government.

During the pre-1975 period, land tenure was not uniform throughout the country. In the northern parts of Ethiopia, where settled agriculture had been practiced for millennia, customary land systems were dominant. In these northern areas, members of a particular lineage owned large areas of land, a claim that could be made through either matrilineal or patrilineal lines and a system wherein both males and females were eligible to inherit land (Kebede, 2002). The highlands were controlled by a revolving set of kings and their representatives, who allocated land as they wanted, creating a deep historical sense of land insecurity (Pankhurst, 1966).

In southern and eastern Ethiopia (which was not incorporated fully into the state until the nineteenth century), multiple tenure systems existed. The empires centered in eastern Ethiopia, such as Harar, and southern Ethiopia, such as Jimma, were oriented toward the laws of Islam and influenced by its jurisprudence relating to property rights (Sait and Lim, 2006). The pastoral Somali and Afar peoples, also influenced by Islamic law, practiced customary systems wherein groups collectively shared areas of land (Gebre Mariam, 1991; Helland, 2006; Hundie and Padmanabhan, 2008; Roth, 1988). In other parts of the country, such as in Kembatta, a king owned all the land and distributed land with obligations of taxes, tributes, labor and contributions to war efforts (Kebede, 2002).

The diversity of tenure systems that were practiced in the south formally ended with the conquest of those lands and their incorporation into the Ethiopian state, although many customary systems continue informally. One example of how informal customary systems continue to predominate in decision-making is inheritance. Ethiopian land laws stipulate that men and women have equal right to land acquisition and daughters are entitled to inherit land, however, according to Bezu and Holden (2014), as of 2012 only 3% of all landholders in Ethiopia were young women (15-29), and a vast majority of (male) household heads say that women will not inherit land from them (Bezu and Holden, 2014). In one district in Wolaita only 6% of household heads voiced the intention to bequeath land to their daughters (Bezu and Holden, 2014). Much more research is needed to better understand gendered land inheritance and holdings, and in some ways the new land certification makes this more challenging as multiple holders are listed. Qualitative research is needed to better assess the extent to which these changes have altered norms or the protection of rights.

The Marxist-inspired land reform implemented by the Derg was similar to the collectivization and redistribution policies implemented in other countries, such as in China and the Soviet Union, with each having its own unique manifestations (Barnett, 1953; Lin, 1990; Nolan, 1976). In the Ethiopian experience, the Derg redistributed land to all people, regardless of lineage, in an effort to end the feudal systems built upon entrenched and institutionalized discrimination. In addition to redistributing land held by large landholders, the reform sought to make the laws of landholding equal, whereas in the past members of religious and/or ethnic groups were barred from living, or owning property, in certain areas (Ahmad, 2000; Wolde Mariam, 1986). At the same time, customary forms of land tenure, some of which included institutionalized redistribution practices, were also barred. The Derg deemed that land transfers were only permitted from one family member to another, while leases, rentals, exchanges, mortgages and sales were prohibited. Additionally, land size was restricted to 10 hectares and the use of laborers was prohibited (Bahru, 1991; Kebede, 2002). Community associations, also called Peasant Associations, were created by the Derg and utilized to redistribute land throughout the country. These associations continue to operate as the lowest level of government administration in Ethiopia.

Critics of the Derg land reform argue that redistribution led to instability, was inefficient and inhibited the development of a land market (Rahmato, 2004). While redistribution offered a degree of land ownership equality, it also increased land insecurity as the idea of regular land redistribution processes took root. Landholders realized that the government could take and redistribute land at will—a process largely based on household size, which is constantly changing (Adem, 2019;

Holden and Yohannes, 2001). Indeed, many land redistribution processes did take place, turning this fear of land loss into a reality (e.g., Ege, 1997). However, many of the criticisms of the Derg relate not to the regime's ideas but to the way it implemented them. While the Derg successfully reformed land ownership throughout much of Ethiopia, it increasingly adopted violent tactics to achieve its objectives. Furthermore, those who were given redistributed land were not given permanent or secure tenure to the land, a situation that discouraged investments (it would not be until 1998 that the first land use certificate was issued, which was still not a right to land but at least recognized the user of it, as discussed more later in this chapter).

When the EPRDF overthrew the Derg they retained state ownership of land and made only minor adjustments to the tenure system. Some of these changes included the permissibility of short-term land rental and a reduction of land redistribution activities. While the government sought to retain ownership of all land, it also had to deal with problems that resulted from a lack of individual ownership such as conflict and irresponsible land use that has resulted in deforestation as well as soil degradation and erosion, and the discouragement of investment in land management due to a lack of tenure security. The Ethiopian Constitution continues to forbid the sale or exchange of land. However, regional states (Tigray in 1998, Amhara in 2003, and Oromia and SNNPR in 2004) have introduced land certification systems which allow individuals to gain the right of land use. While the system does not grant ownership rights and thus secure tenure, it does offer a greater degree of land security (Mekonnen, 2012).

While the land certification program was primarily aimed at reducing tenure insecurity and alleviating the resulting negative impact on investment (Deininger et al., 2003; Deininger et al., 2007), there were other reasons to make these changes, such as seeking a resolution to land conflict and finding a way to counter negative impacts on the land. Investment has increased since implementation and a number of other direct and indirect benefits have been realized: conflicts have been reduced, women's control of land has moderately improved and yields have risen (Bezabih, Holden and Mannberg, 2016; Deininger, Ali and Alemu, 2009; Deininger et al., 2007; Gebre-Egziabher, 2013; Hagos and Holden, 2013a; Hagos and Holden, 2013b; Holden, Deininger and Ghebru, 2011).

The existing tenure system, which only allows for direct family inheritance and prohibits changes to the land tenure system toward privatization, slows the urbanization process because if the land is left unused it returns to the government. A particularly strict policy was instituted in Tigray Regional State where only those dependent upon their parents can inherit land from them; those with land of their own or other sufficient livelihood options (e.g., government employment) are ineligible (Rahmato, 2004). As a result of the inheritance system, families do not move to urban areas as units. Households have members of the family stay in the rural area in order to retain control of the family land. The explicit aim of the inheritance laws is to restrict the means by which land can be transferred (although informal markets are common; Holden, Bezu and Tilahun, 2016; Holden and Ghebru, 2016). The indirect outcome works to slow urbanization and maintain family ties to rural communities. The land tenure system suits the interests of the Government of Ethiopia as it has recognized that rapid urbanization poses significant challenges, one of which is the high rate of urban unemployment (Mains, 2012; Serneels, 2007).

Several studies suggest that rural residents prefer the current system of public ownership to private ownership (Nega, 2002), including one study showing increasing resistance to the legalization of land sales (Holden and Bezu, 2016). Similarly, there is a relatively high level of support for the land certification program, which continues public ownership while offering a greater degree of tenure security to the individuals using the land (Berhane et al., 2014; Berhane, Hoddinott and Kumar, 2014; Gilligan, Hoddinott and Taffesse, 2009, IFPRI, 2013). The land certification program has had positive impacts for rural farmers. For instance, the land certificate can be used to access credit, which was previously difficult for farmers who had little collateral that could be leveraged to obtain loans.

Amidst this general support, based on research on many other government programs, it is worth questioning the extent to which rural community members view the program as a political tool. One way of answering this question could be assessing such attitudes in relation to the areas of resistance to land certification from a perspective of rejecting government control, even if there are benefits embedded in the certification process. As far as I am aware, no such study has been conducted with an objective to analyze areas of weaker implementation of land certification and its potential causes. Research I have conducted in Amhara suggests that farmers view the process of implementing the land certification system as one that enforces tax collection rather than strengthening tenure (Cochrane and Hadis, 2019). Similarly, the broader laws of land tenure have only partially been implemented, often at the discretion of local administration (Chinigo, 2013). As outlined by Berhanu and Poulton (2014: S197), many of the rural services and programs are driven by the "twin imperatives" of economic growth and political control. Due to the politicization of nearly all services and programs, a refusal to engage is considered a political act of opposition to the ruling government (Cochrane and Tamiru, 2016). One explanation of why some individuals refuse to engage or participate is what Scott (1985) describes as everyday acts of peasant resistance, such the lack of interest of some to update their land certificates after an inheritance or other transfer takes place. Other reasons for resistance to certification include the desire to avoid taxation (Cochrane and Hagos, 2019).

Social Safety Net

Ethiopia experienced famines resulting in large losses of life during the 1950s, 1960s, 1970s and 1980s (de Waal, 1991; Gill, 2010; Graham, Rashid and Malek, 2012; Sen and Dreze, 1999; Wolde Giorgis, 1989). Improvements were made in reducing famine-related deaths after the 1984/85 famine. For example, in 2002 the government took note of early warning signs of a pending famine, which by 2003 was projected to affect an estimated 14 million people, making it potentially one of the worst famines in history. For context, the globally publicized famine of 1984 affected an estimated eight million people (Gill, 2010). Due to proactive measures taken by the government and support from international partners in 2003, the loss of life was limited to a few hundred, with one assessment finding it remarkable that there was no measurable increase in child mortality during this widespread drought (de Waal, Taffesse and Carruth, 2006). The improved emergency response was not the only differentiating factor, however. In 1984 there was limited infrastructure, forced resettlement programs and conflict, all of which contributed to the deepening of famine conditions.

Although humanitarian responses have improved, in the 1990s and early 2000s the Government of Ethiopia and its partners recognized that emergency activities, such as those in 2002/03, were costly and unsustainable. The Government of Ethiopia, in discussion with its international partners, began a move to more proactive programming. One of the outcomes of this was the (re)establishment of resettlement programs, which the ruling government had largely halted since coming to power. The government set a goal to resettle over two million people (IRIN, 2004). A second outcome was the planning and establishment of the Productive Safety Net Program, launched in 2005. The Safety Net sought to reduce risk and transfer goods to food-insecure households, and it would do so in a way that supported the retention of assets. In turn, these assets could support recovery and resilience in response to food insecurity and drought (Cochrane and Tamiru, 2016).

The Safety Net supports food-insecure individuals and households with predictable, multi-year transfers that are tailored to match the needs of each regional state where it operates. Research suggests its targeting processes (focusing on specific districts and using community-based selection modalities) are well-designed and well-implemented (Fisseha, 2014; Kassa, 2013). Also, it more effectively targets the intended beneficiaries than the average global safety net program (Coll-Black et al., 2012). Studies indicate that the program efficiently achieves its objectives (IFPRI, 2013; Katane, 2013) and has resulted in positive impacts, such as improved child nutrition (Debela, Shively and Holden, 2014). Research also suggests that the program has supported agricultural livelihoods with no known disincentives (Bezu and Holden, 2008). However, it appears that the program has mainly had a stabilizing effect and is not effectively supporting people to overcome poverty (Maxwell et al., 2013; Rahmato, 2013; Siyoum, 2013). As a result, the program may have limited impact in effecting long-term change, unless it is combined with other initiatives (Gebremariam et al., 2013).

There are two political considerations that should be kept in mind when evaluating the success of the Safety Net. First, the Government of Ethiopia recognizes food insecurity as a threat to political stability. A critical assessment of the Safety Net might suggest that it is primarily a self-serving political effort whereby enhanced food security strengthens stability and prevents unrest. The selective regional coverage of the Safety Net, which does not align with the areas in greatest need, is one indication of this political purpose (FAO and WFP, 2008; see Figure 11). The exclusion of the food-insecure regions of Gambella and Somali in particular marks a continuation of marginalization experienced by certain ethno-linguistic groups in Ethiopia (e.g., Khalif and Doornbos, 2002) and an entrenchment of the "emerging" status of their regions (see discussion in Chapter 2). A second political purpose of the Safety Net is the entrenchment of political power and control in rural areas. As demonstrated by Cochrane and Tamiru (2016: 662), while the program has had a positive impact on the included households, its implementation was politicized as an "intentional means of enhancing administrative power and control while maintaining the appearance of accountability and participation for the donor community." The implementation of the Safety Net effectively disincentivizes political neutrality and political dissent. Any form of community participation or citizen engagement that is not sanctioned by or in support of the current EPRDF government is opposed; some of those who have participated in these activities have been labeled as anti-peace or anti-government.

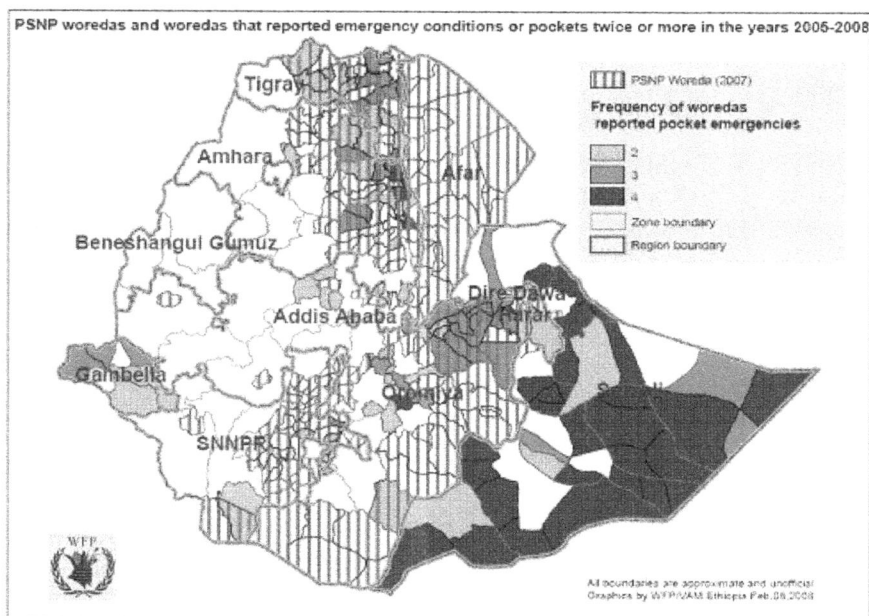

Figure 11. *Safety Net (blue) and Reports of Emergency Conditions (red) in Ethiopia, 2005-2008*
Source: FAO and WFP, 2008.

The politicization of program design and implementation is not new or unique to the Safety Net. De Waal (2015: 69) writes that these processes have long been a political tool in rural Ethiopia: "Party members had preferential access to state-allocated benefits, ranging from enrolment in higher education to subsidized fertilizer and small-scale credit. Sometimes they were the only ones who could get these benefits." Similar political purposes have been identified as primary for the agricultural extension program (Berhanu, 2012; Berhanu and Poulton, 2014; Planel, 2014; Pausewang, 2002), resettlement program (Hammond, 2008), decentralization initiatives (Chinigo, 2013) and rural development programs more broadly (Segers et al., 2008). In this regard, the findings of Cochrane and Tamiru (2016) about the Safety Net are in line with a range of largely qualitative studies that identify the politicization of rural programs and services. Outside of Ethiopia, the political use of policy and programming has long been identified as a tool for entrenching political control through incentivizing political support and disenfranchising people who oppose those in power (Bates, 1981).

The government established the Safety Net as one of the means to address inequalities and chronic food insecurity. In many ways, this program has been successful in preventing famine, reducing malnutrition and supporting households to maintain assets and increase income (Coll-Black et al., 2012; Debela, Shively and Holden, 2014; IFPRI, 2013; Katane, 2013). However, the program's dual purpose, of also entrenching political control and eliminating options for citizen engagement and participation in decision-making, should also be kept in mind (Cochrane and Tamiru, 2016). The politicization of programming is a theme that runs throughout this chapter, one which remains an understudied and undervalued component of development activity (despite strong research on the topic, such as by Autessere (2010), Ferguson (1990), Starn (1991) and Uvin (1999)).

Agricultural Foreign Direct Investment and "Land Grabs"

As noted in Chapter 2, the Government of Ethiopia has viewed agriculture as a means for development as well as ensuring national food security. The prioritization of large-scale commercial agriculture has been justified in that such operations would increase productivity and create jobs. The most recent manifestation of this is the government seeking foreign investment in the agricultural sector, granting large tracts of land to investors to develop commercial operations. During the 2006-2013 period the Government of Ethiopia actively promoted international investment in the agricultural sector (Lavers, 2012). Investors were offered tax breaks, very low rental rates—as low as US$1.15 per hectare—and a range of other incentives, such as credit facilities (Bossio et al., 2012; Rahmato, 2019). However, the potential benefit of large-scale land acquisitions relies upon an array of other government policies and enforcement thereof. These policies include those related to capital inflows, technology transfer, environmental regulation, water use, employment and interactions with smallholder farmers (Hallam, 2013). This section investigates whether the aspirations of the government (job creation, technology transfer, increased productivity) are materializing through this form of agricultural "modernization." In addition, as the government expropriates land, it becomes increasingly important to inquire whose land is being granted for the "public good" of the nation.

Foreign direct investment in the agricultural and livestock sectors in Ethiopia did not begin in 2007. However, that year marked a significant shift, largely in the form of a rapid increase of large-scale land leases which attracted global media and activist attention as part of a rising tide of transnational "land grabs." The figures on the extent of how much land has been leased to international actors vary significantly (in hectares): 602,760 (Cotula et al., 2009), 2,412,562 (Land Matrix, 2013), 3,524,000 (Friis and Reenberg, 2010), 3,619,509 (Oakland Institute, 2011). These discrepancies arise because some figures include the amount of land available for lease, while others include only land leased or committed to leased. As the FAO reports (Hallam, 2013), actual land leases are fewer and smaller than often reported. However, the issue is politically charged. Advocates and NGOs tend to gain more attention when they report alarming trends backed by large figures. This may explain why an American activist NGO, Oakland Institute, lists the largest figure.

A common narrative in news headlines and espoused by activists suggests that oil-rich Gulf nations are buying up agricultural land in developing nations. However, this does not accurately describe the situation in Ethiopia (for more, see Cochrane and Amery, 2017). The foreign nationals and companies acquiring the most agricultural land in Ethiopia between 2000 and 2009 were from India (32.4%), followed by the EU (21.2%), while Saudi Arabia accounted for only 3% (Oakland Institute, 2011). In many countries the largest portion of investors are citizens of that country, either living domestically or in the diaspora. The trends differ by region, however. In one study of Amhara Regional State, for example, of 960 land leases only three were held by foreign investors; however, they leased almost a quarter of the land (Bossio et al., 2012). In contrast, in Oromia Regional State, where many foreign investments are taking place, almost a quarter of investments were foreign and accounted for over 90% of leased land (Bossio et al., 2012). Although the amount of land put up for potential lease and that has been actually leased is large, smallholder farmers continue to be dominant in Ethiopian agriculture as they work more than 90% of the cultivated land (Taffesse, Dorosh and Gemessa, 2012).

After leasing hundreds of thousands, if not millions, of hectares of land, the Ethiopian Ministry of Agriculture realized that many leases had been made on a speculative basis amid a rapid rise of food commodity prices. On up to a third of leases no agricultural operations began at all (Africa Intelligence, 2013). Other studies suggest only 20% of the land involved in these investments has been used (Hallam, 2013). Further evidence for this speculative push in land leases is that a large portion of investment took place in 2008-09 during a major global price spike for food commodities. Moreover, many land lease investors were not agricultural companies (Hallam, 2013). For investments that have started operating, another important factor in Ethiopian land leases, is the boom-and-bust role of biofuels driven by foreign policies. The interest in biofuels was initially driven by European Union alternative energy targets (Busck et al., 2012). Indeed, during these early years it was suggested that biofuels may encompass up to 40% of all global agricultural deals (Kugelman and Levenstein, 2013). However, many of these investments failed as global production and demand changed, including the investment in Wolaita discussed later in this section.

Competing interests for local resources, particularly access and control of water, play an important role in large-scale agricultural investments, which may run counter to the interests of smallholder farmers. In most cases the power dynamics are unequal, and the government gives priority to investors (Bues and Theesfeld, 2012). Standard lease agreements offered by the Government of Ethiopia allow investors to build dams and boreholes for irrigation, after approval by the respective authorities (Bossio et al., 2012). Lavers (2012) finds the only major gain from the land-lease development strategy is an increase in foreign exchange earnings, with the drawback being a greater potential for domestic food insecurity as self-sufficiency is substituted for an emphasis on food commodities produced for international markets.

The impacts of large-scale land leasing are diverse, and thus it is challenging to draw conclusions about the experience as a whole. Rather than offer a statement that attempts to encompass the diversity of impacts, I will focus on a single case study that took place in Wolaita Zone, as described by Chinigo (2015). The case study is not a positive example, and there is selection bias in choosing to tell this story. To counter this, following this case study I make note of positive cases as well (for a more detailed assessment of the national situation, see Dejene and Cochrane, 2021; Cochrane and Legault, 2020). Beginning in 2007, Global Energy Ethiopia, an Israeli company, took a contract-farming approach, establishing agreements with over 10,000 farmers to grow castor trees for biofuels. The expected yields were greatly overestimated by the investor, suggesting outputs up to 10 times higher than typical for Wolaita. The investor promoted the scheme to farmers based on this calculation portraying unrealistic revenues. Government agricultural extension workers were utilized to organize training and connect farmers with the investor. Due to the politicization of government activities "many farmers felt compelled" to respond positively, even when a crop previously used only for fencing was touted as an important new source of income (Chinigo, 2015: 202).

By 2012, the investor had left Wolaita and the business was deemed unviable. Farmers were upset that promises were not kept and contracts were broken. As with many failed agricultural investments, the government gained moderate revenues, companies lost their initial investment capital, and farmers lost their yields and income. The Israeli company behind this scheme was not the first to attempt to enter the biofuels market using land in Wolaita, nor was it the last. Ventures such as this one place significant risk and burden on smallholder farmers. This case study sheds light on one of the ways in which foreign investment in the agricultural sector has affected households in Wolaita Zone.

Not all investors take this approach, and not all investments follow this trajectory. Other research in Ethiopia finds that the integration of biofuel production as one component of agricultural livelihoods can have positive impacts on food security (Negash and Swinnen, 2013). Due to the diversity of outcomes, few generalizations can be drawn; thorough assessments need to be conducted for each location, crop and market to determine its potential viability and usefulness for smallholder farmers.

More importantly, the protection of rights for landholders requires strengthening. Large-scale land leases are not aimed to support people in overcoming poverty, but the Government of Ethiopia has justified them as a means to foster economic growth, technology transfer and the creation of jobs. In many instances, the government-promoted benefits are suggested to be greatest for rural residents, which would translate into improved wellbeing, including strengthened food security. As the example from Wolaita demonstrates, if food security is to be strengthened amidst agricultural investment, the government must take a more proactive role to ensure contracts with farmers are upheld. Policy reforms in 2013 effectively ended foreign investment into large areas of agricultural land (Dejene and Cochrane, 2021). However, large tracts of land have already been leased. Moreover, much of what the government called "unused" land, which was granted to investors, is often located in areas home to minority ethnic groups or those engaged in livelihoods not valued by the government (e.g., pastoralism in the lowlands). As of 2020, a revised federal land proclamation was being reviewed by parliament which would grant more rights to smallholders to reject land expropriation and contest justifications of "public good" rationales. If adopted, this would improve the security of tenure rights for rural residents.

The incentives encouraging foreign direct investment could be shifted in order to better support the smallholder base of the economy. An example is encouraging investment in upstream agricultural production operations that would be supplied by smallholder farmers. For example, rather than expropriating land and seeking investors to grow crops, the government might instead incentivize processing of crops that farmers grow, as value-addition processes for domestic consumption and export (e.g., mango, avocado). This is supported by other research that suggests greater land size is not correlated with greater productivity; rather, it is the practice of efficient farming that should be prioritized (Deininger, Nizalov and Singh, 2013). Although robust studies are few, Shete and Rutten (2015) analyzed one investment in Oromia Regional State that contracted with smallholder farmers and found that due to competing land use needs household food security for community members declined, as did their income. Rahmato (2019) makes a convincing case of how large-scale agricultural investments contributed to the state being challenged and to the mass protests starting in 2015, as lives and livelihoods were negatively impacted as it appeared that the government was prioritizing investors over residents. The mass protests were not only about agricultural investment, however they contributed to the movement. Other land-related sparks of outrage related to the Addis Ababa Master Plan, which was proposed in 2014. Years of mass protest culminated in the resignation of the Prime Minister in 2018.

Ethiopian Commodity Exchange

While large-scale land acquisitions by foreign investors have attracted much attention, most rural residents practice smallholder agriculture as their primary livelihood activity. One of the challenges smallholders face as producers of relatively small quantities of crops for the market is getting a fair price for their crops due to a lack of access to market price information. In recognizing that farmers were not being given a fair price for their crops (due to limited market access and little price information), the government was a key driver in the transformation of the marketplace such that farmers were given the tools to gain a greater share of the value of their crops. While a range of ways exist to improve market access (e.g., Attwood, 2007; Holden, Shiferaw and Pender, 2005), the government sought to create a standardized market system that would facilitate increased exports and thereby generate greatly needed foreign currency. These two objectives are not necessarily opposed to one another, however, an assessment of the implementation of the marketplace transformations can suggest which of these objectives has been prioritized.

In 2008, the Ethiopian Commodities Exchange (ECX) began operations. It was commissioned by a government proclamation with the objective of developing an efficient, modern trading system that protects the rights of sellers, buyers and intermediaries (FDRE, 2007). The ECX attempts to address a number of challenges faced by the agricultural sector. In addition, the absence of national market integration resulted in a lack of quality control and regulation. The ECX is owned by a partnership of market stakeholders and the Government of Ethiopia. Since establishment, it has expanded rapidly. The ECX currently has more than 50 physical warehouses throughout the country, and by 2011 the ECX surpassed US$1 billion in annual trading. Although the types of commodities the ECX handles has expanded over time, it remains focused on a limited selection of exported agricultural commodities.

The ECX acts as a link between different market actors (e.g., government, ECX members, exchange warehouses, clearing banks and the trading system). Members of the ECX can deposit their products at a regional warehouse. Smallholder farmers engage with this system as members of cooperatives and unions or by selling to traders, as the ECX deals only in large quantities (there are five-ton minimum contributions). As described by Mheen-Sluijer (2010), the ECX samples, grades, weighs and certifies the products, and trading takes place at the ECX center in Addis Ababa. As per government direction, it was declared mandatory to sell all coffee on the ECX in 2009 and all sesame seed in 2010. These are two of the country's most important export products (Mheen-Sluijer, 2010).

In order to improve farmers' access to information, particularly in rural areas, commodity price display sites were established throughout the country. Hundreds of thousands of farmers gained access to commodity prices via mobile phones, and prices are advertised on radio, TV and print media (Dabre-Madhin, 2011). In peak seasons, the ECX toll-free call-in service has received more than a million calls monthly, 70% of which are from rural users (Dabre-Madhin, 2011). As a result, sellers are getting better prices for their products; for coffee sales farmers now receive 70% of the final price, whereas they received only 38% before the introduction of the ECX (Dabre-Madhin, 2011). The new system also ensures payment, which provides stability in the marketplace.

Since smallholder farmers' primary source of income is from their agricultural yields, it is important that they receive the best price possible for their commodities. However, many farmers currently face two main challenges in relation to the ECX that prevent them from maximizing their share of the price of their commodities. First, smallholder farmers cannot directly sell to the ECX, and therefore the average rural household, even if a regional warehouse exists, cannot interact with the exchange as direct sellers (in order to meet minimum contribution requirements, traders and cooperatives buy or collect from individual farmers and sell to the ECX). Second, limited cellular network coverage restricts the number of farmers able to benefit from the price information provision services. Thus, while the ECX has increased commodity price share for sellers, it appears that smallholder farmers have benefited only marginally and indirectly. Instead, intermediaries and traders have accrued most of the benefits of the exchange as they are best able to utilize real time prices, hold stock for higher prices and negotiate lower prices with farmers. As a development intervention, which the ECX does not claim to be, the enhancement of regional and national markets offers minimal benefit to rural farmers. Rather, it is more affluent farmers—those with more land and assets and thus higher yields and greater negotiating power—who have most benefited from the establishment of the ECX.

In theory, rural cooperatives, which have been supported for decades by the government's agricultural extension program and workers, would give rural community members the power to engage with the ECX and take advantage of the opportunities it offers. However, as outlined by Tefera, Bijman and Slingerland (2017), the farmers with the least financial resources and assets tend to be excluded from cooperative membership and the impact on smallholder livelihoods depend on which smallholder farmers are considered. Farmers in Wolaita suggest that community-level institutions, such as buying and selling cooperatives, are ineffective and largely non-functional. In many ways this reflects Ethiopia's historical experience with rural cooperatives, as one assessment of them in the 1960s and 1970s found that cooperatives "failed to serve the people for whom they were destined" (Belay, 2003: 56). Far too often these historical experiences are not used to make more informed decisions about how best to support smallholder farmers, resulting in mistakes and failures being repeated.

The ECX also must confront a larger structural challenge. As an economy mostly based on agricultural exports, which are the commodities the ECX controls, there is the potential for the ECX to act as a means to further extract resources from rural areas to fund different government initiatives, an issue raised decades ago by Bates (1981). As the ECX has expanded it has required that all trading of certain cash crop commodities be done via its platform. As a result, the ECX has monopolized the marketplace and thus restricted options for farmers. Potentially, this opens up opportunities for the government to set purchase and sale prices in ways that seek to raise national revenues and foreign earnings through exports, rather than as a means to support the majority of smallholder farmers. As the ECX develops and expands, further research will be needed to assess who benefits from it, how, when and why.

Adoption of programs and services

The literature on adoption of rural agricultural programs and services in Ethiopia suggests that adoption rates are low and many of those who do participate eventually drop out of these programs and services (Bonger, Ayele and Kuma, 2004; EEA/EEPRI, 2006; Gebrehiwot and van der Veen, 2014; Spielman, Mekonnen and Alemu, 2012; Taffesse, Dorosh and Gemessa, 2012). Compared to the experience of other countries, this finding is not unusual. In Rwanda, for example, one evaluation found that only 70 of 4,000 farmers (~2%) had implemented the full agricultural development program (Uvin, 1999: 134). Part of the challenge, as outlined in the history of the Ethiopian experience (as well as that of Rwanda), was that agricultural extension focused on a limited number of export cash crops, which were not the priority of smallholder farmers (Uvin, 1999: 130; Belay, 2003). The top-down approach has consistently been ineffective. In the Rwandan experience, it was in the 1980s that the failure of insufficient participation became apparent (Uvin, 1999: 132), as it was elsewhere in Africa (Bates, 1981). In Ethiopia, it was not until the mid to late 1990s that participation was considered (as discussed already, a questionable form thereof), meaning that farmers would theoretically have had the opportunity to select crops and seeds within the extension packages. Programs nonetheless continued to be offered as packages without the participatory element of farmer choice and these continued to experience low adoption (Limenih and Tefera, 2014). In many instances, in and beyond agricultural extension services, the Government of Ethiopia speaks of "participation" as agreement and adoption rather than as an ability to be involved in the design, format or implementation of a program (Cochrane and Skjerdal, 2015).

This chapter has also challenged the idea that agricultural extension services are failing. More nuanced study identifies components that have been relatively successful (e.g., fertilizer and improved seed) and also those that have not (e.g., microcredit and agricultural training). Community members emphasize that average adoption rates do not apply equally to all the promoted agricultural practices and vary from crop to crop. In some instances, the "traditional" seeds are maintained (e.g., cabbage and enset) and for others improved seeds are used (e.g., maize). Fertilizer and pesticide use similarly vary by crop, indicating how typical household questionnaires make invisible the intricate and informed choices that smallholder farmers make within their agricultural practices. Farmers also discussed the crops and inputs they did adopt in relation to power relations and political expectations. It was clear in Wolaita that agricultural extension services cannot be viewed simply as development activities, but also as a means of entrenching power and control in rural Ethiopia.

One of the key insights drawn from understanding vulnerabilities to food insecurity is that few generalizations can be made and that rural livelihoods exist within dynamic and complex environments wherein households make unique choices based on their respective priorities, opportunities, constraints and challenges. The assessment of adoption rates in Wolaita similarly finds that few viable generalizations can be made. Rather than offering simplistic generalizations about adoption broadly, this research suggests that some extension activities experience relatively high levels of adoption, such as fertilizer, pesticide and improved seed, while others experience lower levels, such as microcredit and agricultural extension training. We see that the situation is even more complex when we look at how farmers make choices on a crop-by-crop basis, rather than an all-or-nothing basis. For example, in Wolaita improved seeds are used for maize but not for cabbage; pesticides are used for vegetables and teff but not for sorghum; planting methods advocated by extension workers are used for maize but not for teff; some fertilizer is purchased only due to political pressure and then resold at a loss. Even these crop-specific and input-specific generalizations fail to hold true when walking from house to house, as each farmer brings their own experiences, priorities, options and barriers to the table.

Farmers are aware of the vulnerabilities they encounter. They are also aware of the faults of the programs, policies and services they engage with. One might wonder, therefore, if they have advocated improvements to their local or regional government representatives. With regard to agricultural programs, policies and services, this has largely not occurred. The next chapter seeks to explore how, when and why citizen-driven change occurs, and what insights different theories might offer for why collective action calling for change to agricultural programs, policies and services has been largely absent.

CHAPTER SEVEN

ENGAGING CHANGE

Food security in Ethiopia needs to be strengthened. Some programs, policies and services are not working as efficiently or effectively as they could. In some instances, those in most need of support are completely missed. This chapter critically analyzes some of the assumptions that have been presented in this book: the importance of participation as a key route to enabling positive change. This idea sits within broader thinking about "how change happens", with participatory approaches being one of many theories that have been proposed for understanding positive change, and planning for undertaking it. This chapter analyzes a range of other theories, alongside bottom-up community-based participatory ones. In so doing it presents critical reflections for positive change within rural agricultural contexts in Ethiopia. In addition to assessing what we know about food security and how we know that, the third objective of this book is understanding what changes might result in positive impacts and how those might be arrived at. This chapter explores the processes of enabling change while Chapter 8 presents some of the activities and outcomes that could be pursued.

Participatory approaches to understanding food security offer a wealth of important insights into how programs and services could work better. It is tempting to assume that participatory approaches would be similarly as important for efforts to bring about positive change as many of the proponents of collective action have argued. Indeed, many people suggest that participatory approaches can lead "to actions which support mutual aid and collective action at the grassroots" (IDS, 2016: 1). The new knowledge obtained, it is argued, facilitates collective action for positive social change. Yet, knowledge does not always result in action, and collective action does not always result in change. While participatory, people-driven change is undoubtedly possible (see attempts of participatory change in Kenya (Thiongo, 1986) in Rwanda (Smith and Webb, 2011) as other examples), we need to look more closely at this assumption that this form of collective action is the most viable pathway to foster the changes needed to strengthen food security in Ethiopia.

There is a large literature that focuses on change driven by citizen participation and a variety of terminologies used to describe it including grassroots change, social movements, bottom-up change, citizen action, poor people's movements and civil resistance (Chenoweth and Stephan, 2011; Gaventa and McGee, 2010; Piven and Cloward, 1977; Schock, 2015). Rather than viewing power as something held by decision-makers, these theorists and practitioners argue that people, when acting collectively, can create power and force change. Acemoglu and Robinson (2006) argue that inclusive economic and political institutions develop when people demand their inclusion and leave decision-makers no choice but to support change. They conclude that "Inclusive economic and political institutions do not emerge by themselves. They are often the outcome of significant conflict between elites resisting economic growth and political change and those wishing to limit the economic and political power of existing elites" (Acemoglu and Robinson, 2006: 332). By contrast, the anti-colonial activist Fanon (1952, 1963) forcefully argued that decolonization would only come about through the complete transformation of society and not by patient, pragmatic reform, which would only result in a continuation of exploitation. Cabral, one of Africa's leading anti-colonial leaders, similarly argues that "we have to destroy in order to construct a new life" (1977: 77). Transforming society, Cabral (1977: 77) explains, means destroying everything that stands against equality of rights, opportunities and flourishing. Drawing upon Fanon, Mbembe suggests working with the elite who are engaged in oppression is like "becoming the accomplice of castration" (2016: 5). What unites these thinkers is the view that the masses and those in power have divergent interests and that revolutionary transformation is the only pathway to real change.

Embedded within the theory of participatory people-driven change is the idea that the majority of individuals are disempowered because of their willingness to cooperate with elites who disempower them. This is the expression of power and control which seeks to shape individuals so that they willingly comply. However, the continuation of a system by the fear of force is fragile. If people act as a collective contrary to what is expected of them, they have the power to facilitate change, to confront power and to resist the control being exerted by those in power. The foundation of action, therefore, is grassroots activity: education, awareness-building, mobilization, training, capacity building and inclusive participation (Stachowiack, 2009; 2013). The collective power of citizen action and engagement has the ability to effectively change governments, policies and programs, as history attests (Chenoweth and Stephan, 2011; Piven and Cloward, 1977). An example Acemoglu and Robinson (2012: 457) provide is in Brazil, where inclusive institutions did not emerge as a result of planned government development activity, or government-driven policy, or a "natural outcome of modernization." Rather, these institutions emerged because individuals and groups within society advocated for change. In the struggles against oppression in African contexts—from Cape Verde to Cape Town—transformation necessitated revolution.

Radical revision of society, as described by Fanon, Cabral and Amin (1976), is rooted in a restoration of dignity. Fanon explained that as "soon as you and your fellow men are cut down like dogs there is no other solution but to use every means available to reestablish your weight as a human being. You must therefore weigh as heavily as possible on your torturer's body so that his wits, which have wandered off somewhere, can at least be restored to their human dimension" (1963: 221). In many regards, anti-colonial thinkers (and as Kwame Nkrumah argued, also those fighting against "sham" independent states) believed that societal and institutional transformation was required, by tearing down what exists and creating anew. In other streams of collective action thought, there is advocacy for reform, or changing society and institutions in their current forms. In both of these perspectives, participation may be an effective means for change, but it is also a process of ensuring the dignity and rights of all are respected and protected, without which democratic processes are impossible.

In "development" activity, there is a growing list of people advocating for greater emphasis in grassroots, participatory civil society activity (Dwyer, 2015; Eyben, 2014; Roy et al., 2016). Yet, in this wave of enthusiasm there is a neglect of the potential for civil society to entrench inequality, or ways in which people are different in society, and thereby be unable to enable positive social change to happen (Bahru, 2002). Ndegwa (1996) expresses this as the "two faces" of civil society. Drawing upon case studies from Kenya, he concludes that there is "nothing inherent about civil society organizations that makes them opponents of authoritarianism and proponents of democracy" (1996: 6). Civil society cannot, he writes, "be assumed to be congenial to or supportive of democratic pluralism by its mere existence, expansion or level of activity" (1996: 7). While Ndegwa focused on national NGOs, his findings are applicable to a broad array of collective action activities—be they international or community-based, formal or informal. Shivji (2007) warns us that "development" actors, often with the best intentions, can easily perpetuate disempowering ideologies and act to legitimize a government that marginalizes and oppresses. If dignity and rights are not prioritized, we may render exclusion invisible.

Participation in community organizations is not in itself a guarantee of efforts to advance positive and inclusive social change. Consider informal organizations common to rural Ethiopia, such as *iddir* (funerary associations), *equb* (savings groups) or *mehaber* (community or group associations), which could be spaces where self-organized community members advocate for change. In some urban instances where *iddir* organizations have overlapped with union activity, members have engaged in activism. While there are suggestions that informal organizations were instrumental for some resistance movements (e.g., *Maccaa fi Tuulamaa* and its connection to the founding of the Oromo Liberation Front), these remain exceptions to the norm. In rural settings, where *iddir* are a much more recent phenomenon, community-based organizations tend to align with government activity rather than standing in opposition to it (e.g. Pankhurst, 2008). As noted in Chapter 2, rural *iddir* associations tend to replicate existing power structures rather than oppose them. The replication of social associations is even more the case for rotational savings groups (*equb*), due to the high level of trust members need to have in informal groups. In other words, ethno-linguistic or religious minorities that are excluded from social and familial associations are similarly excluded from these informal associations. *Mehaber* are also informal associations and vary significantly in type, although they are commonly religious associations often associated with the Ethiopian Orthodox Church. All of these community-based institutions play important functions in disseminating information in the community, but in my experience (and in consultation with other scholars who have studied informal institutions, which is important given the diversity of informal organizations throughout Ethiopia), they have not been in and of themselves institutions that lead opposition or resistance or act as driving forces in activism.

Participation in efforts to advance positive social change is also limited or enabled by institutional factors. The degree to which long-term participation in these efforts is enabled, facilitated or restricted is influenced by available resources and time. Gaining access to information can be particularly problematic; barriers of access and literacy may prevent the most marginalized from participating and engaging in collective action. These challenges are not insurmountable but require purposeful engagement by all involved that acknowledges and grapples with the diverse ways barriers manifest. Addressing questions of inclusion is important. However, in doing so we continue to assume that participatory approaches are the most viable means to strengthening food security in rural Ethiopia. This assumption contains a further assumption that collective action will materialize around food security. It may be that the issue does not affect the majority of Ethiopians and requires a different approach to bring about change. Consider the gender discrimination that was embedded in the family code, criminal code and nationalities law: it was a small group of activist lawyers in in the 1990s that spent years advocating and rallying for change before broader support began to materialize (Cochrane and Betel, 2019). By the early 2000s, with broad support, all of these laws had been revised and much of the discrimination eliminated.

Can a participatory and community-based assessment of vulnerability to food insecurity facilitate the improvement of agricultural extension services? The potential exists. However, in rural Ethiopia there are very few examples of participatory action regarding agricultural politics, programs and services. This raises a number of questions—is the lack of participatory-driven change specific to Ethiopia? Is it specific to rural areas? Is it specific to agriculture? We do not have definitive answers to these questions, but we have some indications.

Given that we know participatory action can work, the first question to ask is whether there is something specific to the Ethiopian context that prevents this type of mobilization. The answer here appears clear: Ethiopians are willing and able to use the power of the people. A couple of examples will suffice. During the 1990s, despite severe government opposition, people in southern Ethiopia rallied together and successfully pushed for the retraction of a language policy that amalgamated three similar but distinct local languages in the education system (Cochrane and Bekele, 2019). In the late 1990s and early 2000s, the work and advocacy of a small group of female lawyers gained popular support and resulted in the changing of discriminatory laws already mentioned (Cochrane and Betel, 2019; Smith, 2008). More recently, in 2018, people exerted their collective power to force the resignation of the former Prime Minister Hailemariam Desalegn. There are also many more examples from history (see McCann, 1987). Thus it is clear that collective power and civil action have been used and have been effective in Ethiopia.

The answer is less clear when we focus on rural participatory action in Ethiopia. It is not that rural residents are complacent but that their action is more often localized, such as the localized demanding of a land redistribution (Ege, 1997). To change policies, programs and services requires engagement at higher levels, where such decisions are made, be that the regional state or the federal level, or both. Change of this kind requires information, networks, alliances and support beyond the local level. These are difficult to muster in isolated rural settings. While it is possible for rural-based participatory action to drive change, it must overcome far more barriers than those that are faced in urban settings (particularly as they seek to rally sufficient number of people to exert mass pressure).

Are participatory theories of change the most suitable for understanding and promoting change to rural agricultural programs and services in Ethiopia? In order to answer this question, at least theoretically, we must explore other theories of change in order to compare the environments in which they function.

Theorizing change

Broad-based positive change can occur in many ways (Stachowiack, 2009; 2013). Rather than seek a generalizable theory of change for all people, places and times, the history of these kinds of people-driven change suggests that a more appropriate approach is to conduct an in-depth assessment of the context in which the desired change will occur and determine the most relevant and appropriate theory of change for the specific context and objectives. In this work, a participatory-driven theory of change was embedded within the Stages of Food Security approach to how we know. This positioning of the importance of participation was largely based on my view of participation as a right and had less to say about how change to rural agricultural policies is most likely to occur. In the Ethiopian context, Wolde Mariam (1986: 18) highlighted several potential barriers to collective engagement: the military might of the government to suppress such activity, a dispersed rural population with irregular communication, the demands of more pressing needs ("attempts to alleviate the nagging daily hunger of themselves and their families"), and a reliance on their "commonsense" informed by past experience of rebellion which "will almost certainly fail to achieve any purpose." Yet, people and movements have overcome these barriers. A comparative assessment of theories enables insight into how these barriers have been overcome.

Understanding theories about change is important because theories often link "description with prescription" (Wolf-Powers, 2014: 202). For example, in describing participatory methodologies as enabling collective action, the description of the methodology has assumed the means through which change is expected to occur (i.e., change happens via collective action by ordinary people). This can result in what Chambers calls a "lock-in," a "paradigmatic syndrome in which there is strong mutually-supporting inflexibility" (2012b: 195). Chambers argues that "concepts, principles, methods, behaviors, relationships and mindsets" (2012b: 196) exist within a particular paradigm and reinforce one another so that minor changes within one area do not challenge the driving paradigm. In these instances, the dominant paradigm is not critically challenged because it is assumed within the description of the methodology and process. In order make this critical assessment, the theories themselves must be analyzed.

In the following sections, I draw on Stachowiak (2009, 2013) to reflect on theories of change that may be well suited for planning, enacting and explaining positive change in rural agricultural policies, programs and services. Stachowiak outlined ten "pathways for change" based on theories about how change happens, focusing largely on advocacy and policy efforts. Based on this work, I have grouped theories of change into three broad categories (situational, elite and targeted). I have not attempted an exhaustive analysis of all theories of change. Instead, I focus on a selection of theories that highlight processes of change that are different from theories that emphasize mass participation. Exploring these alternative theories of change provides insight into the factors that enable and or act as barriers to change and allows for critical reflection on participation as a pathway for change in agricultural settings in rural Ethiopia.

Situational

New evidence or knowledge does not necessarily result in change, nor does extended and robust advocacy. Kingdon (1984) has suggested there are situational windows within which change can occur, which is somewhat similar to what Acemoglu and Robinson (2012) call critical junctures. The factors Kingdon identified (problems, politics, policies) were largely taken up by Baumgartner and Jones (1993) who used them to explain how change happens based on the coalescing of conditions. These authors identify three required conditions: redefining or reframing an issue so that it gains newfound attention, involves new stakeholder groups, and increases levels of media coverage and public attention. They further suggest that a combination of factors must come together to create the right environment for change. These theories also include components that can be facilitated (e.g., via campaigning) but tend to converge in unplanned ways, opening emergent, time-bound opportunities for change. From this perspective, opportunities for change are therefore situational. While Baumgartner and Jones (1993) help to explain why change occurs in sudden shifts, their theory has largely been used to analyze American policy change and may have limited explanatory strength in other socio-political contexts where media and public interest groups do not have the same importance relative to other actors. Kingdon also relied heavily upon the American context in presenting his theory, which includes free media and responsive institutions. This suggests that his theory would need to be adjusted to suit different national environments.

The work of Turner also provides insight into why and how situational change can emerge (Turner, 1982; Turner and Oakes, 1986; Turner et al., 1987). Turner highlighted cohesion and cooperation as the foundation of group formation, which is ncessary for collection action. This is important for the Ethiopian context. The country has over 80 ethno-linguistic groups, and there is no one language that is spoken throughout the country. One of the enabling factors for local-level activism is a "natural" cohesion of language, and often ethnicity and religion. However, this cohesion only exists when the issue at hand affects the entire population in similar ways. For example, the opposition to the language policy in the former North

Omo Zone in southern Ethiopia was strong because it affected all people across economic classes within that particular region. However, when an issue does not affect everyone in a similar way, there may not be cohesion and cooperation, but rather disunity and opposition.

Rural programs and services are not equally (in)effective. Recall that the larger landholders have gained more access to agricultural extension services and that "high potential" areas are prioritized over marginal ones. In effect, those with better land and more resources are benefiting from the status quo. Thus, there is no natural cohesion and cooperation amongst rural residents to encourage them to advocate for the reform of policies, programs and services. In fact, the most powerful residents may work to oppose change. This helps us to understand why participatory action has occurred in some places and times and not others. The use of participatory collective action as an approach to bring about positive social change is built on an assumption of collective interest in the issue. It is therefore possible that in order for collective action to occur, formative work would be necessary to build solidarity across socio-economic classes.

In 1981, Bates identified socio-economic divisions in society as a means for ruling governments to divide and "block the efforts of those who would organize in attempts to achieve structural changes" (1981:117). Bates positions these fractions as barriers to "class action." Bates suggests that we need to recognize how programs, policies and services may be designed to entrench division through the disbursement of benefits, acting as a dividing force in rural society that prevents collective action which spans economic statuses.

Elite

The origin of thinking about elite power in theories of change began with Mills (1956) and has since been incorporated into a range of theories and revived by contemporary scholars (e.g., Domhoff). These theories of change are founded on the idea that power is unequally distributed in society and certain people have a greater ability to enact or prevent change. In direct contrast to the participatory, community-based theories of change, those that focus on elite power advocate that efforts to enact change focus on a limited, targeted set of individuals or institutions. An example of this is the global activism that sought to ensure all people living with AIDS have access to antiretroviral treatment (in the 1990s treatment was prohibitively expensive). Activists targeted specific actors—private companies and international institutions—to push for a market transformation so that all people could access treatment (Kapstein and Busby, 2013).

Ethiopian history attests to the importance of elite power theories, particularly as they relate to politically driven rural agricultural change. McCann outlines how the introduction of plow agriculture in Kaffa in the 17th century was "a result of the royal court's preference for the prestige value of teff and cereals over *qocho* (ensete), yams, and taro, spurring elites to require tributes in cereals" (1995: 47). Similarly, the shift to a mixed coffee and maize agricultural system in Gera from 1850 to 1990 was partly environmental "but [derived] more from policies in the political arena—fixed coffee prices, land reform, and villagization—which projected state power and urban priorities onto the rural landscape" (McCann, 1995: 190). At the same time, however, McCann also provides examples of rural agricultural change occurring outside of elite power and politics, such as the rapid expansion of the "traditional" plow (*marasha*) "reaching peoples of the southern and eastern highlands well before Emperor Menilek II's conquering armies of the late nineteenth century" (McCann, 1995: 5). While essential to consider, these historical examples ought not give the impression that rural agricultural change is primarily the product of elite power and politics. Rather, it is one means by which change has occurred in the past and may again in the future. Indeed, farmers have been the primary drivers of change in their agricultural practices (Cochrane, 2017b).

One approach that seeks to understand the distribution of power in society for assessing how change might occur is the Power Analysis approach, which was developed in a series of workshops run by the Swedish International Development Agency (SIDA) in 2002 and 2003. Contemporary efforts to understand the workings of power in society build upon a range of scholars predating this time, such as work by Patrick Chabal, Naomi Hossain, John Gaventa, Adrian Leftwich, and Mahmoud Mamdani, amongst others. The underlying belief of SIDA's approach is that power asymmetries are crucial in understanding and facilitating change (Nash, Hudson and Luttrell, 2006). The Power Analysis approach tends to highlight the connections between governance, human rights and poverty "through analysis of informal and formal power actors, structures and relations" (OECD, 2005:3). In the Power Analysis approach, power is defined in a unique way according to the needs and context in which the approach is carried out. According to Hyden, Power Analysis "is a valuable complement to other types of analysis by placing policy in its rightful political context" (2005:1). SIDA does this by posing three questions: Who sets the policy agenda? Who gets what, when, and how? Who knows whom, why and how? As outlined by Hyden (2005), these questions respectively evaluate the decision-making environment, the formal institutional arrangement and informal power relations (Vaughan and Tronvoll, 2003). Although its focus on power is unique, SIDA concluded that in practice many outcomes of the Power Analysis approach were not as distinctive as originally hoped, when compared to other socio-cultural or political research approaches (SIDA, 2005). Efforts to understand power before the Power Analysis, and those that followed it, encountered challenges not of critically assessing power but in integrating politics and power into action (Yanguas, 2018).

In the case of rural agricultural policies, programs and services in Ethiopia, drawing upon elite theories of change one might consider a targeted campaign and sustained information exchange with a select few powerful decision makers. In Ethiopia, this would consist of decision-makers at multiple levels: local (community chairman and development agents), district (district agricultural office), zonal (zonal administration and zonal agricultural office), regional (regional agricultural bureau) and federal (Ministry of Agriculture). From one perspective, this approach is practical and pragmatic as it directly engages those who have the ability to make changes to policy, program and service design and implementation. Doing so requires critical engagement, as Berhanu and Poulton (2014) argue that there are "twin imperatives" at work in these programs. They argue that often decisions are made to entrench control and strengthen elite power. The politicization of rural programs and services has been identified in agricultural extension (Berhanu and Poulton, 2014), in land reform (Chingo, 2013) and in the safety net (Cochrane and Tamiru, 2016). This suggests elite power advocacy may have limited impact because decisions might be made to serve objectives different from those publicly stated. The "art of the impossible," as Havel (1997) has called it, is the process of engaging political elite and enabling a reimaging of horizons such that policy change is for the collective good.

Politicization aside, a central difficulty in elite power theories of change is that they are reliant upon the identification of the right individuals who are then targeted for tailored and sustained advocacy for each desired change. While this approach has the potential to be effective, it is limited in scope, often to a specific issue or specific set of actors. In contrast, if instead of targeting elites efforts are focused on the cultivation of critical consciousness (Freire, 1970) so that there is broad-based support to re-shape political and economic systems to be more inclusive, this can lead to sustained and transformative collective action as it can be applied to new contexts by individuals and communities as they see fit. Rather than taking an issue-specific approach which focuses on elites, the cultivation of critical consciousness suggests a deepening of participatory approaches to alter society as a whole from the bottom up.

Coalitions

One way to bring together the strengths of participatory and elite power theories is to build a coalition of diverse stakeholder groups, each with different activities, coordinated to achieve a specific change. Coalition thinking has been developed by Sabatier and Jenkins-Smith (Sabatier, 1988; Sabatier and Jenkins-Smith 1993; 1999). Rather than focus on specific activities, this theory of change relies upon the alignment of core beliefs and objectives—resulting in "unlikely allies" to work together to effect positive change. In order to establish and maintain the alignment of beliefs and objectives there may be a need for a different type of engagement, one that coordinates and brokers between and within organizations (Weible and Sabatier, 2006).

Coalition building for improving agricultural programs and services could align strong international research agencies (e.g., International Food Policy Research Institute), national research agencies (e.g., Agricultural Transformation Agency), non-governmental research bodies (e.g., Forum for Social Studies), key donors and finance agencies (USAID, DFID, World Bank), implementing agencies (e.g., One Acre Fund and Concern) and community-based organizations (e.g., Wolaita Development Association and Terepeza Development Association). In certain contexts coalition building may only influence change if the work is done collectively with government agencies (see Stone, 1993), which in the case of Ethiopia would include the Federal Ministry of Agriculture, the Regional Agricultural Bureau, Zonal Agricultural Office and District Agricultural Office. My experience working with multi-stakeholder initiatives in Ethiopia is that often the government partners inadequately engage with the process, resulting in parallel activities, with little government response to coalitions of non-governmental and community-based alliances. However, the government is the only actor that has the ability to change policies, programs and services.

If governments are not interested to participate in or respond to coalitions, it may require approaching the issue from a different perspective. Kahneman and Tversky (1979; Tversky and Kahneman, 1981; 992) argue that individuals, including decision-makers in the government, do not make rational decisions. Rather, decisions are made based on how issues are framed. Issues can be presented and framed in diverse ways and these affect how people respond to them (Cochrane and Skjerdal, 2015). Influencing change, therefore, might not necessarily be driven by coalitions or advocacy, but by targeting action based on a strategic framing and appropriate presentation.

Assuming that decision-makers in the Ethiopian government are at least partially driven by the objective to entrench rural control, one could strategically frame issues such that they (at least appear to) align with the political objectives. This would turn the "twin imperatives" (Berhanu and Poulton, 2014) around, using the allure of politicization and power to affect positive change. For the sake of clarity, Kahneman and Tversky do not advocate the manipulation of decision-makers in this fashion, rather they outline how framing influences decision-making by distorting "rational" assessments of benefits and costs. Non-governmental organizations regularly reframe activities for the purposes of appeasing the government (or altering the appearance of activities that it would not welcome). For example, the Government of Ethiopia heavily regulates NGO reporting, advocacy and programming on human rights. As a result, organizations simply reframe human rights as wellbeing.

For the purposes of effecting positive change in rural settings to agricultural policies, programs and services, my experience is that reframing would have limited impact because the decision-makers are well aware of the reasons they make choices. For example, one government worker, a community chairman, openly said that despite knowing the requirements of a rural program which he oversaw and the rights of beneficiaries, he argued that community members have "no right" to question or speak about who gets benefits from the government and who does not (Cochrane and

Tamiru, 2016). It was his decision, and if anyone dared speak up there would be consequences. Since the reasoning is well known (but unwritten and therefore invisible), the potential for change driven by reframing appears limited. However, in the long-term, the collective raising of consciousness can alter what is considered acceptable by the majority. The power of changes in collective consciousness can be seen in the mass protests that resulted in the resignation of the Prime Minister in 2018.

This brief survey of theories of change has identified various reasons why the participatory approach may not work for rural agricultural policies, programs and services. It has also identified potential arenas for future action. Engaging in this critical reflection process has enabled us to check our assumptions. This does not negate the ideas I hold about participation as a right, participation as an effective and critical means to producing knowledge and participation as a means for enacting positive social change. Rather, critical analysis helps us to analyze specific issues, at specific times and within specific contexts and how we might be more informed on our courses of action. This is reflective of the Stages of Food Security methodology already discussed—participation is not applied in all steps and within all processes. Instead, participation was used in an informed and strategic way. We ought to approach participation similarly when seeking to change rural agricultural policies, programs and services.

Dealing with complexity

There is a clear need to strengthen rural food security by reducing vulnerabilities and ensuring rights are protected. Current trends suggest that the food security situation will worsen due to population growth and land fragmentation, increasingly unpredictable rainfall, depleting soil fertility and soil loss due to erosion (Meijer et al., 2015). Because rural lives and livelihoods are complex, the way in which we conduct and analyze research renders invisible much of the lived realities that farmers experience. Theories of change similarly make assumptions and generalizations, and thus there appears to be a role for complexity-based analyses, learning approaches and adaptive processes.

The recognition that objects of study exist within interconnected, non-linear and dynamic systems has a long history in philosophy and economics, but this recognition only began to influence the research process and enable the development of new theories in the early 1900s (von

Bertalanffy, 1972). In recent decades, complexity-based approaches have influenced a broader range of issues, including those within development studies (Meadows et al., 1974; Meadows, 2008). Such frameworks offer an alternative to understand change. Rather than seeing change as a function of grassroots activity, elite power or targeted activity, inquiry and action to understand social change are based on assessing dynamic interactions and interconnected relationships within a complex adaptive system.

The complexity of why change occurs in rural agricultural contexts is demonstrated in a study conducted by Wubeneh and Sanders (2006), who found that primary drivers differed based on the context of the challenges being grappled with. While access to information, soil type, farmer perceptions and rainfall risk influenced the adoption of new seed and crop varieties, it was the availability of labor, farm size, manure use and soil type that were important factors affecting fertilizer adoption. A unique analysis done by Ersado et al. (2004) suggests that non-agricultural factors such as the length of time farmers are ill or the length of time spent caring for the ill and problems associated with access to healthcare have significant negative effects on the adoption of agricultural practices. Further, Ersado et al. (2004) find that some agricultural innovations, such as micro-dams, may not only decrease adoption of other new technologies but also increase health challenges (such as malaria) and reduce availability of work time due to illness. Segers et al. (2008) find that the level of engagement with one program and its lack of effectiveness may be unrelated to the quality of that intervention entirely but due to a completely different concurrent activity, such as NGO activities unrelated to government extension services. These diverse factors tend not to be considered as linked, and if they are considered analysts often apply theories of change to understand the overall situation rather than examining individual cases. Even more challenging, yet often unaddressed in studies, is how advocacy for change by different government and non-governmental agencies can be contradictory and yet seek to influence the same households. Ahmed (2015) highlights how this is the case in Ethiopia with the promotion of chemical inputs and government-certified seed, which contrasts with natural resource management practices rooted in agroecology using natural manures and composts (the former common to government extension services and the latter more commonly advocated by NGOs).

Participatory approaches can make visible complexities that might not otherwise be seen, particularly as it relates to traditional ecological knowledge and local contextualization of information. The binary positions (e.g., between external chemical inputs for production and agroecology for sustainability) are commonly driven by value-based positions advocated in opposition to the other. Farmers, on the other hand, may not view this as an either-or decision, and find innovative ways for integrating them. Laekemariam and Gidago (2012), for example, in a study of Wolaita, find that the highest yields occurred when farmers mixed natural and chemical systems as opposed to relying exclusively on one or the other. The authors do not specify how farmers decided on the different options, but one wonders if this was influenced by pre-research farmer-led experimentation as has been identified in other locations as farmers respond to externally advocated change (Cochrane, 2017b). Farmer-led experimentation of this nature is common, such as for potato planting, with farmers planting above and below the government recommendations for row spacing (Abrha, Belew and Woldegiorgis, 2014). Local innovations can be more effective (e.g., in planting methodologies and tools), particularly as they are more appropriate to contexts they are used within, such as considering access to resources and technologies (Biazin, Sterk and Temesgen, 2014; Waters-Bayer et al., 2015).

The above research highlights how engaging with complexity requires integrating knowledge beyond technical research. The understanding and assumptions of actors involved, including as agricultural extension works, can result in biases and blinders. In many instances, these "experts" disregard traditional knowledge, and thus are not interested in learning from farmers. For instance, while in Amhara Regional State in 2013 I asked an extension worker why the fields in one particular area contained so many rocks. The agricultural specialist's response alluded to assumptions about farmers being lazy and stubborn, as they were unwilling to follow guidance given by extension workers to clear the rocks. Farmers saw things differently and understood why they farmed the ways that they did. Innovative research, such as that done by Jan Nyssen, has shown that traditional practices have a range of positive impacts. One of those studies included comparing plots with different levels of rock fragments. It found that the presence of rocks reduced soil loss and concluded that farmers' experience is a key source of knowledge (Nyssen et al., 2001). McCann (1995) notes how "traditional" storage systems were not only effective in storing food but had the added advantage of concealing food stores, which protected valuable resources from being raided during times of unrest. At the same time, however, McCann (1995) provides examples of how "traditional" practices, such as the use of fallows or burning, became less viable due to demographic and environmental changes.

Ramalingam (2013) is one of the most influential advocates of complexity-based analyses of development. In making a case for complexity, Ramalingam shares examples such as the Balinese agricultural terracing systems. Based on research conducted by Lansing et al. (2006), Ramalingam explains how external development agencies aimed to "modernize" the Balinese system, but instead caused a complete failure. Lansing et al. (2006) identified that assessments failed to recognize the interconnected nature of the broader system. Drawing upon such examples, Ramalingam (2013) makes a strong case for the importance of thinking about actors and objects as existing within complex adaptive systems. But in doing so, he offers few options for the practical implementation of the idea. For example, it is not clear how much needs to be known (or can be known) in order to sufficiently understand the dynamics of non-linear systems, which are themselves embedded within layers of uncertainties (Levy, 2000). Meijer et al. (2015) attempted to develop a framework for agricultural adoption and concluded "it is almost impossible to understand the influence of all possible factors involved as well as their interdependencies" (Meijer et al., 2015: 11). In response, learning approaches and adaptive processes have been developing in response to the challenges of how to practically utilize complexity-based approaches (Burns and Worsley, 2015).

As opposed to researching systems to understand their complexity, learning approaches and adaptive processes seek to operate in an iterative way, whereby the interactions and interconnections within the system continuously inform how activity is conducted. Burns and Worsley (2015) provide examples of how this operates in practice, and USAID (2016) has developed resources for adaptive processes for its entire program cycle. In reflecting on theories of change, the learning approaches and adaptive processes offer an alternative to the plan- and theory-based models that predetermine which forms of action ought to be prioritized. Effective use of these alternatives requires different modalities of funding and design, whereby there is greater flexibility in adapting the program as it evolves (Burns and Worsley, 2015; Cundill et al., 2018; Jones et al., 2018).

Where, when and why more adaptive processes are useful is an emerging area of research. Sometimes, top-down approaches that are driven by measurement and evidence are highly effective. In other instances they are not. Honig (2018) suggests that more flexible approaches, what he called "navigation by judgement," are more effective in particular operational environments, such as those where there is a high level of uncertainty. There also appears to be sectors that are more conducive to measurement- and evidence-driven top-down approaches such as in health and education (Cameron, Mishra and Brown, 2016), whereas activities seeking to advocate for behavior change or policy reform are highly context specific and seem more suited to adaptive processes. There is much yet to learn about how to effectively develop, selectively use and appropriately evaluate adaptive processes. This is one potential space where practice-based activities, either led by innovative organizations or through action research approaches, could provide new insights into more effective ways of working.

In the rural agricultural contexts of Ethiopia, complexity could be integrated into the design of extension services by creating flexible and adaptive processes through genuine decentralization of decision-making (as earlier noted, much of the current decentralization has worked to entrench central power). Examples of decentralized decision-making, such as land certification piloting in Tigray region (see Chapter 6), suggest policies, programs and services that are designed within specific contexts, that are problem-based, and have the space to innovate can enable broader policy reform throughout the country. At the federal level, the government is also exploring how to better enable multi-sector engagement. For instance, the National Nutrition Program, started in 2008, is problem-based and fosters collaboration between federal ministries to better engage the myriad of factors affecting nutrition.[22] There are also federal-level successes that are worth highlighting as positive practices in innovation such as the unique design of urban, rural and pastoral health extension services (whereas in many countries the modality is uniform). In the agricultural sector, there are strong community-government-university partnerships emerging

---

22   Signatories include the State Minister of Health, State Minister of Education, State Minister of Industry, State Minister of Water and Energy, State Minister of Trade, State Minister of Agriculture, State Minister of Labor and Social Affairs, State Minister of Finance and Economic Development, and State Minister of Women, Children and Youth Affairs

throughout the country (which are disconnected but are beginning to collaborate through the Ag2Nut Ethiopia Community of Practice). There are also many (albeit disconnected) NGO-led programs developing multi-sectoral programs to consider a broad range of needs as well as the systems within which services exist. Learning emerging from projects funded by USAID, Global Affairs Canada and other donors presents reason for optimism that new approaches are emerging. While we can point to examples of positive new directions, there remain significant barriers to challenging the status quo and finding new ways of working that use complexity- and system-based approaches to engage new directions and envision new horizons.

CHAPTER EIGHT

DISCUSSION

At the end of a book on food security one might expect a set of clear recommendations on ways to strengthen food security in rural Ethiopia. I hesitate to do so. Far too often recommendations are idealistic, presented without sufficient context and done without due consideration of constraints. At the same time, there is important knowledge being developed about how we might reduce vulnerabilities and strengthen food security. I position the ideas presented in this concluding chapter as reflections and options. I position my comments thusly because the notions of reflections and options, as opposed to judgments and prescriptions, are sensitive to the challenging and uncertain decisions that individual farmers and decision makers have before them.

There is no single recipe for how food security in southern Ethiopia can be strengthened. The challenges are far too complex. Some of the options that I explore are specific, such as adjustments to existing programs and services, while others are broader and require systemic change, such as reforming modalities of governance. The options I present are clustered into five themes. The first theme covers options related to governance and specifically the potential consequences of a continuation of the status quo compared to the opportunities afforded by more inclusive systems. The second theme outlines options for making programs and services more appropriate, efficient and effective. The third theme addresses infrastructure, with a focus on water. The last two themes cover issues related to finance and the private sector. In presenting these options, I recognize the limitations of my own knowledge as well as the difficulties that decision makers face with respect to resource constraints and competing priorities.

My experience in rural and remote areas of Ethiopia has taught me that people do not refuse pragmatic change but recognize that widespread transformative change is required to surmount the challenges they encounter. One could frame many of the challenges rural Ethiopians encounter as violations of individual human rights, which the government has a responsibility to protect (e.g., the right to health, education, water, housing, food and social security). Our envisioning of policies, programs and services should not be limited to what is politically palatable or what current resources allow. If we confine ourselves to what is "pragmatic" we may fail to consider outside-the-box transformations and redirections. While many of the options I present are pragmatic, I have not limited myself to pragmatism in considering options.

Governance

For decades Ethiopia has been one of the largest recipients of international development aid (Feyissa, 2011; OECD – DAC, 2016). During this period, concerns have consistently been expressed about ethnic-based favoritism and party-affiliated patronage that have marginalized, excluded and disenfranchised significant portions of the population. Until recently, anyone who joined opposition parties or used their constitutional rights to challenge authority would encounter brutality and imprisonment, with indirect penalties of lost government jobs, services and goods. In 2002, Pausewang (2002: 100) concluded, that rural Ethiopians desiring change should "expect resistance from the people wielding authority in the local administration" and "will have to be prepared for a fight, which might cost them dearly."

Food security is one facet of this broader governance challenge. Sen (1990) argued that famine does not occur in countries where there are diverse political freedoms. Food security is political, and we must view strengthening food security as political action. The eminent Ethiopian social scientist Dessalegn Rahmato (2008: 43) wrote that famine:

> ... is a measure of the vulnerability of the peasant world as well as of its resilience, a reflection of the nature of class relations as well as of the relations between the state and peasantry. Famines do not occur if [the] peasant economy is robust, if the popular classes in the rural areas have a tradition of social assertiveness

and resistance, or if the state is in some manner accountable to the people.

Being more explicitly political is necessary. While the rise of a new Prime Minister and promises of free and fair elections (although delayed due to the coronavirus pandemic) are positive indicators, there are serious governance concerns. Millions of people have been displaced due to conflict while religious, ethnic and political conflict have increased to very concerning levels (Yusuf, 2019). The future directions of the country, as envisioned by a broad spectrum of political elites, suggest that unless governance is reformed, the outcomes look bleak (Destiny Ethiopia, 2020). Sundaram (2016: 42) argues that the "promotion of participation, inclusion and voice of poor people is crucial to overcoming some of the political and structural determinants of poverty and its perpetuation." The research presented in this study demonstrates how governance systems that exclude citizen participation result in programs and services that are ineffective in strengthening food security for the most vulnerable. Inclusive political and economic systems are necessary for ensuring that feedback mechanisms exist and a broader sense of public ownership is fostered.

For international actors, donors and NGOs, it is important to reflect on the fact that "the way development (aid) is defined and implemented interacts with processes of elite reproduction, social differentiation, political exclusion, and cultural change" (Uvin, 1999: 6). Current programs and services operate in rural Ethiopia in ways that entrench elite power, marginalize the poor, disincentivize citizen participation and contribute to rising inequality. The result is deepening ethnic, religious and political division. Donor governments have enabled and facilitated these divisions in supporting these same programs and services, and the broader system within which they function.

Acemoglu and Robinson criticize the cycles of failed foreign assistance as follows:

The idea that rich Western countries should provide large amounts of "developmental aid" in order to solve the problem of poverty in sub-Saharan Africa, the Caribbean, Central America, and South Asia is based on an incorrect understanding of what causes poverty. Countries such as Afghanistan are poor because of their extractive institutions—which result in lack of property rights, law and order, or well-functioning legal systems and the stifling dominance of national and, more often, local elites over political and economic life. (Acemoglu and Robinson, 2012: 452-453)

Astute as this complaint may be, it offers little in the way of concrete action. Humanitarian crises emerge and donors are compelled to act. The call to thinking and working politically is not new, yet, it has been insufficiently heeded, and thus it is necessary to repeat it. All actors—from international donors and international agencies to (I)NGOs and community organizations—need to better situate themselves and their activities within in broader political processes. Doing so could result in donors and agencies taking principled positions. *Medecins sans Frontieres*, for instance, denounced the Ethiopian government's misuse of aid and criticized the practice of forced resettlement, which resulted in the organization being expelled from the country in 1985. Better recognition of broader political process could also result in donors and agencies confronting governments and/or withholding funding. In practice, these actions are problematic as they may run counter to the 2005 Paris Declaration on Aid Effectiveness, which prioritizes recipient countries' abilities to set their own priorities.

The theoretical foundations of this research rest on human rights, and I argue that decision-making that navigates these development dilemmas ought to prioritize human rights. Farmer (2005: 229, emphasis original) forcefully argues this point: "It's not acceptable for those of us fortunate enough to have ties to universities and other 'resource-rich' institutions to throw up our hands and bemoan the place-to-place complexity. Underlying this complexity are a series of very simple first principles regarding human rights... Our commitments, our loyalties, must be *primarily* to the poor and the vulnerable." At the same time, I am also cognizant that, as de Waal has noted (2000), external humanitarian and development assistance can be an obstacle to the development of inclusive political and economic systems as they prop us dysfunctional ones. In addition to utilizing human rights as a guide for decision-making, I echo de Waal (1990: 23) in arguing that all activities taking place within the sphere of international aid need to explicitly promote democratic governance and ensure that human rights are protected.

In Ethiopia, calls for democratization and participatory governance have long been made. One of the most forceful, and still relevant, of such was made by Wolde Mariam in 1986 in his book analyzing vulnerabilities to famine in Ethiopia. He argues that progress can be made "by allowing the peasant masses to articulate their own problems and priorities, and by restoring to them their self-confidence and self-respect in order to mobilize their energy and resources to improve their own conditions of living" (1986: 179). Furthermore, Wolde Mariam reasons that it

"is idle to expect the rural people of Ethiopia to cooperate whole-heartedly in a plan or project that they rightly or wrongly believe is outside the realm of their pressing needs. In such instances, they can only become passive spectators, or, at the most, reluctant participants who will forget the whole thing as soon as the pressure is off them. This is why it is necessary for the new administrators to work with the people by allowing them a large measure of involvement in identifying problems, in setting priorities, in allocating resources, and in deciding the course of action" (1986: 185).

This vision of governance for Ethiopia, made by a leading Ethiopian academic, was outlined over three decades ago and remains pertinent to the present time.

Thinking and acting politically, however, requires us to think well beyond political apparatuses. Inequality occurs within and beyond formal political and economic systems. And thus, as Uvin (1999) suggests, we may need to reconsider what developmental activities should be prioritized (or at least included). This may include peacebuilding and conflict resolution programs that would foster greater trust across divides in the socio-cultural sphere. Improvements in this regard will have direct impacts on food security as well as on long-term stability and political and economic inclusivity. Wossen et al. (2016) demonstrate that households with greater social capital are better able to overcome food insecurity challenges. As ethnic and religious divisions run deep in Ethiopia, the need for more inclusive political and economic institutions also requires more inclusive socio-cultural systems. Social networks based on ethnicity, religion and political affiliation may further entrench inequalities, and inroads for inclusiveness are needed to foster change from the bottom up.

Experts from conflict and peace studies may offer more specific options to improve the inclusiveness of the governance system. One potential path emerging from the agricultural realm is research in rural Ethiopia concerning the introduction of new ideas and the altering of individual aspirations, which has shown that encountering new ideas can enable new ways of living and working (Bernard et al., 2014). Communication tools, such as telephone networks, radio scripts and television programs, may be relatively low-cost mechanisms to more explicitly promote social cohesion. Regionally tailored communications could address specific challenges faced in particular locales, with an aim to counter commonly held negative assumptions about others and promote a greater sense of national unity. In putting this option forward, I am fully cognizant that ethnic and religious divisions have long existed and in many ways are reinforced by administrative boundaries and language policies. Focusing on what development experts call the "low-hanging fruit", or relatively straight-forward or low cost interventions, in rural development has the appeal of producing relatively cost-effective and short-term results (e.g., mass malaria net distribution or vaccinations). But it is the nebulous and daunting tasks, such as enhancing social cohesion, that offer potential for more transformative and sustained change.

Appropriate and Efficient Services

The Sustainable Development Goals make explicit, more so than any other international objectives, the idea that success lies with serving the poorest, most marginalized and difficult to reach individuals and communities. Consider the first two goals. Goal 1 states: "End poverty in all its forms everywhere" (UN, 2016: 1). Goal 2 states: "End hunger, achieve food security and improved nutrition and promote sustainable agriculture" (UN, 2016: 1). These goals are important as they will continue to shape government and donor funding, however these goals cannot and be met by status quo programming (Cimadamore, Koehler and Pogge, 2016; Sundaram, 2016). While many of the ideas in the Sustainable Development Agenda are conducive to positive change, the design and implementation of activities working to achieve them may further marginalize the poorest and increase inequality. As discussed in earlier chapters, Ethiopian rural agricultural programs are not reaching those who need them most: those well served by agricultural extension programs tend to be the relatively better off, the inputs and credit needed by the most food-insecure are inaccessible to them due to cost and/or program design, and the safety net program stifles citizen engagement and entrenches elite power.

It is not the case that Ethiopian rural agricultural programs are ineffective for everyone. As was discussed in Chapter 6, The relatively food-secure are gaining access to inputs, training and credit. They are also better positioned to take advantage of technology to obtain a greater share of the crop price when selling. Those with livestock to support the transportation of goods to market are able to sell directly rather than to traders. The Ethiopian Commodity Exchange, agricultural extension services and microfinance institutes have facilitated these positive changes. The essential question that often goes unasked, however, is who is not benefiting from these programs and services, and what impact has this on them. The vulnerability that emerges from exclusion, as well as the benefits accrued from inclusion, has fostered increasing rural inequality. Additional attention is need to better understand the ways in which multiple forms of inequality multiply, such as the challenges not only living in rural areas but also being a member of a minority ethno-linguistic group and engaging in a livelihood practice that is not valued by the government, such as pastoralism (ISSC, IDS and UNESCO, 2016). Seasonal malnutrition, seasonal school absenteeism and dropout, distress migration, lack of access to programs and services, and socio-cultural and political exclusion are all interconnected. Inequality runs much deeper and is much broader than a simple measure of income—both averaged as a figure of GDP and as a direct measure of individuals and their households.

Improving policies, programs and services cannot rely on aggregates and averages. This will not meet the 2030 Agenda objective of "leaving no one behind." However, analyzing existing data in new ways also presents limitations, we need to ask new questions, and we need new ways of answering those questions. Knowledge co-production is one new way asking and answering questions, which can complement existing evidence by adding new perspectives and voices. This option has the potential to identify avenues for more inclusive programs and services as well as options that disproportionately benefit the most food insecure and marginalized— what Gutierrez (1973; Farmer and Gutierrez, 2013) calls the preferential option for the poor, or what Chambers (1983) calls putting the last first.

Extension packages experience low rates of uptake and relatively high rates of discontinuation. As discussed in Chapter 6, some components of packages were broadly used by farmers and reasons why this was the case were presented. The government could better support the most food insecure farmers by reducing its emphasis on promoting the adoption of packages and instead focus on supporting a component-specific, demand-driven system for inputs. This, however, remains a theoretical option as the programs and services have "twin imperatives" that are not limited to supporting food insecure households. Nonetheless, this shift would offer multiple benefits. First, a component-specific, demand-driven system would be more responsive to the needs and priorities of users, and therefore a more effective use of public resources.

Second, a demand-driven system would allow the government to support farmer-led experimentation. Farmer experimentation and "traditional" practices can be more efficient than government-mandated practices, or they can be used in combination with new inputs and methods in unplanned ways. Innovations such as a farmer-developed teff seed planter that enabled row planting (Cochrane, 2017b) is one example of many that demonstrate the potential of farmers to experiment and innovate when they are supported rather than required to follow extension demands.

Third, through a demand-driven system the government could better target its programs and services in each region based on farmer demand, making the program more cost-efficient as extension workers are not forced to promote inputs and methods that farmers have no interest in. This would also act as a feedback mechanism for monitoring where programs and services are not functioning. This is not yet the case. The extension system enforces policies—from the method of planting teff, to the utilization of inputs—sometimes with penalties for those who do not comply. While programs are currently tailored to regions and agricultural research centers support locally relevant studies, the processes remain top-down and have no mechanisms for upward learning (if anything there are disincentives for suggesting or advocating alternatives).

Shifting to a demand-driven model of agricultural extension components would require a significant overhaul of the agricultural extension program. Ethiopia would not be the first country to attempt such a transformation, and much can be learned from the experience of other nations such as India and Uganda (e.g., Birner and Anderson, 2007; Parkinson, 2009). There are other options that would improve the existing system within its current operational modality. Farmers should not be required or forced to purchase inputs. A change to the reporting system, which puts pressure on lower levels of government to meet certain distribution targets, could improve this situation and reduce the pressure experienced by farmers. Microfinance repayment schedules need to be made more flexible in order that farmers who might experience less-than-ideal harvests would not face losing their land because of debt. The development of public research in agriculture, via the regional research centers, has the potential to significantly support farmers. The choice of crop in which research is invested can help to strengthen food security for the most vulnerable, such as engaging in research on crops important for local food security, such as enset, which have received limited research funding. Additional funding for research on these locally important crops, as was done with taro in southern Ethiopia, has the potential to offer significant benefits of improving yields or addressing challenges of pest and disease. Furthermore, providing additional funding through national institutions retains public ownership of innovations and thus complications associated with corporate control of seed and supply chains are avoided.

Even with the governmental promotion of cereal crops, research indicates that increases in the yields of different crops benefit different segments of society. For example, while a 12% to 14% yield increase in teff offers the greatest benefit to urbanites, particularly the urban poor, the economic benefits of a similar increase in maize yields accrue to rural residents (Benson, Engida and Thurlow, 2014). These differences in benefits are due to the nature of producer and consumer markets for the crops. Therefore, the crops in which the government chooses to invest affects who benefits. In Wolaita, cereals are not the most productive crop; many farmers prefer to grow root crops instead, which may have five times more yield than cereals. However, cereals have been prioritized in government-supported research, training and input provision. In some parts of Ethiopia, the government's prioritization of cereal crops aligns with the interests of farmers, but in Wolaita it does not. There is significant potential to realign research, training and extension in a way that would strengthen food security of the most food insecure by focusing upon the crops (like enset, for example) most important to this segment of society.

Beyond adjusting the current modality of implementation for agricultural extension services, there is a need to rethink its purpose. In the past, services were directed specifically at "high potential" areas and larger operations such as state farms. While the objectives have changed, the modus operandi has not. Smallholder farmers are viewed as key to agricultural growth, but the design and implementation of the programs and services disproportionately benefit those with greater assets and land. Thus, the food-insecure are entrenched in a position of chronic food insecurity or experience vulnerability to it. The poorest and most food-insecure households experience many forms of exclusion from rural programs and services: fertilizer access, seed access (and therefore public research into seed breeding), access to extension support (and therefore research on methodologies), credit access and resulting asset accumulation, and new opportunities in livestock (poultry) and agriculture (fruit trees) due to financial limitations and opportunity costs. These households also experience poverty penalties for accessing healthcare and education.

It is essential that programs and services be more inclusive and that they align with the needs, priorities and opportunities identified by farmers. But even more radical rethinking may be required. Research which shows that input-driven growth can increase yields tends to be based on high-potential areas and not marginal lands. Kassie et al. (2010) find that sustainable land management practices (such as minimum tillage and "traditional" practices) outperform chemical fertilizers in low-potential areas. In communities such as those in Wolaita, which are home to different agroecological settings than the highlands, farmer-developed practices may be more productive than those tested in research centers. Conducting numerous studies on farmer practices has led Nyssen to suggest that we ought to prioritize farmer knowledge rather than enforce changes that may not be the most effective or appropriate for local communities (Nyssen et al., 2001).

On a more pragmatic note, according to Handino (2014) Ethiopian farmers do not seek aid and are not aid-dependent. In times of difficulty they opt for a range of adjustments to their lives and in their livelihoods (e.g., adjusting food consumption, seeking off-farm opportunities). When these adjustments and alternatives are not sufficient and there is no external support, then farmers have no choice but to sell assets. It is at this point that farmers cross the famine threshold. What is notable is that there is low dependency on the government for emergency food relief, despite multiple Ethiopian governments fearing such a relationship. Moreover, this finding is not new for rural contexts in other countries (Watts, 1983).

Based on this finding of low dependency, policymakers should recognize that when people in rural communities do seek help, this may indicate that the most vulnerable are on the brink of a serious food insecurity situation that requires immediate attention. In theory, the safety net program has emergency allotments, but these are not made available when needed nor are they accessible when sought (Cochrane and Tamiru, 2016). More could be done to align the safety net with the early warning systems such as that run by FEWS Net. Donors and NGOs can be important mediators in these shifts toward enabling better food security, but finding a path to be an effective agent of change in government systems is a task that few external actors have successfully managed.

Before closing this section, it merits noting that programs and services specific to agriculture are just one part of the interconnected lives of smallholder families. In fact, Banerjee et al. (2015) demonstrate that integrated approaches to supporting livelihoods, which took a more holistic and multi-sectoral approach to development planning, have positive immediate and long-term impacts on poverty reduction. The current coverage of healthcare beyond basic health posts, education beyond the primary years, veterinary services, and fruit tree nurseries remain far too low. The Government of Ethiopia has made significant progress in expanding coverage and increasing accessibility of these services. However, much more work is required to improve the quality of these services. Veterinary services are a good example: in many cases a building exists but is understaffed, lacks medications and does not have a functional cold chain system for vaccines and other temperature sensitive commodities. That said, it is easy to criticize the poor quality of existing services but much more difficult to offer specific advice within the bounds of existing resource and capacity constraints.

Infrastructure

Infrastructure plays an important role in strengthening food security. This includes transportation, markets, irrigation, electricity and mobile phone networks, and the buildings to expand access to education, healthcare and water. Expanding infrastructure is not a novel recommendation. Gibson also advocates for "investments in agricultural infrastructure, roads, markets, water harvesting devices, institutions and credit" (2012: 498). Rather than offer a list of essential needs, the focus of this section will be on options related to irrigation and drinking water, building on the transformative impacts discussed in Chapter 6.

The current situation of irrigation infrastructure in Ethiopia demonstrates both its potential and the opportunities it presents. Exact figures on access to irrigation in Ethiopia are rare due to poor information regarding which irrigation systems are functional and which are not. However, available data suggests only a small percentage of smallholder farmers have access to irrigation. For example, in 2006, the World Bank (2006) found that only 5% of Ethiopia's total potential land for irrigation (3.7 million hectares) was irrigated. The Ministry of Water, Irrigation and Energy has stated that as of 2010 irrigation coverage was less than 3% (Birhan, 2013). A significant portion of the irrigated land was state-owned or home to commercial operations. The available data makes clear that small- and medium-scale irrigation can contribute to significantly strengthening food security (Agide et al., 2016; Ahmed, Mume and Kedir, 2014; Beyene and Engida, 2016; Gebrehiwot, Mesfin and Nyssen, 2015; Kelilo, Ketema and Kedir, 2014; Ven Den Berg and Ruben, 2006). Irrigation should be understood not only as a potential means to increase yields and income but also as an important means for income and food security stabilization, allowing households to reduce the risks associated with seasonality and annual rainfall fluctuations (Masset, 2012). At the same time, while irrigation offers opportunities, it is not feasible in all places and at all times, and thus it should be seen as one option among others based on the local context (Dereveux, Sabates-Wheeler and Longhurst, 2012).

The broad recommendation for irrigation expansion has been recognized by the Government of Ethiopia, and it is working with its partners to address it. For example, the Ministry of Water, Irrigation and Energy explicitly seeks to expand irrigation coverage and has planned to construct medium- and large-scale irrigation schemes. However, improving irrigation infrastructure must also take into account issues of equity and capacity, which Yami (2016) identified as hindering the effectiveness of existing irrigation projects in Ethiopia. Irrigation projects designed to serve commercial interests may further increase inequalities. If food security is the government's goal, it must develop and convey explicit objectives whereby smallholder farmers are prioritized in public sector investments. The government also must regulate commercial enterprises as they develop their own irrigation infrastructure lest smallholder farmers lose access to existing water resources (Bues, 2011). Additionally, regulation of government and private sector investments should consider broader impacts and unintended negative consequences such as higher rates of malaria (Ersado et al., 2004; Kibret et al., 2014). Rehabilitation and expansion of irrigation infrastructure should also integrate monitoring systems to identify unknown threats related to improved and expanded irrigation that may emerge.

Furthermore, while investment is needed to support new irrigation coverage, there are key areas where improvements can be made in the delivery and management of existing water systems. In particular, focus should be on reducing water loss, particularly on-farm water loss, and enhancing management to improve fairness of distribution (Agide et al., 2016). Repairing or improving existing irrigation schemes would be a relatively low-cost means to enhancing smallholder access to irrigation.

Also related to water infrastructure is improved access to drinking water. The literature makes clear the linkages between food security and access to clean water in the realms of nutrition, sanitation, hygiene, health and time (Dereveux, Sabates-Wheeler and Longhurst, 2012). A study in Ethiopia conducted by Aklilu (2013) has demonstrated the impact that improved access to drinking water has on strengthening food security. As with irrigation infrastructure, there is significant room for cost-efficient rehabilitation of existing water infrastructure. An estimated 50,000 water supply infrastructure units are in a state of disrepair across Africa (Ramalingam, 2013). Figures for all of Ethiopia are unknown but non-functioning water supply points are a common phenomenon throughout rural areas. Within Wolaita, Zonal Administration data suggests that one-fifth of hand-dug wells with hand pumps, more than half of shallow wells with hand pumps, 69% of deep wells and 11% of springs are not functional. In addition to rehabilitating existing infrastructure, management plans must address the reasons for widespread disrepair and put in place a strategy to ensure the continued functionality of water supply infrastructure.

Finance

Smallholder farmers frequently need access to credit, and the options available to them are limited, with high interest rates and inflexible repayment terms (see Chapter 6). The extent of borrowing and debt found within Wolaita was well beyond what many Ethiopian researchers anticipated, those findings provide new knowledge on the dynamics of the rural financial market (Cochrane and Thornton, 2017). It is important to note that the majority of borrowing was done to ensure basic needs are met (healthcare, education and food), suggesting that borrowed funds for the most part are not being invested. Rather, what we are witnessing is households which are vulnerable to minor shocks borrowing to survive through the year.

One option that can support a shift in financial service delivery is expanding the use of mobile-based cash transfers (conditional or unconditional), which are slowly emerging in Ethiopia but continue to be hindered by restrictive financial regulation. Programs such as Bolsa Familia in Brazil have shown that systems can be created that reduce "financial leakage" (i.e., corruption and politicization) and effectively redistribute funds to the most vulnerable. The challenges of limited telecommunication coverage and illiteracy in parts of Brazil were overcome by experimental, localized solutions, such as branchless banking for remote areas. Other systems, such as offering e-vouchers instead of e-transfers, have been put into practice in Nigeria. My research does not offer a specific recommendation that is most suitable for rural Ethiopia. Rather, it suggests that a relatively minor amount of national resources can be utilized to reduce costly humanitarian responses using effective, targeted mobile-based transfers.

Reducing vulnerability to shocks and the need to borrow to meet necessities are only one side of a broader financial challenge. Significant opportunities exist for rural smallholder households to gain a greater share of the value of their sold yields, to invest in new businesses (e.g., livestock fattening and sale), and to improve their land and livelihood through positive diversification and land management. These opportunities are not being facilitated by the existing microfinance system, except for a few individuals. The largest barrier identified by community members in Wolaita was the program's design, specifically the inflexible payment options combined with the fear of losing their land as a consequence of being unable to repay. If the government seeks to enable microfinance opportunities, it must (1) change the program design, (2) alter the repayment terms, and (3) allow alternative, non-governmental options to develop. Informal savings groups (*equb*) and recent self-help development activities revolving around savings groups present alternatives for people to gain access to credit in a way that is self-organized. While there is potential to scale these activities to broaden access to credit, if they are not well managed, there is a potential to replicate existing forms of existing forms of inequality in society (e.g., members may be less willing to accept members who are considered "risky" for defaulting on loans, which may be one means of exclusion, as are other forms of group-based identity), as was discussed in Chapter 7.

With respect to point three above, the development of alternative, non-governmental options, the international NGO One Acre Fund operates throughout East Africa and one of its services is credit provision. However, due to financial regulations in Ethiopia, One Acre Fund is not able to provide credit in the country. As a result of these regulations, smallholder farmers have few options to select from. Due to existing regulations, government services do not have to be competitive with other service providers, nor have they created an environment where innovation and creativity would be rewarded. The result is ineffective services continuing to operate unchallenged alongside informal options with predatory repayment terms. Rather than call for an overhaul of the financial system and its regulations, specific policies can be developed that allow registered non-profit organizations to offer credit services. This minor shift will have an important impact while not requiring lengthy discussions about the national financial regulatory system.

On the subject of finance, a large amount of interest has been generated by smallholder farmer insurance programs in Ethiopia (the large amount of emerging research cannot be summarized here, one study will be noted, as it makes connections to government services, particularly the Safety Net). For instance, Oren (2013) found that Ethiopian farmers, despite an apparent need for it, did not adopt rainfall index insurance offered by two well-known companies, Dashen (bank) and Nyala (insurance company). Although this was a pilot in one region (Amhara), the author argues that the evidence suggests that demand for insurance is lower in places where the safety net operates. Oren also argues that the study shows that the "perception of government credibility drives behavior because individuals consider the government to be a reliable source of aid" (Oren, 2013: 27). Although this was a quantitative study and few contextual factors were taken into account, the author speculates that "it may be that the government rewards supporters" by prioritizing them for the safety net. A wealth of examples and qualitative studies have been noted throughout this book that show this to be the case, at least in some contexts. Theoretically, smallholder farmer insurance (crop, weather, rainfall) offers great potential to overcome the challenges of unpredictable rainfall and seasonality, but it could quite easily have little to no impact if it is not designed and implemented to meet the needs and priorities of smallholder farmers.

Private Sector

Rural development programming insufficiently takes into account the important role of the private sector in smallholder farmer livelihoods. The private sector provides credit, purchases crops and transports goods to markets. It is one means of accessing inputs and livestock and/or fruit trees. It is the private sector that engages with local markets and in so doing supports the expansion of employment opportunities. Although not covered in detail in this research, the expansion of khat production and trade throughout Ethiopia is an example of a rapidly expanding agricultural market almost entirely driven by the private sector and one that has created a range of new forms of employment throughout the supply chain (Cochrane and O'Regan, 2016).

There are some scholars who place a heavy emphasis on private sector job creation. For instance, Uvin (2009: 119) argues strongly that "job creation is the only key to development. Nothing else matters. Any way to promote job creation must be pursued: decentralized vocational training that builds on local economic dynamics and resources; the transformation of primary products; economic networks that bring to the growing cities the food, artisanal, and other products they need; intermediate technologies that use local resources, including in the field of recycling and trash removal; public works that create employment during low economic periods at the same time maintaining infrastructure; training in basic business skills for young men and women, as well as simplified and preferably non-corrupt procedures for establishing small businesses." Rahmato (2007) shares an enthusiasm for job creation, and both of their examples are ones that balance social services (e.g., education and training) with economic growth. Amidst this promotion, however, I argue that we must be careful in promoting economic development and job creation by any means as we have seen that some efforts to create jobs have resulted in lost land and livelihoods. They may also increase inequality and deepen vulnerability as the new jobs are short-term and low-paid.

Research by Bedemo et al. (2014) finds that rural labor markets can contribute significantly to household resources and income. However, this general finding requires further clarification as not all forms of private sector investment are equal, nor do they equally offer opportunity for those who need such employment. For example, foreign direct investment (FDI) in agriculture has the potential to create jobs, but the approach of large-scale land leases has been shown to provide marginal and temporary employment opportunities (Alamirew et al., 2015). Rather than encourage FDI in the form of large-scale land leases, the government could offer incentives for upstream investments in the agricultural sector, such as in processing and packaging for domestic and international markets. Investments of this nature support smallholder agricultural livelihoods rather than compete with them for land and water as well as in the markets. As the government has enabled the rapid expansion of the manufacturing base, low-skill entry jobs are also not equally available to those who need them, often due to unintended impacts of other policies, such as regional language policies resulting in people not speaking federal or regional languages.

A final note on private sector investment is that investment touted as "pro-poor" may not be as beneficial for smallholder farmers as suggested. For example, a study on Fairtrade ventures in Ethiopia and Uganda found they are "not effective in protecting the rights of or improving the welfare of poor rural wage workers" when compared to alternative "institutional settings" for export commodities (Cramer et al., 2017: 841). There are potential responses to Fairtrade's failure to generate positive impacts for the poorest members of society. For example, the Fairtrade market is driven by consumers choosing to pay a higher price for products based on the assumption that producers receive a more just payment for their labor and products. If producers are not seeing these benefits, consumers need to put pressure on Fairtrade companies to ensure their practices have the positive impact that they advocate. Cramer et al. (2017) suggest that relatively smaller firms, like these Fairtrade companies, face a range of unique wage and labor challenges when engaging in competitive export markets when compared to larger and more established companies. Another challenge for Fairtrade as a means to reshape the market is scale. While the Fairtrade market is growing substantially, it remains a niche market and there needs to be a recognition that the majority of crops grown and sold by smallholder farmers do not enter it. Rather than await a consumer market driven by social-justice minded consumers and investors motivated by redistribution, the Government of Ethiopia will need to take a proactive role in seeking investors in sectors that complement smallholder farmer activities in the agricultural sector and ensuring that investors are regulated so that contracts are upheld and environmental regulations are followed.

Clarifications

Some readers might ask why I have chosen to focus only on these five areas for options to improve food security? Before ending this book, I will attempt to clarify my reasons for prioritizing these five areas by discussing potential options not considered here. Specifically, I want to address three areas where priority has been made by others scholars in the development of policy and programs to strengthen food security: (1) food loss and waste, (2) urbanization and migration, and (3) land rights. These topics are important; the clarifications that follow will situate them within the broader argument made in this chapter and offer some reflections on why they have not been prioritized in this book.

A sizable literature has been devoted to food loss and waste in recent years. The estimates of the amount of food loss and waste demonstrate why the issue has received so much attention. The Food and Agriculture Organization estimates that 1.3 billion tons of food is wasted or lost, directly costing US$750 billion annually, and indirectly costing much more in misused resources and negative impacts on the environment (FAO, 2013a). However, studies in rural Ethiopia suggest that post-harvest losses for smallholder farmers are relatively modest—between 2.2% and 3.3% for the main cereal teff (McCann, 1995; Minten, Engida and Tamru, 2016). This does not take into account pre-harvest losses, which vary significantly from year to year. Undoubtedly, reducing any loss improves smallholder farmer income and food security. Available research indicates that the magnitude of the potential gains is relatively small when compared to other potential intervention areas. To reiterate, I am not arguing that food waste and loss are unimportant but rather that other supports for smallholder farmers have a greater potential for improving food security.

A second clarification concerns migration and urbanization. As land fragmentation continues and landholdings fall short of the minimum threshold of what is required to be self-sufficient in an average year, increasingly there is talk about supporting a shift away from smallholder livelihoods. Rahmato (2007) has suggested that because smallholder farming in parts of the country cannot adequately support large numbers of people, rural inhabitants should be assisted to move to urban areas through facilitated migration. This was a trend that was predicted to occur across the continent (Bryceson, 1997). Arguably, the Government of Ethiopia is facilitating this transition, with its strong emphasis on building industrial parks and its aim of creating a manufacturing industry. To support such a transition, Rahmato argued that there is a need for appropriate and accessible training and education aligned with the needs of the job market to enable a transition that aligns with existing and anticipated future jobs rather than adding to already high levels of unemployment. Yet, in this process we ought not lose sight of justice and human rights. As Bettini, Nash and Gioli (2017) point out, a discourse that views migration as a viable adaptation option can neglect the human rights of the individuals involved and instead place greater burdens on them as they are pressured to migrate, find work and compete in challenging labor markets. While I do not oppose migration, these processes should be based on respect and dignity rather than trying to relocate "surplus people" from challenging rural contexts into equally challenging urban settings with high levels of unemployment. Before advocating for migration away from agriculture, we ought to advocate the equitable distribution of national resources (Ferguson, 2015) or, at a bare minimum, that basic services be provided.

A third clarification is required with regard to land rights and land tenure. Since the late 1990s the government has been implementing a land certification program and this has had a range of positive impacts for smallholder farmers. The first phase of the land certification program was paper-based and is largely complete, while the second phase, an electronic certification system, remains an expensive pilot with limited demand. Improved tenure has positive impacts. However, I am less confident that the second phase of certification will add significant value for smallholder farmers relative to its cost. Nor I do I anticipate it will address some of the ongoing challenges, particularly those related to land rights for women and for commonly held property. In promoting improved land rights it must be recognized that legal shifts alone will be insufficient (Ossome, 2014). Research indicates that legal reform has had limited impact on traditional norms and attitudes (Tura, 2014). Despite significant progress in land certification and legal reform, Bezu and Holden (2014) find that only 3% of landholders are young women and only 6% of families are even considering bequeathing land to daughters. Based on these experiences, and the anticipated impacts of the second phase of the land certification program, it is clear that changes to socio-cultural norms are needed to ensure that land certification and legal changes translate into more equitable and inclusive tenure.

Final Words

More than a decade ago Rahmato (2007) argued that the future of rural agricultural livelihoods in places like Wolaita had become less viable. Farmers were vulnerable to even the smallest of shocks and emergency situations were recurrent. More recent studies suggest that even if the poorest farmers were to adopt all advocated practices and inputs this would not be sufficient to uplift them from poverty (Kotu and Admassie, 2015). I grappled with these difficult and worrisome findings as I weighed focusing on pragmatic reforms or calls for transformative revolution. I have attempted to strike a balance between the two, not by simply offering options on design and implementation adjustments but by attending to systemic questions of governance and justice.

As I have argued throughout this book, to improve research and practice aimed at strengthening food security in rural areas, particularly for the most food-insecure, we must rethink evidence. Available data based on household surveys, designed to obtain particular types of information, may make important details invisible. We must rethink evidence—how we obtain it, what constitutes useful knowledge, and how we act on it—in decision-making processes. As noted in this book, there are some positive examples of these already occurring (e.g., problem-based, multi-sectoral approaches; innovative approaches to program delivery), however these remain exceptions to the status quo. Enabling these transformations requires thinking and acting politically. This includes explicitly investigating and acting on information that shows who is excluded, marginalized and disenfranchised, such as evidence that shows disproportionate under-investment in basic healthcare, education and livelihood support services. It requires envisioning change beyond the compartments of agricultural extension and credit such as facilitating citizen participation, free speech and freedom of the press. The impact of inclusive political and economic systems on food security cannot be understated, yet many food security programs and services are implemented as if they are apolitical and compartmentalized. While there is much enthusiasm about the new Prime Minister, time will tell if this marks a new beginning, or in his phraseology if a new horizon is upon us, or not. Undoubtedly, Ethiopia is making progress in creating new programs and expanding the coverage of services, yet significant challenges remain. With almost half of all children under the age of five experiencing stunted growth due to malnutrition, the need for action is urgent lest another generation be denied the opportunity to fulfill its potential because it has been limited by food insecurity.

BIBLIOGRAPHY

Aadland, O. (2002). Sera: Traditionalism or Living Democratic Values? A Case Study of the Sidama in Southern Ethiopia (p. 29-44). In *Ethiopia: The Challenge of Democracy from Below*, edited by Bahru Zewde and Siegfried Pausewang. Forum for Social Studies: Addis Ababa.

Aalen, L. (2011). *The Politics of Ethnicity in Ethiopia*. Brill: Leiden.

Abate, G. T., Rashid, S., Borzaga, C. and Getnet, K. (2016). Rural Finance and Agricultural Technology Adoption in Ethiopia: Does the Institutional Design of Lending Organizations Matter? *World Development* 84: 235-253.

Abbink, J. (2006). Discomfiture of Democracy? The 2005 Election Crisis in Ethiopia and its Aftermath. *African Affairs* 105(419): 173-199.

Abdulla, A. M. (2015). Determinants of Household Food Security and Coping Strategies: The Case of Bule-Hora District, Borana Zone, Oromia, Ethiopia. *European Journal of Food Science and Technology* 3: 30-44.

Abebe, S. G. (2016). *The Last Post-Cold War Socialist Federation: Ethnicity, Ideology and Democracy in Ethiopia*. Routledge: New York.

Abebe, N., Kebede, T. and Addise, D. (2017). Diabetes in Ethiopia 2000-2016 – Prevalence and Related Acute and Chronic Complications; A Systematic Review. African Journal of Diabetes Medicine 25(2): 7-12.

Abegaz, B. (2011). *Political Parties in Business*. Working Paper 113. Department of Economics, College of William and Mary: Williamsburg.

Abraham, A. (2013). Toward a Workable Biosafety System for Regulating Genetically Modified Organisms in Ethiopia. *GM Crops & Food: Biotechnology in Agriculture and the Food Chain* 4: 28-35.

Abraham, K. (1994). *Ethiopia From Bullets to the Ballot Box: The Bumpy Road to Democracy and the Political Economy of Transition*. Red Sea Press: Lawrenceville, NJ.

Abrha, H., Belew, D. and Woldegiorgis, G. (2014). Effect of Inter and Intra Row Spacing on Seed Tuber Yield and Yield Components of Potato (Solanum tuberosum L.) at Ofla Woreda, Northern Ethiopia. *African Journal of Plant Science* 8(6): 285-290.

ACCRA. (2011). *Preparing for the future? Understanding the influence of development interventions on adaptive capacity at the local level in Ethiopia.* http://oxfamilibrary.openrepository.com/oxfam/bitstream/10546/18829 0/3/rr-accra-ethiopia-development-adaptive-capacity-report-271011- en.pdf.

Acemoglu, D. and Robinson, J. A. (2006). *Economic Origins of Dictatorship and Democracy.* Cambridge University Press: New York.

Acemoglu, D. and Robinson, J. A. (2012). *Why Nations Fail: The Origins of Power, Prosperity, and Poverty.* Crown Business: New York.

Adedeji, A. (1989). *Interaction between Structuralism, Structural Adjustment and Food Security Policies in Development Policy Management.* European Centre for Development Policy Management: Maastricht.

Adem, T. A. (2019). Land Tenure and Tenure Policy in Ethiopia, 1950-2000. In Oxford Handbook of the Ethiopian Economy edited by F. Cheru, C. Cramer and A. Oqubay. Oxford University Press: Oxford.

Africa Intelligence. (2013). *Ethiopia: Land policy revisited.* http://farmlandgrab.org/post/view/22621

Africa Leadership Forum. (1989). *The Challenges of Agricultural Production and Food Security in Africa.* Conference Report 27-30 July 1989, Ota, Nigeria.

Agarwal, B. (2013). *Food Security, Food Sovereignty and Democratic Choice: Addressing Potential Contradictions.* Presented at Agrarian Studies Conference, Yale University, September 14-15.

Agide, Z., Haileslassie, A., Sally, H., Erkossa, T., Schmitter, P., Langan, S. and Hoekstra, D. (2016). *Analysis of Water Delivery Performance of Smallholder Irrigation Schemes in Ethiopia: Diversity and Lessons Across Schemes, Typologies and Reaches.* International Livestock Research Institute: Nairobi.

Ahmad, A. H. (2000). Muslims of Gondar 1864-1941. *Annales d'Ethiopie* 16: 161-172.

Ahmed, A. (pen name: DRAZ) (2017). *Erkab nna Menber.* Self-Published: Unknown.

Ahmed, B., Mume, J. and Kedir, A. (2014). Impact of Small-scale Irrigation on Farm Income Generation and Food Security Status: The Case of Lowland Areas, Oromia, Ethiopia. *International Journal of Economics and Empirical Research* 2(10): 412-419.

Ahmed, M. H. (2015). Adoption of Multiple Agricultural Technologies in Maize Production of the Central Rift Valley of Ethiopia. *Studies in Agricultural Economics* 117: 162-168.

Aklilu, A. Z. (2013). *Water, Smallholders and Food Security – An Econometric Assessment of the Effect of Time Spent on Collecting Water on Households' Economy and Food Security in Rural Ethiopia.* Master's thesis,

Environmental Economics and Management, Swedish University of Agricultural Sciences.

Aklilu, H. A., Alemkinders, C. J., Udo, H. M. and va der Zijpp, A. J. (2007). Village Poultry and Marketing in Relation to Gender, Religious Festivals and Market Access. *Tropical Animal Health Production* 39: 165-177.

Alamgir, M. and Arora, P. (1991). *Providing Food Security for All. International Fund for Agricultural Development*. New York University Press: New York.

Alamirew, B., Grethe, H., Siddig, K. H. and Wossen, T. (2015). Do Land Transfers to International Investors Contribute to Employment Generation and Local Food Security? Evidence from Oromia Region, Ethiopia. *International Journal of Social Economics* 42(12): 1121-1138.

Alemu, G. (2009). *A Case Study of Aid Effectiveness in Ethiopia: Analysis of the Health Sector Aid Architecture*. Brookings Institute: Washington.

Alinsky, S. D. (1971). *Rules for Radicals*. Vintage: New York.

Altieri, M. A. (1995). *Agroecology: Creating the Synergisms for a Sustainable Agriculture*. UNDP Guidebook Series: New York.

Amin, S. (1976). *Unequal Development: An Essay on the Social Formations of Peripheral Capitalism*. Monthly Review Press: New York.

Aminaw, W. and Seyoum, Y. (2017). Increasing Prevalence of Diabetes Mellitus in a Developing Country and its Related Factors. *PloS One* 12(11): e0187670.

Amnesty International. (2016). *Ethiopia: Dozens Killed as Police Use Excessive Force Against Peaceful Protesters*. www.amnesty.org/en/latest/news/2016/08/ethiopia-dozens-killed-as-police-use-excessive-force-against-peaceful-protesters/

Anderson, B. (1983). *Imagined Communities*. Verso: New York.

Andrews, M. (2013). *The Limits of Institutional Reform in Development: Changing Rules for Realistic Solutions*. Cambridge University Press: Cambridge.

Andrews, N. (2009). Foreign Aid and Development in Africa: What the Literature Says and What the Reality Is. *Journal of African Studies and Development* 1: 8-15.

Attwood, D. (2007). Small is Deadly, Big is Wasteful. In *Waterscapes* edited by A. Baviskar. Permanent Black Press: New Delhi.

Bahru Z. (1991). *A History of Modern Ethiopia 1855-1991*. Addis Ababa University Press: Addis Ababa.

Bahru Z. (2002). Introduction (p 7-16). In *Ethiopia: The Challenge of Democracy from Below*, edited by Bahru Zewde and Siegfried Pausewang. Forum for Social Studies: Addis Ababa.

Bahru Z. (2014). *The Quest for Socialist Utopia: The Ethiopian Student Movement c. 1960-1974*. Addis Ababa University Press: Addis Ababa.

Bailey, R. and Willoughby, R. (2013). *Edible Oil: Food Security in the Gulf.* Chatham House Briefing Paper EEP BP 2013/03. Chatham House: London.

Ballard, T. J., Kepple, A. W. and Cafiero, C. (2013). *The Food Insecurity Experience Scale: Development of a Global Standard for Monitoring Hunger Worldwide.* Technical Paper. Food and Agriculture Organization: Rome.

Banerjee, A., Duflo, E., Goldberg, N., Karlan, D., Osei, R., Pariente, W., Shapiro, J., Thuysbaert, B. and Udry, C. (2015). A Multifaceted Program Causes Lasting Progress for the Very Poor: Evidence from Six Countries. *Science* 348(6236): 1260799-1 (p. 1-17).

Barder, O. (2012). *What is Development?* Center for Global Development: http://www.cgdev.org/blog/what-development

Barker, D. (2007). *The Rise and Predictable Fall of Globalized Industrialized Agriculture.* The International Forum on Globalization: San Francisco.

Barnes, C. (2006). *Ethiopia: A Sociopolitical Assessment.* A report commissioned by the United Nations High Commissioner for Refugees, Status Determination and Protection Information Section (DIPS).

Barnett, A. D. (1953). China's Road to Collectivization. *Journal of Farm Economics* 35(2): 188-202.

Barraclough, S. and Utting, P. (1987). *Food Security Trends and Prospects in Latin America.* Working Paper No. 99, Helen Kellog Institute for International Studies, University of Notre Dame.

Barrett, C. (2010). Measuring Food Insecurity. *Science* 327: 825-828.

Barrett, C., Reardon, T. and Webb, P. (eds) (2001). Income Diversification and Livelihoods in Rural Africa: Cause and Consequence of Change. *Food Policy* 26(4), Special Issue.

Barth, F. (1964). Capital Investment and Social Structure of a Pastoral Nomad Group in South Persia. In *Capital, Savings and Credit in Peasant Societies from Asia, Oceania, the Caribbean and Middle America* edited by R. Firth and B. Yamey. Aldine Publishing Company: Chicago.

Bates, R. H. (1981). *Markets and States in Tropical Africa: The Political Basis of Agricultural Policies.* University of California Press: Berkeley.

Baumgartner, F. and Jones, B. (1993). *Agendas and Instability in American Politics.* University of Chicago: Chicago.

Bayart, J.-F. (1989). *L'Etat en Afrique: La Politique du Ventre.* FAYARD: Paris.

BBC. (1984). *Extent of Ethiopia Famine Revealed.* http://news.bbc.co.uk/2/hi/8315248.stm

Bedemo, A., Getnet, K., Kassa, B. and Chaurasia, S. (2014). The Role of the Rural Labor Market in Reducing Poverty in Western Ethiopia. *Journal of Development and Agricultural Economics* 6(7): 299-308.

Belay, K. (2003). Agricultural Extension in Ethiopia: The Case of Participatory Demonstration and Training Extension System. *Journal of Social Development in Africa* 18: 49-84.

Bellu, L. (2011). *Development and Development Paradigms: A (Reasoned) Review of Prevailing Visions*. Food and Agriculture Organization: Rome.

Benson, T., Engida, E. and Thurlow, J. (2014). *The Economywide Effects of Teff, Wheat, and Maize Production Increases in Ethiopia: Results of Economywide Modeling*. Working Paper 01366, International Food Policy Research Institute: Washington.

Berhane, G., Gilligan, D., Hoddinott, J., Kumar, N. and Taffesse, A. (2014). Can Social Protection Work in Africa? The Impact of Ethiopia's Productive Safety Net Programme. *Economic Development and Cultural Change* 63: 1-16.

Berhane, G., Hoddinott, J. and Kumar, N. (2014). *The Productive Safety Net Programme and the Nutritional Status of Pre-School Children in Ethiopia – Preliminary Results*. Presentation at DFID, Addis Ababa, 14 August 2014.

Berhanu, K. (2012). *The Political Economy of Agricultural Extension in Ethiopia: Economic Growth and Political Control*. Working Paper 042. Future Agricultures: Brighton.

Berhanu, K. and Poulton, C. (2014). The Political Economy of Agricultural Extension Policy in Ethiopia: Economic Growth and Political Control. *Development and Policy Review* 32(S2): S197-S213.

Bernard, T., Dercon, S., Orkin, K. and Taffesse, A. S. (2014). *The Future in Mind: Aspirations and Forward-looking Behaviour in Rural Ethiopia*. CSAE Working Paper WPS/2014-16.

Bernstein, H. (2013). *Food Sovereignty: A Skeptical View*. Presented at Agrarian Studies Conference, Yale University, September 14-15.

Berry, L. and Ofcansky, T. (2004). *Ethiopia a Country Study*. Kessinger Publishing: Whitefish.

Bettini, G., Nash, S. L. and Gioli, G. (2017). One Step Forward, Two Steps Back? The Fading Contours of (In)justice in Competing Discourses on Climate Migration. *The Geographic Journal* 183(4): 348-358.

Beyene, B. M. (2014). The Effects of International Remittances on Poverty and Inequality in Ethiopia. *Journal of Development Studies* 50: 1380-1396.

Beyene, L. M. and Engida, E. (2016). Public Investment in Irrigation and Training, Growth and Poverty Reduction in Ethiopia. *International Journal of Microsimulation* 9: 86-108.

Beyene, Y., Botha, A-M. and Myburg, A. A. (2005). Genetic Diversity in Traditional Ethiopian Highland Maize Accessions Assessed by AFLP Markers and Morphological Traits. *Biodiversity and Conservation* 15: 2655-2671.

Bezabih, M., Holden, S. and Mannberg, A. (2016). The Role of Land Certification in Reducing Gaps in Productivity between Male- and Female-owned Farms in Rural Ethiopia. *Journal of Development Studies* 52: 360-376.

Bezu, S. and Barrett, C. B. (2010). *Activity Choice in Rural Non-farm Employment (RNFE): Survival Versus Accumulative Strategy.* MPRA Paper No. 55034. https://mpra.ub.uni-muenchen.de/55034/2/MPRA_paper_55034.pdf

Bezu, S. and Holden, S. (2008). Can Food-for-work Encourage Agricultural Production? *Food Policy* 33: 541-549.

Bezu, S. and Holden, S. (2014). Are Youth in Ethiopia Abandoning Agriculture? *World Development* 64: 259-272.

Bhattacharya, J., Currie, J. and Haider, S. (2004). Poverty, Food Insecurity, and Nutritional Outcomes in Children and Adults. *Journal of Health Economics* 23: 839-862.

Biazin, B., Sterk G. and Temesgen, M. (2014). Participatory Planning of Appropriate Rainwater Harvesting and Management Techniques in the Central Rift Valley Dry Lands of Ethiopia. *Environment and Natural Resources Research* 4(3): 123-139.

Birhan, D. (2013). *Ethiopia's Ministry of Water & Energy to Add Irrigation.* http://debirhan.com/?p=1583

Birner, R. and Anderson, J. R. (2007). *How to Make Agricultural Extension Demand Driven? The Case of India's Agricultural Extension Policy.* IFPRI: Washington.

Bonger, T., Ayeke, G. and Kuma, T. (2004). *Agricultural Extension, Adoption, and Diffusion in Ethiopia.* Ethiopian Development Research Institute: Addis Ababa.

Bossio, D., Erkossa, T., Dile, Y., McCartney, M., Killiches, F. and Hoff, H. (2012). Water Implications of Foreign Direct Investment in Ethiopia's Agricultural Sector. *Water Alternatives* 5(2): 223-242.

Bowen, G. (2008). Naturalistic Inquiry and the Saturation Concept: A Research Note. *Qualitative Research* 8: 137-152.

Braukamper, U. (1992). Aspects of Religious Syncretism in Southern Ethiopia. *Journal of Religion in Africa* 22(3): 194-207.

Brown, L. (2012). Diverting Corn and Grain to Biofuels Increases Food Insecurity. In *At Issue: Food Insecurity*, Edited by L. Gerdes. Greenhaven Press: New York.

Bryceson, D. F. (1997). De-Agrarianisation in Sub-Saharan Africa: Acknowledging the Inevitable. In *Farewell to Farms: De-Agrarianisation and Employment in Africa* edited by D. F. Bryceson and V. Jamal. Routledge: New York.

Bues, A. (2011). *Agricultural Foreign Direct Investment and Water Rights: An Institutional Analysis from Ethiopia.* International Conference on

Global Land Grabbing, 6-8 April, Institute of Development Studies, University of Sussex.

Bues, A. and Theesfeld, I. (2012). Water Grabbing and the Role of Power: Shifting Water Governance in the Light of Agricultural Foreign Direct Investment. *Water Alternatives* 5(2): 266-283.

Burke, M. and Lobell, D. (2010). Food Security and Adaptation to Climate Change: What Do We Know? (pp. 133-153). In *Climate Change and Food Security*. Springer: Dordrecht.

Burlando, A. (2015). The Disease Environment, Schooling, and Development Outcomes. Evidence from Ethiopia. *Journal of Development Studies* 51: 1563-1584.

Burnett, K. and Murphy, S. (2013). *What Place for International Trade in Food Sovereignty?* Presented at Agrarian Studies Conference, Yale University, September 14-15.

Burns, D. and Worsley, S. (2015). *Navigating Complexity in International Development: Facilitating Sustainable Change at Scale*. Practical Action Publishing: Rugby, UK.

Busck, M., Meinecke, S., Hansen, S. and Andersen, A. (2012). *Foreign Land Investments for Biofuel Production*. Rosklide University Dissertation.

Butterly, J. and Shepherd, J. (2010). *Hunger: The Biology and Politics of Starvation*. University Press of New England: Lebanon, NH.

Cabral, A. (1977; 2016 translation). *Resistance and Decolonization*. Rowman & Littlefield: London.

Cameron, D. B., Mishra, A. and Brown, A. N. (2016). The Growth of Impact Evaluations for International Development: How Much Have We Learned? *Journal of Development Effectiveness* 8(1): 1-21.

Carletto, C., Jolliffe, D. and Banerjee, R. (2015). From Tragedy to Renaissance: Improving Agricultural Data for Better Policies. *Journal of Development Studies* 51: 133-148.

Carothers, T. and de Gramont, D. (2013). *The Almost Revolution: Development Aid Confronts Politics*. Carnegie Endowment: Washington.

Central Statistical Agency. (2004). *Agricultural Sample Survey 2003/2004, Vol. 1: Area and Production of Major Crops*. Addis Ababa: Central Statistical Agency, Federal Democratic Republic of Ethiopia.

Central Statistical Agency. (2005). *Agricultural Sample Survey 2004/2005, Vol. 1: Area and Production of Major Crops*. Addis Ababa: Central Statistical Agency, Federal Democratic Republic of Ethiopia.

Central Statistical Agency. (2006). *Agricultural Sample Survey 2005/2006, Vol. 1: Area and Production of Major Crops*. Addis Ababa: Central Statistical Agency, Federal Democratic Republic of Ethiopia.

Central Statistical Agency. (2007). *Agricultural Sample Survey 2006/2007, Vol. 1: Area and Production of Major Crops.* Addis Ababa: Central Statistical Agency, Federal Democratic Republic of Ethiopia.

Central Statistical Agency. (2008). *Agricultural Sample Survey 2007/2008, Vol. 1: Area and Production of Major Crops.* Addis Ababa: Central Statistical Agency, Federal Democratic Republic of Ethiopia.

Central Statistical Agency. (2009). *Agricultural Sample Survey 2008/2009, Vol. 1: Area and Production of Major Crops.* Addis Ababa: Central Statistical Agency, Federal Democratic Republic of Ethiopia.

Central Statistical Agency. (2010). *Agricultural Sample Survey 2009/2010, Vol. 1: Area and Production of Major Crops.* Addis Ababa: Central Statistical Agency, Federal Democratic Republic of Ethiopia.

Central Statistical Agency. (2011). *Agricultural Sample Survey 2010/2011, Vol. 1: Area and Production of Major Crops.* Addis Ababa: Central Statistical Agency, Federal Democratic Republic of Ethiopia.

Central Statistical Agency. (2012). *Agricultural Sample Survey 2011/2012, Vol. 1: Area and Production of Major Crops.* Addis Ababa: Central Statistical Agency, Federal Democratic Republic of Ethiopia.

Central Statistical Agency. (2013). *Agricultural Sample Survey 2012/2013, Vol. 1: Area and Production of Major Crops.* Addis Ababa: Central Statistical Agency, Federal Democratic Republic of Ethiopia.

Central Statistical Agency. (2014). *Agricultural Sample Survey 2013/2014, Vol. 1: Area and Production of Major Crops.* Addis Ababa: Central Statistical Agency, Federal Democratic Republic of Ethiopia.

Central Statistical Agency. (2015). *Agricultural Sample Survey 2014/2015, Vol. 1: Area and Production of Major Crops.* Addis Ababa: Central Statistical Agency, Federal Democratic Republic of Ethiopia.

CFS (Committee on World Food Security). (2018). *Connecting Smallholders to Markets.* http://www.fao.org/cfs/home/activities/smallholders/en/

CGD. (2014). *Mapping the Impacts of Climate Change.* http://www.cgdev.org/page/mapping-impacts-climate-change

Chamberlin, J. and Schmidt, E. (2012). Ethiopian Agriculture: A Dynamic Geographic Perspective. In *Food and Agriculture in Ethiopia* edited by P. Dorosh and S. Rashid. University of Pennsylvania Press: Philadelphia.

Chambers, R. (1983). *Rural Development: Putting the Last First.* John Wiley & Sons: New York.

Chambers, R. (1995). Poverty and Livelihoods: Whose Reality Counts? *Environment and Urbanization* 7:173-204.

Chambers, R. (2006). *Poverty Unperceived: Traps, Biases and Agenda.* IDS Working Paper 270.

Chambers, R. (2008). *Revolutions in Development Inquiry*. Earthscan: London.

Chambers, R. (2012a). Forward (p. xv-xviii). In *Seasonality, Rural Livelihoods and Development* edited by S. Devereux, R. Sabates-Wheeler and R. Longhurst. Earthscan: New York.

Chambers, R. (2012b). *Provocations for Development*. Practical Action Publishing: Warwickshire.

Chang'a, L. B., Yanda, P. Z. and Ngana, J. (2010). Indigenous Knowledge in Seasonal Rainfall Prediction in Tanzania: A Case of South-western Highland of Tanzania. *Journal of Geography and Regional Planning* 3(4): 66-72.

Chenoweth, E. and Stephan, M. J. (2011). *Why Civil Resistance Works: The Strategic Logic of Nonviolent Conflict*. Columbia University Press: New York.

Cheru, F., Cramer, C. and Oqubay, A. (2019). *The Oxford Handbook of the Ethiopian Economy*. Oxford University Press: New York.

Chinigo, D. (2013). Decentralization and Agrarian Transformation in Ethiopia: Extending the Power of the Federal State. *Critical African Studies* 6: 40-56.

Chinigo, D. (2015). Historicising Agrarian Transformation. Agricultural Commercialisation and Social Differentiation in Wolaita, Southern Ethiopia. *Journal of Eastern African Studies* 9(2): 193-211.

Chirwa, E. W., Dorward, A. and Vignen, M. (2012). Seasonality and Poverty: Evidence from Malawi (p. 97-116). In *Seasonality, Rural Livelihoods and Development* edited by S. Devereux, R. Sabates-Wheeler and R. Longhurst. Earthscan: New York.

Ciampalini, R., Billi, P., Ferrari, G. and Borselli, L. (2008). Plough Marks as a Tool to Assess Soil Erosion Rates: A Case Study in Axum (Ethiopia). *Catena* 75: 18-27.

Ciampalini, R., Billi, P., Ferrari, G., Borselli, L. and Follain, S. (2012). Soil Erosion Induced by Land Use Changes as Determined by Plough Marks and Field Evidence in the Aksum Area (Ethiopia). *Agriculture, Ecosystems and Environment* 146: 197-208.

Cimadamore, A. D., Koehler, G. and Pogge, T. (2016). Poverty and the Millennium Development Goals: A Critical Look Forward (p. 3-25). In *Poverty and the Millennium Development Goals* edited by A. Cimadamore, G. Koehler and T. Pogge. Zed Books: London.

CNN. (2017). *We Spend Billions on Lottery Tickets. Here's Where All that Money Goes*. https://money.cnn.com/2017/08/24/news/economy/lottery-spending/index.html

Cochrane, L. (2011). Food Security or Food Sovereignty: The Case of Land Grabs. *Journal of Humanitarian Assistance*. Feinstein International Center, Tufts University.

Cochrane, L. (2017a). Stages of Food Security: A Co-produced Mixed Methods Methodology. *Progress in Development Studies* 17(4): 291-306.

Cochrane, L. (2017b). Worldviews Apart: Agriculture Extension and Ethiopian Smallholder Farmers. *Journal of Rural Social Sciences* 32: 98-118.

Cochrane, L. (2017c). *Strengthening Food Security in Rural Ethiopia.* Doctoral dissertation (Interdisciplinary Studies) submitted to the University of British Columbia.

Cochrane, L. (2018). Food Security in Ethiopia: Review of Research, 2005-2016. *Ethiopian Journal of Applied Sciences and Technology* 9:1-11.

Cochrane, L. (2019). *Ethiopia: Social and Political Issues.* Nova: New York.

Cochrane, L. and Adem, T. A. (2017). Debates, Knowledge Gaps, and Opportunities for Future Research on Ethiopian Food Security and Agriculture. *Ethiopian Journal of Applied Science and Technology* 8(2): 33-41.

Cochrane, L. and Amery, H. A. (2017). Gulf Cooperation Council Countries and the Global Land Grab. *Arab World Geographer* 20: 17-41.

Cochrane, L. and Bekele, Y. (2018a). Average Crop Yield (2002-2017) in Ethiopia: Trends at National, Regional and Zonal Levels. *Data in Brief* 16: 1025-1033.

Cochrane, L. and Bekele, Y. (2018b). Contextualizing Narratives of Economic Growth and Navigating Problematic Data: Economic Trends in Ethiopia (1999-2017). *Economies* 6(64): 1-16.

Cochrane, L. and Bekele, Y. (2019). Contested Identities: Language, Politics and Power in Southern Ethiopia. *Language Matters* 50(3): 26-45.

Cochrane, L. and Betel B. B. (2019). Pathways of Legal Advocacy for Change: Ethiopian Women Lawyers Association. *Forum for Development Studies* 46(2): 347-365.

Cochrane, L. and Cafer, A. (2018). Does Diversification Enhance Community Resilience? A Critical Review. *Resilience* 6(2): 129-143.

Cochrane, L. and Gecho, Y. (2016). The Dynamics of Vulnerability and Adaptive Capacity in Southern Ethiopia (p. 139-148). In *Responses to Disasters and Climate Change: Understanding Vulnerability and Fostering Resilience*, edited by M. Companion and M. Chaiken. CRC Press: Boca Raton.

Cochrane, L. and Hadis, S. (2019). Functionality of the Land Certification System in Ethiopia: Exploratory Evaluation of the Process of Updating Certificates. *Land* 8(10): 149 (1-14).

Cochrane, L. and Legault, D. D. (2020). The Rush for Land and Agricultural Investment in Ethiopia: What We Know and What We Are Missing. *Land* 9(5): 167.

Cochrane, L. and O'Regan, D. (2016). Legal Harvest and Illegal Trade: Trends, Challenges and Options in Khat Production in Ethiopia. *International Journal of Drug Policy* 30: 27-34.

Cochrane, L. and Rao, N. (2019). Is the Push for Gender Sensitive Research Advancing the SDG Agenda of Leaving No One Behind? *Forum for Development Studies* 46(1): 45-65. doi: 10.1080/08039410.2018.1427623

Cochrane, L. and Skjerdal, T. (2015). Reading the Narratives: Resettlement, Investment and Development in Ethiopia. *Forum for Development Studies* 42(3): 467-487.

Cochrane, L. and Tamiru, Y. (2016). Ethiopia's Productive Safety Net Program: Politics, Power and Practice. *Journal of International Development* 28(5): 649-665.

Cochrane, L. and Thornton, A. (2017). A Socio-Cultural Analysis of Smallholder Borrowing and Debt in Southern Ethiopia. *Journal of Rural Studies* 49: 69-77.

Cochrane, L. and Thornton, A. (2018). The Geography of Development Studies: Leaving No One Behind. *Forum for Development Studies* 45: 167-175

Cochrane, L. and Vercillo, S. (2018). Youth perspectives on migration, poverty and the precarious future of farming in rural Ethiopia. In *Gender and Youth Migration: A Global Survey*. Polity Press.

Cohen, J. and Isaksson, N. (1987). Villagisation in Ethiopia's Arsi Region. *The Journal of Modern African Studies* 25(3): 435-464.

Coll-Black, S., Gilligan, D. O., Hoddinott, J., Kumar, N., Taffesse, A. S. and Wiseman, W. (2012). Targeting Food Security Interventions in Ethiopia: The Productive Safety Net Programme. In *Food and Agriculture in Ethiopia: Progress and Policy Challenges* edited by P. Dorosh and S. Rashid. University of Pennsylvania: Philadelphia.

Committee to Protect Journalists. (2015). *Conflating Terrorism and Journalism in Ethiopia.* https://cpj.org/2015/04/attacks-on-the-press-conflating-terrorism-and-journalism-in-ethiopia.php

Cooke, B. and Kothari, U. (2001). *Participation: The New Tyranny?* Zed Books: London.

Coppock, D. L. (1993). Grass Hay and Acacia Fruits: A Local Feeding System for Improved Calf Performance in Semi-Arid Ethiopia. *Tropical Animal Health and Production* 25(1): 41-49.

Cotula, L. (2013). *The Great African Land Grab? Agricultural Investments and the Global Food System.* Zed Books: New York.

Cotula, L., Vermeulen, S., Leonnard, R. and Keeley, J. (2009). *Land Grab or Development Opportunity? Agricultural Investment and the International Land Deals in Africa.* Food and Agriculture Organization: Rome.

Coulson, A. (1982). *Tanzania: A Political Economy.* Oxford University Press: Oxford.

Cramer, C., Johnston, D., Mueller, B., Oya, C. and Sender, J. (2017). Fairtrade and Labour Markets in Ethiopia and Uganda. *Journal of Development Studies* 53(6): 841-856

Cronon, W. (1992). A Place for Stories: Nature, History, and Narrative. *Journal of American History* 78(4): 1347-1376.

CSA, EDRI and IFPRI. (2006). *Atlas of the Ethiopian Rural Economy.* Central Statistical Agency: Addis Ababa.

CSA. (1996). *The 1994 Population and Housing Census of Ethiopia.* Central Statistical Agency: Addis Ababa.

CSA. (2000). *Ethiopia Demographic and Health Survey.* Central Statistical Agency: Addis Ababa.

CSA. (2007). *Population and Housing Census.* Central Statistical Agency: Addis Ababa.

CSA. (2011). *Demographic and Health Survey.* Central Statistical Agency: Addis Ababa.

CSA. (2013). *Population Projection of Ethiopia for All Regions at Wereda Level from 2014 – 2017.* Central Statistical Agency: Addis Ababa.

Cundill, G., Harvey, B., Tebboth, M., Cochrane, L., Currie-Alder, B., Vincent, K., Lawn, J., Nicolls, R. J., Scodanibbio, L., Prakash, A., New, M., Wester, P., Leone, M., Morchain, D., Ludi, E., DeMaria-Kinney, J., Khan, A. S. and Landry, M. (2018). Large-Scale Transdisciplinary Collaboration for Adaptation Research: Challenges and Insights. *Global Challenges* doi: 10.1002/gch2.201700132.

D'Andrea, A. C., Manzo, A., Harrower, M. J. and Hawkins, A. L. (2008). The Pre-Aksumite and Aksumite Settlement of NE Tigrai, Ethiopia. *Journal of Field Archeology* 33: 151-176.

Dabre-Madhin, E. (2011). *A Market for Abdu: Creating a Commodity Exchange in Ethiopia.* International Food Policy Research Institute: Washington.

Dalelo, A. and Stellmacher, T. (2012). *Faith-based Organizations in Ethiopia: The Contribution of the Kale Heywet Church to Rural Schooling, Ecological Balance and Food Security.* Bonn University Press: Goettingen.

Davison, W. (2015). *Yes, Ethiopia has problems – but this drought is no 1984 return.* https://www.theguardian.com/commentisfree/2015/nov/11/ethiopia-drought-1984-economic-growth-safety-net

de Waal, A. (1990). *Democratic Political Processes and the Fight Against Famine.* Working Paper 107. Institute of Development Studies: Brighton.

de Waal, A. (1991). *Evil Days: 30 Years of War and Famine in Ethiopia.* Human Rights Watch: New York.

de Waal, A. (1997). *Famine Crimes: Politics & the Disaster Relief Industry in Africa.* Indiana University Press: Bloomington.

de Waal, A. (2015). *The Real Politics of the Horn of Africa: Money War and the Business of Power.* Polity: Malden.

de Waal, A. (2018). *Mass Starvation: The History and Future of Famine.* Polity Press: Cambridge.

de Waal, A., Taffesse, A. S. and Carruth, L. (2006). Child Survival during the 2002-2003 Drought in Ethiopia. *Global Public Health* 1(2): 125-132.

Debela, B. L., Shively, G. and Holden, S. T. (2014). *Does Ethiopia's Productive Safety Net Program Improve child nutrition?* Centre for Land Tenure Studies Working Paper 01/14, Norwegian University of Life Sciences.

Decron, S. and Singh, A. (2011). *From Nutrition to Aspirations and Self-Efficacy: Gender Bias over Time among Children in Four Countries.* Working Paper No. 71. Young Lives, Department of International Development, University of Oxford: Oxford.

Deininger K., Ali, D., Holden, S. and Zevenbergen, J. (2007). *Rural Land Certification in Ethiopia: Process, Initial Impact, and Implications for Other African Countries.* Policy Research Working P. 4218. World Bank: Washington.

Deininger, K., Ali, D. and Alemu, T. (2011). *Productivity Effects of Land Rental Markets in Ethiopia: Evidence from a Matched Tenant-landlord Sample.* Policy Research Working Paper 5727. World Bank: Washington.

Deininger, K., Ali, D., and Alemu, T. (2009). *Impacts of Land Certification on Tenure Security, Investment, and Land Markets: Evidence from Ethiopia.* EfD Discussion Paper 09-11. Environment for Development and Resources for the Future: Washington.

Deininger, K., Jin, S., Anenew, B., Gebre-Selassie, S., and Nega, B. (2003). *Tenure Security and Land-related Investment.* Policy Research Working P. 2991. Working Bank: Washington.

Deininger, K., Nizalov, D. and Singh, S. K. (2013). *Are Mega Farms the Future of Global Agriculture? Exploring the Farm Size-productivity Relationship for Large Commercial Farms in Ukraine.* Policy Research Working Paper 6544. World Bank: Washington.

Dejene, M. and Cochrane, L. (2021). The Power of Policy and Entrenching Inequalities in Ethiopia: Reframing Agency in the Global Land Rush (Chapter 9). In *The Transnational Land Rush in Africa: A Decade After the Spike,* edited by L. Cochrane and N. Andrews. Palgrave: New York.

Derbew, D. (2013). *Ethiopia's Renewable Energy Power Potential and Development Opportunities.* Presentation in Abu Dhabi, UAE, 22 June.

Dercon, S. and Krishnan, P. (2000). Vulnerability, Seasonality and Poverty in Ethiopia. *Journal of Development Studies* 36(6): 25-53.

Dercon, S., Hoddinott J. and Woldehanna, T. (2012). Growth and Chronic Poverty: Evidence from Rural Communities in Ethiopia. *Journal of Development Studies* 48(2): 238-253.

Destiny Ethiopia. (2020). *Four Scenarios.* http://destinyethiopia.com/

Devarajan, S. and Khemani, S. (2016). *If Politics is the Problem, How Can External Actors be Part of the Solution?* Policy Research Working Paper 7761. World Bank Group: Washington.

Devereux, S. (2009). Why Does Famine Persist in Africa? *Food Security* 1: 25-35.

Devereux, S., Ed. (2006). *The New Famines: Why Famines Persist in an Era of Globalization.* Routledge: New York.

Devereux, S. and Guenther, B. (2009). *Agriculture and Social Protection in Ethiopia.* Growth & Social Protection Working Paper 03, Future Agricultures.

Devereux, S. and Sharp, K. (2006). Trends in Poverty and Destitution in Wollo, Ethiopia. *Journal of Development Studies* 42(4): 592-610.

Devereux, S. Vaitla, B. and Hauenstein-Swan, S. (2008). *Seasons of Hunger.* Pluto Press: London.

Devereux, S., Sabates-Wheeler, R. and Longhurst, R. (Eds) (2012). *Seasonality, Rural Livelihoods and Development.* Earthscan: New York.

DHS. (2011). *Demographic and Health Survey.* Central Statistical Agency: Addis Ababa.

DHS. (2016). *Demographic and Health Survey.* Central Statistical Agency: Addis Ababa.

Di Falco, S., Yesuf, M., Kohlin, G., Ringler, C. (2011). Estimating the Impact of Climate Change on Agriculture in Low-income Countries: Household Level Evidence from the Nile Basin, Ethiopia. *Environmental and Resource Economics* 52(4): 457—478.

Di Nunzio, M. (2014). 'Do Not Cross the Red Line': The 2010 General Elections, Dissent, and Political Mobilization in Urban Ethiopia. *African Affairs* 113(452): 409-430.

Donini, A. (Ed.) (2012). *The Golden Fleece: Manipulation and Independence in Humanitarian Action.* Kumarian Press: Sterling.

Dorosh, P. and Rashid, S. (2012). *Food and Agriculture in Ethiopia.* University of Pennsylvania Press: Philadelphia.

Dreze, J. 2018. Evidence, Policy, and Politics. www.ideasforindia.in/topics/miscellany/evidence-policy-and-politics.html

Dubale, B., Solomon, A., Geremew, B, Sethumadhava, R. G. and Waktole, S. (2014). Mycoflora of Grain Maize (Zea mays L.) Stored in Traditional Storage Containers (Gombisa and Sacks) in Selected Woredas of Jimma

Zone, Ethiopia. *African Journal of Food, Agriculture, Nutrition and Development* 14(2): 8676-8694.

Dwyer, A. (2015). *The Anatomy of Giving*. Stratford Press: Toronto.

Edkins, J. (2007). The Criminalization of Mass Starvations: From Natural Disaster to Crime Against Humanity. In *The New Famines: Why Famines Persist in an Era of Globalization*, edited by S. Devereux. Routledge: New York.

EEA/EEPRI (Ethiopian Economic Association / Ethiopian Economic Policy Research Institute). (2006). *Evaluation of the Ethiopian Agricultural Extension with Particular Emphasis on the Participatory Dimension and Training Extension System*. EEA/EEPRI: Addis Ababa.

Ege, S. (1997). Peasant Participation in Land Reform: The Amhara Land Redistribution of 1997. In *Ethiopia: The Challenge of Democracy from Below* edited by B. Zewde and S. Pausewang. Forum for Social Studies: Addis Ababa.

Ege, S., Ed (2019). *Land Tenure and Security: State-Peasant Relations in the Amhara Highlands, Ethiopia*. James Currey: Martlesham.

Elias, A., Nohmi, M., Yasunobu, K. and Ishida, A. (2015). Farmers' Satisfaction with Agricultural Extension Service and its Influencing Factors: A Case Study in North West Ethiopia. *Journal of Agricultural Science and Technology* 17: 1-15.

Eneyew, A. and Bekele, W. (2012). Causes of Household Food Insecurity in Wolayta: Southern Ethiopia. *Journal of Stored Products and Postharvest Research* 3: 35-48.

Eriksen, P. (2008). What is the Vulnerability of a Food System to Global Environmental Change? *Ecology and Society* 13(2): 14 (1-18).

Ersado, L., Amacher, G. and Alwang, J. (2004). Productivity and Land Enhancing Technologies in Northern Ethiopia: Health, Public Investments, and Sequential Adoption. American *Journal of Agricultural Economics* 86(2): 321-331.

Escobar, A. (1988). Power and Visibility: Development and the Invention and Management of the Third World. *Cultural Anthropology* 3(4): 428-443.

Escobar, A. (1994). *Encountering Development: The Making and Unmaking of the Third World*. Princeton University Press: Princeton.

Evans, A. (2012). *Resources, Risk and Resilience: Scarcity and Climate Change in Ethiopia*. Center on International Cooperation, New York: New York University.

Eversole, R. and Johnson, M. (2014). Migrant Remittances and Household Development: An Anthropological Analysis. *Development Studies Research* 1: 1-15.

Eyasu, E. (2000). Soil Enrichment and Depletion in Southern Ethiopia. In *Nutrients on the Move: Soil Fertility Dynamics in African Farming Systems*, edited by T. Hilhorst and F. Muchena. IIED: London.

Eyasu, E. (2002). *Farmers' Perception of Soil Fertility Change and Management.* SOS-Sahel: Addis Ababa.

Eyben, R. (2014). *International Aid and the Making of a Better World: Reflexive Practice.* Routledge: New York.

Fanon, F. (1952). *Black Skin, White Masks.* Grove: New York.

Fanon, F. (1963). *The Wretched of the Earth.* Grove: New York.

FAO and WFP. (2008). *Special Report: FAO/WFP Crop and Food Security Assessment Mission to Ethiopia (Phase 2).* Food and Agriculture Organization: Rome / World Food Programme: Rome.

FAO. (2003). *Trade Reforms and Food Security.* Food and Agriculture Organization: Rome.

FAO. (2006). *Food Security.* Food and Agriculture Organization: Rome.

FAO. (2008a). *FAO/WFP Crop and Food Security Assessment Mission to Ethiopia (Phase 2).* Food and Agriculture Organization: Rome.

FAO. (2008b). *State of Food Insecurity in the World.* Food and Agriculture Organization: Rome.

FAO. (2009a). *Food Security Policy - Formulation and Implementation.* Food and Agriculture Organization: Rome.

FAO. (2009b). *Declaration of the World Summit on Food Security.* World Summit on Food Security, November 16-18, Rome.

FAO. (2010). *State of Food Insecurity in the World.* Food and Agriculture Organization: Rome.

FAO. (2012a). *Part 3 – Feeding the World.* Food and Agriculture Organization: Rome.

FAO. (2012b). *The Global Forum on Food Security and Nutrition: Online Discussions that Make a Difference.* Food and Agriculture Organization: Rome.

FAO. (2013a). *Food Waste Harms Climate, Water, Land and Biodiversity – New FAO Report.* http://www.fao.org/news/story/en/item/196220/icode/

FAO. (2013b). *Mainstreaming the Right to Food into Sub-national Plans and Strategies.* http://www.fao.org/righttofood/our-work/current-projects/rtf-district-level/en/

FAO. (2016). *About Right to Food.* http://www.fao.org/righttofood/about-right-to-food/en/

FAO. (2017). State of Food Security and Nutrition in the World. Food and Agriculture Organization: Rome.

FAO. (2020). *Hunger and Food Insecurity.* http://www.fao.org/hunger/en/

Farmer, P. (1999). *Infections and Inequalities: The Modern Plagues.* University of California Press: Berkeley.

Farmer, P. (2005). *Pathologies of the Power: Health, Human Rights, and the New War on the Poor.* University of California Press: Berkeley.

Farmer, P. and Gutierrez, G. (2013). *In the Company of the Poor: Conversations between Dr. Paul Farmer and Father Gustavo Gutierrez.* Orbis: Maryknoll.

Fasil, M. (2015). *An Ethiopian Court Jailed Muslim Leaders, Activists to Lengthy Terms.* http://allafrica.com/stories/201508032408.html

FDRE. (2007). *Proclamation No. 551/2007.* Federal Negarit Gazeta of the Federal Democratic Republic of Ethiopia: Addis Ababa.

Ferguson, J. (1990). *The Anti-politics Machine: "Development," Depoliticization, and Bureaucratic Power in Lesotho.* Cambridge University Press: New York.

Ferguson, J. (2015). *Give a Man a Fish: Reflections on the New Politics of Distribution.* Duke University Press: Durham.

FEWS NET. (2010). *Food Security Outlook Update: November 2010.* FEWS NET: Washington.

FEWS NET. (2011a). *Food Security Outlook Update: August 25, 2012.* FEWS NET: Washington.

FEWS NET. (2011b). *Food Security Outlook Update: November 2011.* FEWS NET: Washington.

FEWS NET. (2011c). *Food Security Outlook: October 2010 to March 2011.* FEWS NET: Washington.

FEWS NET. (2011d). *Food Security Outlook: January to June 2011.* FEWS NET: Washington.

FEWS NET. (2012a). *Food Security Outlook: March to June 2013.* FEWS NET: Washington.

FEWS NET. (2012b). *Food Security Outlook: July to December 2013.* FEWS NET: Washington.

FEWS NET. (2013). *Food Security Outlook Update: March 2013.* FEWS NET: Washington.

FEWS NET. (2014). *Food Security Outlook Update: March 2014.* FEWS NET: Washington.

Feyissa, D. (2011). Aid Negotiation: The Uneasy "Partnership" between EPRDF and the Donors. *Journal of Eastern African Studies* 5(4): 788-817.

Fisseha, K. (2014). *Food Security and the Relative Importance of Various Household Assets: The Case of Farm Households in Southern Ethiopia.* Master's Thesis, Department of Urban and Rural Development, Swedish University of Agricultural Sciences.

Foucault, M. (1977). *Discipline and Punish: The Birth of the Prison.* Random House: New York.

Foucault, M. (1979). Governmentality. *Ideology and Consciousness* 6: 5-21.

Freire, P. (1970). *Pedagogy of the Oppressed.* Continuum International: New York.

Friis C. and Reenberg, A. (2010). *Land Grab in Africa: Emerging Land System Drivers in a Teleconnected World.* University of Copenhagen: Copenhagen.

Gaventa, J. and McGee, R. (2010). *Citizen Action and National Policy Reform: Making Change Happen.* Zed Books: New York.

Gebeyehu, B., Regasa, G. and Tebeje, M. (2015). On-farm Activities and Households Food Security in Wolaita Zone, Ethiopia. *Food Science and Quality Management* 41: 73-78.

Gebre Mariam, A. (1991). Livestock and Economic Differentiation in North East Ethiopia: The Afar Case. *Nomadic Peoples* 29: 10-20.

Gebre-Egziabher, K. A. (2013). Land Registration and Certification as a Key Strategy for Ensuring Gender Equity, Preventing Land Grabbing and Enhancing Agricultural Productivity: Evidence from Tigray, Ethiopia. *International Journal of Africa Renaissance Studies – Multi-, Inter- and Transdisciplinarity* 8(2): 5-22.

Gebrehiwot, N. T., Mesfin, K. A. and Nyssen, J. (2015). Small-scale Irrigation: The Driver for Promoting Agricultural Production and Food Security (The Case of Tigray Regional State, Northern Ethiopia). *Irrigation & Drainage Systems Engineering* 4(2): 1000141 (p. 1-9).

Gebrehiwot, T. and van der Veen, A. (2014). Coping with Food Insecurity on a Micro-scale: Evidence from Ethiopian Rural Households. *Ecology of Food and Nutrition* 53(2): 214-240.

Gebremariam, G. G., Edriss, A. K., Maganga, A. M. and Terefe, A. T. (2013). Labor as a Payment Vehicle for Valuing Soil Conservation Practices in a Subsistence Economy: Case of Adwa Woreda in Ethiopia. *American Journal of Economics* 3(6): 283-290.

Gecho, Y. (2014). *Livelihood Strategies and Food Security of Rural Households in Wolaita Zone, Southern Ethiopia.* Doctoral Dissertation submitted to the College of Agriculture and Natural Resource Management, Haramaya University.

Gecho, Y., Ayele, G., Lemma, T. and Alemu, D. (2014). Rural Household Livelihood Strategies: Options and Determinants in the Case of Wolaita Zone, Southern Ethiopia. *Social Sciences* 3(3): 92-104.

Geleta, E. B. (2016). Microfinance and Women's Empowerment: An Ethnographic Inquiry. *Development in Practice* 26: 91-101.

GFRAS. (2012). *Fact Sheet on Extension Services.* Global Forum for Rural Advisory Services: Lindau.

Gibson, M. (2012). *The Feeding of Nations: Redefining Food Security for the 21ˢᵗ Century*. CRC Press: Boca Raton.

Gill, G. (1991). *Seasonality and Agriculture in the Developing World: A Problem of the Poor and Powerless*. Cambridge University Press: Cambridge.

Gill, P. (2010). *Famine and Foreigners: Ethiopia Since Live Aid*. Oxford University Press: Oxford.

Gilligan, D., Hoddinott, J., Taffesse, A. (2009). The Impact of Ethiopia's Productive Safety Net Programme and its Linkages. *Journal of Development Studies* 45: 1684-1706.

Gitlin, T. (1980). *The Whole World is Watching: Mass Media in the Making and Unmaking of the New Left*. University of California Press: Berkeley.

Glaser, B. and Strauss, A. (1967). *The Discovery of Grounded Theory: Strategies for Qualitative Research*. Aldine: Chicago.

Glover, D., Sumberg, J. and Andersson, J. (2016). The Adoption Problem; or Why We Still Understand to Little about Technological Change in African Agriculture. *Outlook on Agriculture* 45: 3-6.

GoE. (2014). *The Structure and Division of Power*. http://www.ethiopia.gov.et/the-structure-and-division-of-power

Goldman, M. (2005). *Imperial Nature: The World Bank and Struggles for Social Justice in the Age of Globalization*. Yale University Press: New Haven.

Graham, J., Rashid, S. and Malek, M. (2012). Disaster Response and Emergency Risk Management in Ethiopia. In *Food and Agriculture in Ethiopia*, edited by P. Dorosh and S. Rashid. University of Pennsylvania Press: Philadelphia.

Gramsci, A. (1971). *Prison Notebooks: Selections from the Prison Notebooks of Antonio Gramsci*. Edited and translated by Q. Hoare and G. N. Smith. International Publishers: New York.

Gramsci, A. (1975). *Letters from Prison* (translated an edited by L. Lawner). Jonathan Cape: London.

Gray, A. (2018). Ethiopia is Africa's Fastest-Growing Economy. www.weforum.org/agenda/2018/05/ethiopia-africa-fastest-growing-economy/

Grobler, W. C. J. (2016). Perceptions of Poverty: A Study of Food Secure and Food Insecure Households in an Urban Area in South Africa. *Procedia Economics and Finance* 35: 224-231.

Gudina, M. (2003). *Ethiopia: Competing Ethnic Nationalisms and the Quest for Democracy 1960-2000*. Shaker Publishing: Maastricht.

Guest, G., Bunce, A. and Johnson, L. (2006). How Many Interviews are Enough? An Experiment with Data Saturation and Variability. *Field Methods* 18: 59—82.

Guthiga, P. and Newsham, A. (2011). Meteorologists Meeting Rainmakers: Indigenous Knowledge and Climate Policy Processes in Kenya. *IDS Bulletin* 42(3): 104-109.

Gutierrez, G. (1971). *A Theology of Liberation: History, Politics, Salvation.* Orbis: Maryknoll.

Hagos, H. G. and Holden, S. (2013b). *Links between Tenure Security and Food Security: Evidence from Ethiopia.* IFPRI Discussion Paper 01295. IFPRI: Washington.

Hagos, H.G. and Holden, S. (2013a). *Efficiency and Productivity Differential Effectives of Land Certification Program in Ethiopia.* IFPRI Discussion Paper 01295. IFPRI: Washington.

Hallam, D. (2013). Overview. In *The Global Farms Race: Land Grabs, Agricultural Investment and the Scramble for Food Security,* edited by Kugelman and Levenstein. Island Press: Washington.

Hallegatte, S.,Bangalore, M., Bonzanigo, L., Fay, M., Kane, T., Narloch, U., Rozenberg, J., Treguer, D. and Vogt-Schilb, A. (2016). *Shock Waves: Managing the Impacts of Climate Change on Poverty.* Climate Change and Development Series. Washington, DC: World Bank.

Hamm, M. W. and Bellows, A. C. (2003). Community Food Security and Nutrition Educators. *Journal of Nutrition Education* 35: 37-43.

Hammond, L. (2008). Strategies of Invisibilization: How Ethiopia's Resettlement Programme Hides the Poorest of the Poor. *Journal of Refugee Studies* 21(4): 517-536.

Handino, M. L. (2014). *'Green Famine' in Ethiopia: Understanding the Causes of Increasing Vulnerability to Food Insecurity and Policy Responses in the Southern Ethiopian Highlands.* Doctoral thesis submitted to the University of Sussex.

Hardt, M. and Negri, A. (2004). *Multitude: War and Democracy in the Age of Empire.* Penguin: New York.

Hathaway, T. (2008). *What Cost Ethiopia's Dam Boom? A Look Inside the Expansion of Ethiopia's Energy Sector.* International Rivers: Berkeley.

Havel, V. (1997). *The Art of the Impossible: Politics as Morality in Practice.* Knopf: Toronto.

Hawando, T. (1997). *Desertification in Ethiopian Highlands.* RALA Report No. 200. Norwegian Church Aid: Addis Ababa.

Headey, D., Dereje, M. and Taffesse, A. S. (2014). Land Constraints and Agricultural Intensification in Ethiopia: A Village-level Analysis of High-potential Areas. *Food Policy* 48: 129-141.

Headey, D., Dereje, M., Ricker-Gilbert, J., Josephson, A., Taffesse, A. S. (2013). *Land Constraints and Agricultural Intensification in Ethiopia: A Village-Level*

Analysis of High Potential Areas. ESSP Working Paper 58, International Food Policy and Research Institute: Washington.

Headey, D., Taffesse, A. S. and You, L. (2014). Diversification and Development in Pastoralist Ethiopia. *World Development* 56: 200-213.

Heinrich, T., Machain, C. M. and Oestman, J. (2017). Does Counterterrorism Militarize Foreign Aid? Evidence from Sub-Saharan Africa. *Journal of Peace Research* 54(4): 527-541.

Helland, J. (2006). *Pastoral Land Tenure in Ethiopia*. Paper presented at the Colloque International, Les Frontieres de la Question Fonciere – At the Frontier of Land Issues, Montpellier, France.

Hill, R. V. and Porter, C. (2015). *Shocks, Safety-Nets and Vulnerability to Poverty in Ethiopia*. www.researchgate.net/publication/281774460

Hirvonen, K., Taffesse, A. S. and Worku, I. (2015). *Seasonality and Household Diets in Ethiopia*. Working Paper 74. International Food Policy Research Institute: Washington.

Hoddinott, J. (1999). *Operationalizing Household Food Security in Development Projects*. International Food Policy Research Institute: Washington.

Holden, S. and Bezu, S. (2016). Preferences for Land Sales Legalization and Land Values in Ethiopia. *Land Use Policy* 52: 410-421.

Holden, S. and Ghebru, H. (2016). Land Rental Market Legal Restrictions in Northern Ethiopia. *Land Use Policy* 55: 212-221.

Holden, S. and Yohannes, H. (2001). *Land Redistribution, Tenure Insecurity, and Intensity of Production: A Study of Farm Households in Southern Ethiopia*. CAPRi Working Paper No. 21. International Food Policy Research Institute: Washington.

Holden, S., Bezu, S. and Tilahun, M. (2016). How Pro-poor are Land Rental Markets in Ethiopia? Norwegian University of Life Science, Centre for Land Tenure Studies Report.

Holden, S., Deininger, K. and Ghebru, H. (2011). Tenure Insecurity, Gender, Low-cost Land Certification and Land Rental Market Participation in Ethiopia. *Journal of Development Studies* 47(1): 31-47.

Holden, S., Shiferaw, B. and Pender, J. (2005). *Policy Analysis for Sustainable Land Management and Food Security in Ethiopia*. International Food Policy Research Institute: Washington.

Holmes, R. and Jones, R. (2010). *Gender Inequality, Risk and Vulnerability in the Rural Economy*. ESA Working Paper No. 11-13. Food and Agriculture Organization: Rome.

Holmgren, D. (2002). *Permaculture*. Holmgren Design Services: Victoria.

Honig, D. (2018). *Navigation by Judgement: Why and When Top-Down Management of Foreign Aid Doesn't Work*. Oxford University Press: New York.

Holt-Gimenez, E. and Shattuck, A. (2011). Food Crises, Food Regimes and Food Movements: Rumblings of Reform or Tides of Transformation? *Journal of Peasant Studies* 38(1): 109-144.

HRW. (2010a). *"One Hundred Ways of Putting Pressure" Violations of Freedom of Expression and Association in Ethiopia*. Human Rights Watch: New York.

HRW. (2010b). *Development Without Freedom: How Aid Underwrites Repression in Ethiopia*. Human Rights Watch: New York.

HRW. (2012a). *"Waiting here for Death": Displacement and "Villagization" in Ethiopia's Gambella Region*. Human Rights Watch: Washington.

HRW. (2012b). *Prominent Muslims Detailed in Crackdown*. www.hrw.org/news/2012/08/15/ethiopia-prominent-muslims-detained-crackdown

HRW. (2016a). *Ethiopia: No Let Up in Crackdown on Protests*. February 21, Human Rights Watch: Nairobi.

HRW. (2016b). *Such a Brutal Crackdown: Killings and Arrests in Response to Ethiopia's Oromo Protests*. Human Rights Watch: New York.

Hundie, B. and Padmanabhan, M. (2008). *The Transformation of the Afar Commons in Ethiopia*. CAPRi Working Paper No. 87. IFPRI: Washington.

Huntington, S. (1975). Issues in Woman's Role in Economic Development: Critique and Alternatives. *Journal of Marriage and Family* 37(4): 1001-1012.

Hurd, W. (2013). *Understanding Land Investment Deals in Africa: Ignoring Abuse in Ethiopia*. Oakland Institute: Oakland, CA.

Hurlbert, M. and Gupta, J. (2015). The Split Ladder of Participation: A Diagnostic, Strategic, and Evaluation Tool to Assess When Participation is Necessary. *Environmental Science & Policy* 50: 100-113.

Hurni, H. (1988). Degradation and Conservation of the Resources in the Ethiopian Highlands. *Mountain Research and Development* 8: 123-130.

Husmann, C. (2015). Marginality as a Root Cause of Poverty: Identifying Marginality Hotspots in Ethiopia. *World Development* 78: 420-435.

Hyden, G. (2005). *Why Do Things Happen the Way They Do? A Power Analysis of Tanzania*. http://xa.yimg.com/kq/groups/20674633/1114493356/name/Goran%20Hyden_Power%20Analysis_Tanzania.pdf

IDS. (2016). *Using Participatory Action Research to Improve Development Practice*. http://www.ids.ac.uk/events/using-participatory-action-research-to-improve-development-practice

IFAD. (2009). *Food Security: A Conceptual Framework*. International Fund for Agricultural Development: Rome.

IFPRI. (2013). *Highlights of Recent IFPRI Food Policy Research for DFID*. IFPRI: Washington.

IRIN. (2004). *Ethiopia: Rural Resettlement Programme Criticised.* http://www.irinnews.org/Report/48797/ETHIOPIA-Rural-resettlement-programme-criticised

ISSC, IDS and UNESCO. (2016). *World Social Science Report 2016, Challenging Inequalities: Pathways to a Just World.* UNESCO: Paris.

Jerven, M. (2013). *Poor Numbers: How We Are Misled by African Development Statistics and What to Do About it.* Cornell University Press: Ithaca.

Jones, L., Harvey, C., Cochrane, L., Cantin, B., Conway, D., Cornforth, R. J., De Souza, K. and Kirbyshire, A. (2018). Designing the Next Generation of Climate Adaptation Research for Development. *Regional Environmental Change* 18: 297-304.

Josephson, A. L., Ricker-Gilbert, J. and Florax, R. (2014). How Does Population Density Influence Agricultural Intensification and Productivity? Evidence from Ethiopia. *Food Policy* 48: 142-152.

Kahneman, D. and Tversky, A. (1979). Prospect Theory: An Analysis of Decision Under Risk. *Econometrica* 47: 263-292.

Kalanda-Joshua, M., Ngongondo, C., Chipeta, L. and Mpembeka, F. (2011). Integrating Indigenous Knowledge with Conventional Science: Enhancing Localised Climate and Weather Forecasts in Nessa, Mulanje, Malawi. *Physics and Chemistry of the Earth* 36(14-15): 996-1003.

Kant, I. (1781, 2008 reprint). *A Critique of Pure Reason.* Penguin: New York.

Kapstein, E. B. and Busby, J. W. (2013). *AIDS Drugs for All: Social Movements and Market Transformations.* Cambridge University Press: New York.

Karunamoorthi, K., Mohammed, M. and Wassie, F. (2012). Knowledge and Practices and Farmers with Reference to Pesticide Management: Implications on Human Health. *Archives of Environmental & Occupational Health* 67(2): 109-116.

Kassa, T. (2013). The Impact of the PSNP on Food Security in Selected Kebeles of Enebse Sar Midir District East Gojjam Zone, Amhara National Regional State. In *Food Security, Safety Nets and Social Protection in Ethiopia* edited by D. Rahmato, A. Pankhurst and J-G van Uffelen. Forum for Social Studies: Addis Ababa.

Kassie, B. T., Asseng, S., Rotter, R. P., Hengsdijk, H., Ruane, A. C., Van Ittersum, M. K. (2015). Exploring Climate Change Impacts and Adaptation Options for Maize Production in the Central Rift Valley of Ethiopia Using Different Climate Change Scenarios and Crop Models. *Climate Change* 129(1): 145-158.

Kassie, M., Zikhali, P., Pender, J. and Kohlin, G. (2010). The Economics of Sustainable Land Management Practices in the Ethiopian Highlands. *Journal of Agricultural Economics* 61(3): 605-627.

Katane, G. O. (2013). An Assessment of the PSNP in Selected Kebeles of Konso Special Woreda, Southern Nations, Nationalities, and Peoples Regional State. In *Food Security, Safety Nets and Social Protection in Ethiopia* edited by D. Rahmato, A. Pankhurst and J-G van Uffelen. Forum for Social Studies: Addis Ababa.

Kebede, B. (2002). Land Tenure and Common Pool Resources in Rural Ethiopia: A Study Based on Fifteen Sites. *African Development Bank* 113-149.

Kebede, G. (2013). Political Corruption: Political and Economic State Capture in Ethiopia. *European Scientific Journal* 9(35): 250-279.

Kebede, Y., Gunjal, K. and Coffin, G. (1990). Adoption of New Technologies in Ethiopian Agriculture: The Case of Tegulet-Bulga District, Shoa Province. *Agricultural Economics* 4: 27-43.

Kefale, A. (2014). *Federalism and Ethnic Conflict in Ethiopia: A Comparative Regional Study.* Routledge: New York.

Kelilo, A., Ketema, M. and Kedir, A. (2014). The Contribution of Small Scale Irrigation Water Use to Households Food Security in Gorogutu District of Oromia Regional State, Ethiopia. International Journal of Economics and Empirical Research 2(6): 221-228.

Keller, E. J. (1991). *Revolutionary Ethiopia: From Empire to People's Republic.* Indiana University Press: Bloomington.

Kenny, C. (2011). *Getting Better: Why Global Development is Succeeding – And How We Can Improve the World Even More.* Basic Books: New York.

Ketsela, Y. (2006). Attendant Issues in the Current Agricultural Extension Programme. In *Ethiopia: Development Policies, Trends, Changes and Continuities*, edited by K. Berhanu and D. Fantaye. Addis Ababa University Press: Addis Ababa.

Khalif, M. H. and Doornbos, M. (2002). The Somali Region in Ethiopia: A Neglected Human Rights Tragedy. *Review of African Political Economy* 91: 73-94.

Kibret, S., Wilson, G. G., Tekie, H. and Petros, B. (2014). Increased Malaria Transmission around Irrigation Schemes in Ethiopia and the Potential of Canal Water Management for Malaria Vector Control. *Malaria Journal* 13: 360 (1-12).

Kingdon, J. (1984). *Agendas, Alternatives, and Public Policies.* Little, Brown: Boston.

Kneen, C. (2012). *The People's Food Policy Project: Introducing Food Sovereignty in Canada.* Food Secure Canada: Montreal.

Kotu, B. H. and Admassie, A. (2015). *Potential Impact of Improved Varieties on Poverty Reduction: A Case Study of Selected Cereal Crops in Two Districts of Ethiopia.* International Conference of Agricultural Economists, August 8-14, Milan, Italy.

Krishna, A. (2004). Escaping Poverty and Becoming Poor: Who Gains, Who Loses, and Why? *World Development* 32(1): 121-136.

Krishna, A. (2005). *Stages of Progress: A Community-Based Methodology for Defining and Understanding Poverty.* http://www2.sanford.duke.edu/krishna/SoP.pdf

Krishna, A. (2010). *One Illness Away.* Oxford University Press: New York.

Kubik, Z. and Maurel, M. (2016). Weather Shocks, Agricultural Production and Migration: Evidence from Tanzania. *Journal of Development Studies* 52(5): 665-680.

Kugelman, M. and Levenstein, S. (Eds). (2013). *The Global Farms Race: Land Grabs, Agricultural Investment and the Scramble for Food Security.* Island Press: Washington.

La Via Campesina. (2011). *The International Peasant's Voice.* http:// viacampesina. org/en/index.php/organisation-mainmenu-44

La Via Campesina. (2013). *Using the Global Strategic Framework for Food Security and Nutrition to Promote and Defend the People's Right to Adequate Food.* La Via Campesina: Jakarta.

Laekemariam, F. and Gidago, G. (2012). Response of Maize (Zea mays L.) to Integrated Fertilizer Application in Wolaita, South Ethiopia. *Advances in Life Science and Technology* 5: 21-30.

Land Matrix. (2013). *Ethiopia.* http://www.landmatrix.org/

Lansing, J. S., Schoenfelder, J. and Scarborough, V. (2006). Rappaport's Rose: Structure, Agency and Historical Contingency in Ecological Anthropology (p. 325-357). In *Reimaging Political Ecology* edited by A. Biersack and J. B. Greenberg. Duke University Press: Durham.

Lantican, M. A., Dubin, H. J., Morris, M. L. (2005). *Impacts of International Wheat Breeding Research in the Developing World, 1988-2002.* CIMMYT: Mexico.

Lautze, S. and D. Maxwell. (2007). Why do Famines Persist in the Horn of Africa? Ethiopia 1999-2003. In *The New Famines: Why Famines Persist in an Era of Globalization*, edited by S. Devereux. Routledge: New York.

Lavers, T. (2012). Land Grab as Development Strategy? The Political Economy of Agricultural Investment in Ethiopia. *Journal of Peasant Studies* 39(1): 105-132.

Levy, D. L. (2000). Applications and Limitations of Complexity Theory in Organization Theory and Strategy. In *Handbook of Strategic Management*, Second Edition edited by J. Rabin, G. J. Miller and W. B. Hildreth, Marcel Dekker Inc.: New York.

Lewis, A. (1955). *The Theory of Economic Growth.* Unwin Hyman: London.

Li, T. (2007). *The Will to Improve: Governmentality, Development, and the Practice of Politics.* Duke University Press: Durham.

Li, T. (2014). *Land's End: Capitalist Relations on an Indigenous Frontier*. Durham: Duke University Press.

Li, X. (1996). Making Sense of the Right to Food. In *World Hunger and Morality*, *2nd edition*, edited by W. Aiken and H. LaFollette. Prentice-Hall: Upper Saddle River.

Limenih, B. and Tefera, T. (2014). Knowledge Gaps in Potato Technology Adoption: The Case of Central Highlands of Ethiopia. *Journal of Agricultural Extension and Rural Development* 6(8): 339-346.

Lin, J. Y. (1990). Collectivization and China's Agricultural Crisis in 1959-1961. *Journal of Political Economy* 98(6): 1228-1252.

Loening, J. L., Durevall, D. and Birru, Y. A. (2009). *Inflation Dynamics and Food Prices in an Agricultural Economy: The Case of Ethiopia*. Policy Research Working Paper 4949. Washington, D.C.: The World Bank.

Loevinsohn, M. (2012). Seasonal Hunger, Famine and the Dynamics of HIV in Malawi (p. 56-75). In *Seasonality, Rural Livelihoods and Development* edited by S. Devereux, R. Sabates-Wheeler and R. Longhurst. Earthscan: New York.

Lyons, D. and Freeman, A. (2009). 'I'm not Evil': Materializing Identities of Marginalised Potters in Tigray Region, Ethiopia. *Azania: Archeological Research in Africa* 44: 75-93.

Lyons, T. (2019). *The Puzzle of Ethiopian Politics*. Lynne Rienner: Boulder.

Mahadevan, R. and Hoang, V. (2016). Is there a Link between Poverty and Food Security? *Social Indicators Research* 128(1): 179-199.

Mains, D. (2012). *Hope is Cut: Youth, Unemployment and the Future in Urban Ethiopia*. Temple University Press: Philadelphia.

Mandefro, H. (2016). Politics by Numbers: Poverty Reduction Discourse, Contestations and Regime Legitimacy in Ethiopia. *International Review of Sociology* 26(3): 386-406.

Martins, V., Florencio, T., Grillo, L., Franco, M., Martins, P., Clemente, A., Santos, C., Vieira, M. and Sawaya, A. (2011). Long-lasting Effects of Undernutrition. *International Journal of Environmental Research and Public Health* 8(6): 1817-1846.

Masset, E. (2012). The Stabilizing Effect of Irrigation on Seasonal Expenditure: Evidence from Rural Andhra Pradesh (p. 117-130). In *Seasonality, Rural Livelihoods and Development* edited by S. Devereux, R. Sabates-Wheeler and R. Longhurst. Earthscan: New York.

Margulis, M. E. (2013). The Regime Complex for Food Security: Implications for the Global Hunger Challenge. *Global Governance* 19: 53-68.

Maxwell, D., Vaitla, B. and Coates, J. (2014). How Do Indicators of Household Food Insecurity Measure Up? An Empirical Comparison from Ethiopia. *Food Policy* 47: 107-116.

Maxwell, D., Vaitla, B., Tesfay, G. and Abadi, N. (2013). *Resilience, Food Security Dynamics, and Poverty Traps in Northern Ethiopia*. Feinstein International Center, Tufts University: Somerville.

Maxwell, S. and Smith, M. (1992). Household Food Security: A Conceptual Review. In *Household Food Security: Concepts, Indicators, Measurements: A Technical Review* edited by S. Maxwell and T. Frankenberger. IFAD/ UNICEF: Rome/New York.

Mbembe, A. (2016; 2019 translation). *Necropolitics*. Duke University Press: Durham.

McArthur, J. W. (2016). *What Does "Agriculture" Mean Today? Assessing Old Questions with New Evidence*. Brookings Institute: Washington.

McCann, J. C. (1995). *People of the Plow: An Agricultural History of Ethiopia, 1800-1990*. University of Wisconsin Press: Madison.

Meadows, D. (2008). *Thinking in Systems* (edited by Diana Wright). Chelsea Green Publishing Company: White River Junction, VT.

Meadows, D. H., Meadows, D. L., Behrens III, W., Naill, R., Randers, J. and Zahn, E. (1974). *Dynamics of Growth in a Finite World*. Wright-Allen Press: Cambridge.

Meijer, S. S., Catacutan, D., Ajayi, O. C., Sileshi, G. W. and Nieuwenhuis, M. (2015). The Role of Knowledge, Attitudes and Perceptions in the Uptake of Agricultural and Agroforestry Innovations among Smallholder Farmers in Sub-Saharan Africa. *International Journal of Agricultural Sustainability* 13: 40-54.

Mekonen, S., Lachat, C., Ambelu, A., Steurbaut, W., Kolsteren, P., Jacxsens, L., Wondafrash, M., Houbraken, M. and Spanoghe, P. (2015). Risk of DDT Residue in Maize Consumed by Infants as Complementary Diet in Southwest Ethiopia. *Science of the Total Environment* 511: 454-460.

Mekonnen, S. (2012). Rights of Citizens and Foreign Investors to Agricultural Land under the Land Policy and Laws of Ethiopia. *Haramaya Law Review* 1: 31-42.

Mendoza, R. U. (2008). Why do the Poor Pay More? Exploring the Poverty Penalty Concept. *Journal of International Development* 23: 1-28.

Mengistu, A. (2006). *Ethiopia*. Food and Agriculture Organization: http://www.fao.org/ag/AGP/AGPC/doc/counprof/ethiopia/ethiopia.htm

Mesfin, T. and Obsa, T. (1994). Ethiopian Traditional Veterinary Practices and their Possible Contribution to Animal Production and Management. *Scientific and Technical Review of the Office International des Epizooties* 13(2): 417-424.

Messer, E. and M. Cohen. (2007). *The Human Right to Food as a U.S. Nutrition Concern, 1976-2006*. IFPRI Discussion Paper 00731. International Food Policy Research Institute: Washington.

Mezgebe, D. (2015). Decentralized Governance under Centralized Party Rule in Ethiopia: The Tigray Experience. *Regional & Federal Studies* 25(5): 473-490.

MFA, UNCDF and UNDP. (2007). *Emerging Regions Development Programme*. Government of Ethiopia, Ministry of Federal Affairs: Addis Ababa.

Mheen-Sluijer, J. (2010). *Ethiopian Commodity Exchange and Contract Farming Arrangements: Complementing Institutions*. Wageningen International: Droevendaalsesteeg.

Millikan, M. F. and Rostow, W. W. (1957). *A Proposal: Key to an Effective Foreign Policy*. Harper: New York.

Million, T. (2014). Fertilizer Adoption, Credit Access, and Safety Nets in Rural Ethiopia. *Agricultural Finance Review* 74(3): 290-310.

Mills, C. W. (1956). *The Power Elites*. Oxford University Press: New York.

Minten, B., Engida, E. and Tamru, S. (2016). *How Big are Post-harvest Losses in Ethiopia? Evidence form Teff*. ESSP Working Paper 93, International Food Policy Research Institute: Washington.

Minten, B., Taffesse, A. S. and Brown, P., Eds (2018). *The Economics of Teff: Exploring Ethiopia's Biggest Cash Crop*. IFPRI: Addis Ababa.

Mintesinot, B., Verplancke, H. Van Ranst, E. and Mitiku, H. (2004). Examining Traditional Irrigation Methods, Irrigation Scheduling and Alternate Furrows Irrigation on Vertisols in Northern Ethiopia. *Agricultural Water Management* 64: 17-27.

Mintz, S. W. (1985). *Sweetness and Power: The Place of Sugar in Modern History*. Penguin Books: New York.

Mollison, B. (1991). *Introduction to Permaculture*. Tagari Publications: Sisters Creek.

Moyo, D. (2010). *Dead Aid: Why Aid is Not Working and How There is a Better Way for Africa*. Farrar, Straus and Giroux: New York.

Muche, M., Endalew, B. and Koricho, T. (2014). Determinants of Household Food Security among Southwest Ethiopia Rural Households. *Asian Journal of Agricultural Research* 1-11.

Munro-Hay, S. (1991). *Aksum: An African Civilization of Late Antiquity*. Edinburgh University Press: Edinburgh.

Munro-Hay, S. (2002). Ethiopia: The Unknown Land: A Cultural and Historical Guide. I.B. Tauris: New York.

Nash, R., Hudson, A. and Luttrell, C. (2006). *Mapping Political Context: A Toolkit for Civil Society Organizations*. Research and Policy in Development Programme, Overseas Development Institute: London.

Nasir, M. and Hundie, B. (2014). The Effect of Off Farm Employment on Agricultural Production and Productivity: Evidence from Gurage Zone of Southern Ethiopia. *Journal of Economics and Sustainable Development* 5(23): 85-98.

NBE [National Bank of Ethiopia]. (2014). *Annual Report 2013/14*. Addis Ababa: National Bank of Ethiopia.

ND-GAIN. (2016). *Country Rankings: Vulnerability and Readiness*. http://index.gain.org/ranking

Ndegwa, S. (1996). *The Two Faces of Civil Society: NGOs and Politics in Africa*. Kumarian Press: West Hartford.

NEBE. (2015). *Official Results of the 24th May 2015 General Election, National Electoral Board of Ethiopia*. http://www.electionethiopia.org/en/

Nega, B. (2002). *Land Tenure and Agricultural Development in Ethiopia*. Ethiopian Policy Research Institute: Addis Ababa.

Negash, M. and Swinnen, J. (2013). Biofuels and Food Security: Micro-evidence from Ethiopia. *Energy Policy* 61: 963-976.

Ng, F. and Aksoy, M. (2008). *Who are the Net Food Importing Countries?* World Bank Policy Research Working Paper 4457.

Nigatu, A. W., Bratveit, M. and Moen, B. E. (2016). Self-Reported Acute Pesticide Intoxications in Ethiopia. *BMC Public Health* 16: 575 (1-8).

Nino-Zarazua, M., Barrientos, A., Hickey, S. and Hulme, D. (2012). Social Protection in Sub-Saharan Africa: Getting the Politics Right. *World Development* 40: 163-176.

Nolan, P. (1976). Collectivization in China: Some Comparisons with the USSR. *Journal of Peasant Studies* 3(2): 192-220.

Norris, P. (2011). *Democratic Deficit: Critical Citizens Revisited*. Cambridge University Press: New York.

NPC. (2017). *The 2017 Voluntary National Reviews on SDGs of Ethiopia: Government Commitments, National Ownership and Performance Trends*. National Planning Commission: Addis Ababa.

NRF. (2018). *Halloween Headquarters*. https://nrf.com/resources/consumer-research-and-data/holiday-spending/halloween-headquarters

Nyssen, J., Frankl, A., Haile, M., Hurni, H., Descheemaeker, K., Crummey, D., Ritler, A., Portner, B., Nievergelt, B., Moeyersons, J., Munro, N., Deckers, J., Billi, P. and Poesen, J. (2014). Environmental Conditions and Human Drivers for Changes to North Ethiopian Mountain Landscapes over 145 years. *Science and the Total Environment* 485-486: 164-179.

Nyssen, J., Haile, M., Moeyersons, J., Poesen, J. and Deckers, J. (2000). Soil and Water Conservation in Tigray (Northern Ethiopia): The Traditional Daget Technique and its Integration with Introduced Techniques. *Land Degradation & Development* 11: 199-208.

Nyssen, J., Haile, M., Possen, J., Deckers, J. and Moeyersons, J. (2001). Removal of Rock Fragments and its Effect on Soil Loss and Crop Yield, Tigray, Ethiopia. *Soil Use and Management* 17: 179-187.

Oakland Institute. (2011). *Understanding Land Investment Deals in Africa - Country Report: Ethiopia*. Oakland Institute: Oakland.

Oakland Institute. (2013). *Omo: Local Tribes Under Threat*. Oakland Institute: Oakland.

OCHA. (2016). *Ethiopia*. http://www.unocha.org/eastern-africa/about-us/about-ocha-eastern-africa/ethiopia

OEC. (2014). *Ethiopia*. http://atlas.media.mit.edu/en/profile/country/eth/

OECD - DAC. (2016). *Ethiopia*. http://www.oecd.org/dac/stats

OECD. (2005). *Lessons Learned on the Use of Power and Drivers of Change Analyses in Development Co-operation*. http://web.iaincirebon.ac.id/ebook/moon/Econ-Dev/DOC82.pdf

OECD. (2018). *Aid (ODA) Statistics to Resource Flows to Developing Countries*. http://www.oecd.org/dac/financing-sustainable-development/development-finance-data/TAB30e.xls

OPHI. (2017). OPHI Country Briefing 2017: Ethiopia. Oxford Poverty and Human Development Initiative. University of Oxford: Oxford.

Oren, M. (2013). *Too Certain to Invest? Government Credibility and Ethiopian Insurance Markets*. Department of Political Science, UC San Diego.

Ossome, L. (2014). Can the Law Secure Women's Rights to Land in Africa? Revisiting Tensions between Culture and Land Commercialization. *Feminist Economics* 20: 155-177.

Pankhurst, R. (1966). State and Land in Ethiopian History. Haile Sellassie I University and Oxford University Press: Addis Ababa and Nairobi.

Pankhurst, R. (1985). *The History of Famines and Epidemics in Ethiopia Prior to the Twentieth Century*. Relief and Rehabilitation Commission: Addis Ababa.

Pankhurst, R. (1990). *A Social History of Ethiopia. Institute of Ethiopian Studies*. Addis Ababa University: Addis Ababa.

Pankhurst, R. (1997). *The Ethiopian Borderlands: Essays in Regional History from Ancient Times to the End of the 18th Century*. Red Sea Press: Asmara.

Pankhurst, R. (1998). *The Ethiopians: A History*. Blackwell Publishers: Oxford.

Pankhurst, A. (2008). The Emergence, Evolution and Transformations of *iddir* Funeral Associations in Urban Ethiopia. *Journal of Ethiopian Studies* 41(1/2): 143-185.

Pausewang, S. (2002). No Environmental Protection without Local Democracy? Why Peasants Distrust their Agricultural Advisers (p. 87-100). In *Ethiopia: The Challenge of Democracy from Below,* edited by Bahru Zewde and Siegfried Pausewang. Forum for Social Studies: Addis Ababa.

Parkinson, S. (2009). When Farmers Don't Want Ownership: Reflections on Demand-Driven Extension in Sub-Saharan Africa. *The Journal of Agricultural Education and Extension* 15(4): 417-429.

PEN International. (2016). *Freedom of Expression Under Threat Amid Growing Crackdown.* http://www.pen-international.org/newsitems/ethiopia-freedom-of-expression-under-threat-amid-growing-crackdown/

Percy, R. (2000). Capacity Building for Gender-Sensitive Agricultural Extension Planning in Ethiopia. *Journal of Agricultural Education and Extension* 7: 21-30.

Peterman, A., Behrman, J. and Quisumbing, A. (2010). *A Review of Empirical Evidence on Gender Differences in Nonland Agricultural Inputs, Technology, and Services in Developing Countries.* International Food Policy Research Institute: Washington.

Pimbert, M. (2008). *Towards Food Sovereignty: Reclaiming Autonomous Food Systems.* CAFS, IIED and RCC: London.

Piven, F. F. and Cloward, R. A. (1977). *Poor People's Movements: Why they Succeed, How they Fail.* Vintage Books: New York.

Planel, S. (2014). A View of a Bureaucratic Developmental State: Local Governance and Agricultural Extension in Rural Ethiopia. *Journal of Eastern African Studies* 8(3): 420-437.

Powledge, F. (2012). Food Insecurity: An Overview. In *At Issue: Food Insecurity,* Edited by L. Gerdes. Greenhaven Press: New York.

Prendergast, J. and Duffield, M. (1999). Liberation Politics in Ethiopia and Eritrea (p. 35-51). In *Civil Wars in Africa: Roots and Resolutions,* edited by T. Ali and R. Matthews. McGill-Queen's University Press: Montreal and Kingston.

Provost, C. (2013). *Migrants' Billions put Aid in the Shade.* www.theguardian.com/global-development/2013/jan/30/migrants-billions-overshadow-aid

Provost, C. (2014). *Ethiopia Seed Bank's Novel Approach to Preserving Diversity Under Threat.* www.theguardian.com/global-development/2014/feb/19/ethiopia-seed-bank-preserving-diversity-under-threat-g8-new-alliance

Quisumbing, A. R., Meinzen-Dick, R., Raney, T. L., Croppenstedt, A., Behrman J. A. and Peterman, A. (2014). *Gender in Agriculture.* Springer: London.

Ragasa, C., Berhane, G., Tadesse, F. and Taffesse, A. S. (2014). Gender Differences in Access to Extension Services and Agricultural Productivity. *Journal of Agricultural Education and Extension* 19(5): 437-468.

Rahmato, D. (1984). *Agrarian Reform in Ethiopia.* Scandinavian Institute of African Studies: Uppsala.

Rahmato, D. (1992). *The Dynamics of Rural Poverty: Case Studies from a District in Southern Ethiopia.* Monograph 2/92. CODESRIA: Dakar.

Rahmato, D. (1995). Resilience and Vulnerability: Enset Agriculture in Southern Ethiopia. *Journal of Ethiopian Studies* 28(1): 23-51.

Rahmato, D. (2004). *Searching for Tenure Security? The Land System and New Policy Initiatives in Ethiopia.* Forum for Social Studies Discussion Paper No. 12. Forum for Social Studies: Addis Ababa.

Rahmato, D. (2007). *Development Interventions in Wollaita, 1960s-2000s: A Critical Review.* Forum for Social Studies, Monograph No. 4: Addis Ababa.

Rahmato, D. (2008). *The Peasant and the State: Studies in Agrarian Change in Ethiopia, 1950s-2000s.* Custom Books: Addis Ababa.

Rahmato, D. (2011). *Land to Investors: Large-scale Land Transfers in Ethiopia.* Forum for Social Studies: Addis Ababa.

Rahmato, D. (2013). Food Security and Safety Nets: Assessment and Challenges. In *Food Security, Safety Nets and Social Protection in Ethiopia* edited by D. Rahmato, A. Pankhurst and J.-G. van Uffelen. Forum for Social Studies: Addis Ababa.

Rahmato, D. (2019). Land Deals, Rural Unrest and the Crisis of State in Ethiopia. In *Ethiopia: Social, Economic and Political Issues* edited by L. Cochrane. Nova: New York.

Rahmato, D., Pankhurst, A. and van Uffelen, J.-G, eds. (2013). *Food Security, Safety Nets and Social Protection in Ethiopia.* Forum for Social Studies: Addis Ababa.

Ramalingam, B. (2013). *Aid on the Edge of Chaos: Rethinking International Cooperation in a Complex World.* Oxford University Press: Oxford.

Rawls, J. (1958). Justice as Fairness. *Philosophical Review* 67: 164-194.

Rawls, J. (1971). *A Theory of Justice.* Harvard University Press: Cambridge.

Rawls, J. (1999). *The Law of Peoples.* Harvard University Press: Cambridge.

ReliefWeb. (2016). *Ethiopia: Drought – 2015-2016.* http://reliefweb.int/disaster/dr-2015-000109-eth

Riddell, R. (2007). Does Foreign Aid Really Work? Oxford University Press: New York.

Rigg, J. (2006). Land, Farming, Livelihoods, and Poverty: Rethinking the Links in the Rural South. *World Development* 34(1): 180-202.

Rivera, J., Hotz, C., Gonzalez-Cossio, T., Neufeld, L. and Garcia-Guerra, A. (2003). The Effect of Micronutrient Deficiencies on Child Growth: A Review of Results from Community-based Supplementation Trials. *Journal of Nutrition* 133(11): 4010S-4020S.

Rose, P. and Al-Samarrai, S. (2001). Household Constraints on Schooling by Gender: Empirical Evidence from Ethiopia. *Comparative Education Review* 45: 36-63.

Rosenthal, J. E. (1974). Survival in the Sahel. In War on Hunger. Agency for International Development: Washington, D.C.

Rostow, W. W. (1960). *The Stages of Economic Growth: A Non-Communist Manifesto.* Cambridge University Press: Cambridge.

Roth, M. (1988). *Somalia Land Policies and Tenure Impacts.* http://pdf.usaid.gov/pdf_docs/pnabb822.pdf

Roy, A., Negron-Gonzales, G., Opoku-Agyemang, K. and Talwalker, C. (2016). *Encountering Poverty: Thinking and Acting in an Unequal World.* University of California Press: Oakland.

Rubenson, S. (1964). *Wichale XVII: The Attempt to Establish a Protectorate Over Ethiopia.* Haile Sellassie I University and Oxford University Press: Addis Ababa and Nairobi.

Rubenson, S. (1966). *King of Kings: Tewodros of Ethiopia.* Haile Sellassie I University and Oxford University Press: Addis Ababa and Nairobi.

Sabatier, P. A. (1988). An Advocacy Coalition Model of Policy Change and the Role of Policy Oriented Learning Therein. *Policy Science* 21: 129-168.

Sabatier, P. A. and Jenkins-Smith, H. (1993). *Policy Change and Learning: An Advocacy Coalition Approach.* Westview Press: Boulder.

Sabatier, P. A. and Jenkins-Smith, H. (1999). The Advocacy Coalition Framework: An Assessment (p. 117-166). In *Theories of the Policy Process* edited by P. A. Sabatier. Westview Press: Boulder.

Sachs, J. (2005). *The End of Poverty: Economic Possibilities for Our Time.* Penguin: New York.

Sahn, D. (1989). *Seasonal Variability in Third World Agriculture: The Consequences for Food Security.* Johns Hopkins University Press: London.

Sait, S. and Lim, H. (2006). *Land, Law and Islam: Property and Human Rights in the Muslim World, Volume 1.* Zed Books: New York.

Samberg, L. H., Fishman, L. and Allendorf, F. W. (2013). Population Genetic Structure in a Social Landscape: Barley in a Traditional Ethiopian Agricultural System. *Evolutionary Applications* 6: 1133-1145.

Sana, M. Stecklov, G. and Weinreb, A. (2012). *Local or Outsider Interviewer? An Experimental Evaluation.* Submitted to the Annual Meeting of the Population Association of America, San Francisco, 3-5 May 2012.

Sandefur, J. and Glassman, A. (2015). The Political Economy of Bad Data: Evidence from African Survey & Administrative Statistics. *Journal of Development Studies* 51: 116-132.

Schock, K. (2015). *Civil Resistance Today.* Polity: Cambridge.

Scott, J. C. (1985). *Weapons of the Weak: Everyday Forms of Peasant Resistance.* Yale University Press: New Haven.

Scott, J. C. (1998). *Seeing Like a State: How Certain Schemes to Improve the Human Condition Have Failed.* Yale University Press: Yale.

Scott, J. C. (2009). *The Art of Not Being Governed: An Anarchist History of Upland Southeast Asia.* Yale University Press: New Haven.

Segers, K., Dessein, J., Nyssen, J., Haile, M. and Deckers, J. (2008). Developers and Farmers Intertwining Interventions: The Case of Rainwater Harvesting and Food-for-Work in Degua Temben, Tigray, Ethiopia. *International Journal of Agricultural Sustainability* 6(3): 173-182.

Segers, K., Dessein, J., Hagberg, S., Develtere, P., Haile, M. and Deckers, J. (2009). Be Like Bees – The Politics of Mobilizing Farmers for Development in Tigray, Ethiopia. *African Affairs* 108(430): 91-109.

Sen, A. (1981). *Poverty and Famines: An Essay on Entitlement and Deprivation.* Oxford University Press: New York.

Sen, A. (1983). *Choice, Welfare, and Measurement.* Harvard University Press: Cambridge.

Sen, A. (1985). *Commodities and Capabilities.* Oxford University Press: New York.

Sen, A. (1990). *Individual Freedom as a Social Commitment.* New York Review of Books, June 14th.

Sen, A. (1999). Development as Freedom. Anchor Books: New York.

Sen, A. (2009). *The Idea of Justice.* Harvard University Press: Cambridge.

Sen, A. and J. Dreze. (1990). *The Political Economy of Hunger.* Oxford University Press: Oxford.

Sen, A. and J. Dreze. (1999). *The Amartya Sen & Jean Dreze Omnibus.* Oxford University Press: Oxford.

Serneels, P. (2007). The Nature of Unemployment among Young Men in Urban Ethiopia. *Review of Development Economics* 11: 170-186.

Shete, M. and Rutten, M. (2015). Impacts of Large-scale Farming on Local Communities' Food Security and Income Levels – Empirical Evidence from Oromia Region, Ethiopia. *Land Use Policy* 47: 282-292.

Shipton, P. (1990). African Famines and Food Security: Anthropological Perspectives. *Annual Review of Anthropology* 19: 353-394.

Shivji, I. (2007). *Silences in NGO Discourses: The Role and Future of NGOs in Africa.* Fahamu: Oxford.

SIDA. (2005). *Methods for Analysing Power – A Workshop Report*. http://www. sida.se/contentassets/aa2a1e482af44911a07cd217698fde9e/methods-of-analysing-power---a-workshop-report_729.pdf

Siraj, A. S., Santos-Vegam M., Bouma, M. J., Yadeta, D., Ruiz Carrascal, D. and Pascual, M. (2014). Altitudinal Changes in Malaria Indidence in Highlands of Ethiopia and Colombia. *Science* 343(6175): 1154-1158.

Siyoum, A. D. (2013). The Importance of Labour for Food Security: Household Experiences in Ebinat Woreda, Amhara Region. In *Food Security, Safety Nets and Social Protection in Ethiopia* edited by D. Rahmato, A. Pankhurst and J-G van Uffelen. Forum for Social Studies: Addis Ababa.

Smith, A. (1790, 1976 reprint). *The Theory of Moral Sentiments*. Clarendon Press: Oxford.

Smith, L. (2008). The Politics of Contemporary Language Policy in Ethiopia. *Journal of Developing Societies* 24(2): 207-243.

Smith, M., Pointing, J. and Maxwell, S. (1993). *Household Food Security: Concepts and Definitions*. Institute of Development Studies: Sussex.

Smith, S. and Webb, E. (2011). Acting Out of Conflict: Using Participatory Theatre as a Tool of Peacebuilding in Rwanda. *Africa Peace and Conflict Journal* 4(2): 66-80.

Soubbotina, T. (2000). *Beyond Economic Growth: Meeting the Challenges of Global Development*. World Bank: Washington.

Spear, J. (2016). The Militarization of United States Foreign Aid (p. 18-41). In *The Securitization of Foreign Aid*. Palgrave: New York.

Spielman, D., Mekonnen, D. and Alemu, D. (2012). Seed, Fertilizer, and Agricultural Extension in Ethiopia. In *Food and Agriculture in Ethiopia*, edited by P. Dorosh and S. Rashid. University of Pennsylvania Press: Philadelphia.

Stachowiak, S. (2009). *Pathways for Change: 6 Theories about How Policy Change Happens*. Organizational Research Services: Seattle.

Stachowiak, S. (2013). *Pathways for Change: 10 Theories in Inform Advocacy and Policy Change Efforts*. Center for Evaluation Innovation: Washington.

Stamoulis, K. and A. Zezza. (2003). *A Conceptual Framework for National Agricultural, Rural Development, and Food Security Strategies and Policies*. ESA Working Paper No. 03-17, Food and Agriculture Organization of the United Nations.

Starn, O. (1991). Missing the Revolution: Anthropologists and War in Peru. *Cultural Anthropology* 6: 63-91.

Stone, C. N. (1993). Urban Regimes and the Capacity to Govern: A Political Economy Approach. *Journal of Urban Affairs* 15: 1-28.

Sulas, F., Madella, M. and French, C. (2009). State Formation and Water Resources Management in the Horn of Africa: The Aksumite Kingdom of the Northern Ethiopian Highlands. *World Archeology* 41(1): 2-15.

Sumner, A and Tribe, M. (2008). *International Development Studies: Theories and Methods in Research and Practice.* SAGE: London.

Sundaram, J. K. (2016). The MDGs and Poverty Reduction (p. 26-44). In *Poverty and the Millennium Development Goals* edited by A. Cimadamore, G. Koehler and T. Pogge. Zed Books: London.

Taddesse, D., Jamieson, D. and Cochrane, L. (2015). Strengthening Public Health Supply Chains in Ethiopia: PEPFAR Supported Expansion of Access and Availability. *Development in Practice* 25(7): 1043-1056.

Tadesse, M. (2014). Fertilizer Adoption, Credit Access, and Safety Nets in Rural Ethiopia. *Agricultural Finance Review* 74(3): 290-310.

Taffesse, A. S., Dorosh P., Gemessa, S.A. (2012). Crop production in Ethiopia: Regional patterns and trends. In *Food and Agriculture in Ethiopia: Progress and Policy Challenges* edited by P. Dorosh and S. Rashid. University of Pennsylvania: Philadelphia.

Tambo, J. (2016). Adaptation and Resilience to Climate Change and Variability in North-East Ghana. *Risk Reduction* 17: 85-94.

Tamiru, D., Argaw, A., Gerbaba, M., Ayana, G., Nigussie, A. and Belachew, T. (2016). Household Food Insecurity and its Association with School Absenteeism among Primary School Adolescents in Jimma Zone, Ethiopia. *BMC Public Health* 16: 802.

Tareke, G. (2009). *The Ethiopian Revolution: War in the Horn of Africa.* Yale University Press: London.

te Lintelo, D., Munslow, T., Lakshman, R. and Pittore, K. (2016). *Assessing the Policy Impact of 'Indicators': A Process-Tracing Study of the Hunger and Nutrition Commitment Index (HANCI),* Evidence Report Number 185. Institute of Development Studies: Brighton.

Tefera, D. A., Bijman, J. and Slingerland, M. A. (2017). Agricultural Co-operatives in Ethiopia: Evolution, Functions and Impact. *Journal of International Development* 29(4): 431-453.

Tefera, T. (2015). Extension Programme Participation and Smallholder's Livelihood: Evidence from Awassa Zuria District, SNNPR, Ethiopia. *Journal of Agricultural Extension and Rural Development* 7(5): 150-155.

Tefera, T. T., Handoro, F. and Gemu, M. (2013). Prevalence, Incidence and Distribution of Sweet Potato Virus: It's Effect on the Yield of Sweet Potato in Southern Region of Ethiopia. *International Journal of Science and Research* 2(1): 591-595.

Tefera, T., Tesfay, G., Elias, E., Diro, M. and Kooren, I. (2016). *Drivers of Adoption of Agricultural Technologies and Practices in Ethiopia: A Study Report from 30 Woredas in Four Regions*. Capacity Building for Scaling Up of Evidence-based Best Practices in Agricultural Production in Ethiopia Project Report No. NS_DfA_2016_1.

Temesgen, M., Rockstrom, J., Savenije, H. H. G. and Hoogmoed, W. B. (2007). Assessment of Strip Tillage Systems for Maize Production in Semi-Arid Ethiopia: Effects on Grain Yield and Water Balance. *Hydrology and Earth Systems Sciences* 4: 2229-2271.

Terry, F. (2002). *Condemned to Repeat? The Paradox of Humanitarian Action*. Cornell University Press: London.

Tesfahunegn, G. B., Tamene, L. and Vlek, P. L. G. (2011). Evaluation of Soil Quality Identified by Local Farmers in Mai-Negus Catchment, Northern Ethiopia. *Geoderma* 163: 209-218.

Teshome, A., Torrance, J, K., Baum, B., Fahrig, L., Lambert, D. H. and Arnason, J. T. (1999). Traditional Farmers' Knowledge of Sorghum (*Sorghum bicolor* [Poaceae]) Landrace Storability in Ethiopia. *Economic Botany* 53(1): 69-78.

Thiongo, N. (1986). *Decolonizing the Mind*. James Currey: London.

Thome, K., Meade, B., Rosen, S. and Beghin, J. C. (2016). *Assessing Food Security in Ethiopia with USDA ERS's New Food Security Modeling Approach*. Working Paper 16-WP 567, Center for Agricultural and Rural Development, Iowa State University.

Tolossa, D. (2003). Issues of Land Tenure and Food Security: The Case of Three Communities of Munessa Wereda, South-central Ethiopia. *Norwegian Journal of Geography* 57: 9-19.

Tronvoll, K. (2010). The Ethiopian 2010 Federal and Regional Elections: Re-Establishing the One-Party State. *African Affairs* 110(438): 121-136.

Tsegaye, A. and Struik, P. C. (2002). Analysis of Enset (Ensete vventricosum) Indigenous Production Methods and Farm-based Biodiversity in Major Enset-growing Regions of Southern Ethiopia. *Experimental Agriculture* 38: 291-315.

Tsegaye, D., Vedeld, P. and Moe, S. R. (2013). Pastoralists and Livelihoods: A Case Study from Northern Afar, Ethiopia. *Journal of Arid Environments* 91: 138-146.

Tura, H. A. (2014). Woman's Right to and Control over Rural Land in Ethiopia. *Journal of Current Research* 2(4): 81-93.

Turin, C. and Valdivia, C. (2012). Off-farm Work in the Peruvian Altiplano: Seasonal and Geographic Considerations for Agricultural and Development Policies (p. 145-160). In *Seasonality, Rural Livelihoods and Development* edited by S. Devereux, R. Sabates-Wheeler and R. Longhurst. Earthscan: New York.

Turner, J. C. (1982). Towards a Cognitive Redefinition of the Social Group (p 15-40). In *Social Identity and Intergroup Relations*, edited by H. Hajfel. Cambridge University Press: New York.

Turner, J. C. and Oakes, P. J. (1986). The Significance of the Social Identity Concept for Social Psychology with Reference to Individualism, Interactionism and Social Influence. *British Journal of Social Psychology* 25(3): 237-252.

Turner, J. C., Hogg, M. A., Oakes, P. J. and Reicher, S. D. (1987). *Rediscovering the Social Group: A Self-Categorization Theory*. Basil Blackwell: Cambridge.

Tversky, A. and Kahneman, D. (1981). The Framing of Decisions and the Psychology of Choice. *Science* 211: 453-458.

Tversky, A. and Kahneman, D. (1992). Advances in Prospect Theory: Cumulative Representation of Uncertainty. *Journal of Risk and Uncertainty* 5: 297-323.

U.S. State Department. (2007). *Ethiopia: International Religious Freedom Report*. http://m.state.gov/md90097.htm

U.S. State Department. (2014). *Ethiopia: International Religious Freedom Report*. http://m.state.gov/md222049.htm

UN OCHA. (2018). *CERF Releases US$15M to Scale Up Humanitarian Assistance to People Affected by Escalating Inter-communal Violence*. http://www.unocha. org/story/ethiopia-cerf-releases-us15m-scale-humanitarian-assistance-people-affected-escalating-inter

UN. (1975). *Report on the World Food Conference 1974*. United Nations: New York.

UN. (2011). *World Population Prospects: The 2010 Revision*. United Nations: New York.

UN. (2015). *World Population Prospects: The 2015 Revision*, Custom Data Acquired via website. United Nations Department of Economic and Social Affairs, Population Division.

UN. (2016). *Transforming Our World: The 2030 Agenda for Sustainable Development*. https://sustainabledevelopment.un.org/post2015/transformingourworld

UNDP. (2017). *Ethiopia: Human Development Indicators*. http://hdr.undp.org/en/countries/profiles/ETH#

UNEP. (2014). *Assessing Global Land Use: Balancing Consumption with Sustainable Supply*. Working Group on Land and Soils of the International Resource Panel.

UNICEF. (2013). *Progress Shows that Stunting in Children can be Defeated*. http://www.unicef.org/media/media_68734.html

UNICEF. (2016). *Current Stats + Progress*. http://data.unicef.org/child-mortality/under-five.html

Uraguchi, Z. B. (2010). Food Price Hikes, Food Security, and Gender Equality: Assessing the Roles and Vulnerability of Women in Households of Bangladesh and Ethiopia. *Gender & Development* 18(3): 491-501.

USAID. (2016). *Adaptive Management.* https://usaidlearninglab.org/learning-guide/adaptive-management

USDA. (2008). *Food Security in the United States: Measuring Household Food Security.* United States Department of Agriculture: Washington.

Uvin, P. (1999). *Aiding Violence: The Development Enterprise in Rwanda.* Kumarian Press: West Hartford.

Uvin, P. (2009). *Life After Violence: A People's Story of Burundi.* Zed Books: London.

Vaughan, S. (2003). *Ethnicity and Power in Ethiopia.* Doctoral Dissertation submitted to the University of Edinburgh.

Vaughan, S. and Tronvoll, K. (2003). *The Culture of Power in Contemporary Ethiopian Political Life.* SIDA's Information Centre: SIDAStudies No. 10.

Vecchiato, N. L. (1993). Illness, Therapy, and Change in Ethiopian Possession Cults. *Africa* 63(2): 176-196.

Ven Den Berg, M. and Ruben, R. (2006). Small-scale Irrigation and Income Distribution in Ethiopia. *Journal of Development Studies* 42(5): 868-880.

Vervoort, J. M., Palazzo, A., Mason-D'Croz, D., Ericksen, P. J., Thornton, P. K., Kristjanson, P., Forch, W., Herrero, M., Havlik, P., Jost, C. and Rowlands, H. (2013). *The Future of Food Security, Environments and Livelihoods in Eastern Africa: Four Socio-economic Scenarios.* CCAFS Working Paper 63. CGIAR Research Program on Climate Change, Agriculture and Food Security.

Von Bertalanffy, L. (1972). The History and Status of General Systems Theory. *Academy of Management Journal* 15(4): 407-426.

Waters-Bayer, A., Kristjanson, P., Wettasinha, C., van Veldhuizen, L., Quiroga, G., Swaans, K. and Douthwaite, B. (2015). Exploring the Impact of Farmer-led Research Supported by Civil Society Organizations. *Agriculture & Food Security* 4:4 (p. 1-7).

Watts, M. (1983). *Silent Famine: Food, Famine & Peasantry in Northern Nigeria.* University of California Press: Berkeley.

Webb, P. and Braun, J. (1994). *Famine and Food Security in Ethiopia: Lessons for Africa.* Wiley & Sons: New York.

Weber, E. (1976). *Peasants into Frenchmen: The Modernization of Rural France, 1870-1914.* Stanford University Press: Stanford.

Wegner, L. and Zwart, G. (2011). *Who Will Feed the World? The Production Challenge.* Oxfam International: Cowley.

Weible, C. M. and Sabatier, P. A. (2006). A Guide to the Advocacy Coalition Framework (p. 123-136). In *Handbook of Public Policy Analysis: Theory, Politics and Methods* edited by F. Fischer, G. J. Miller and M. S. Sidney. CRC Press: Boca Raton.

Westengen, O. T. and Banik, D. (2016). The State of Food Security: From Availability, Access and Rights to Food Systems Approaches. *Forum for Development Studies* 43(1): 113-134.

WFP. (2009). *Comprehensive Food Security & Vulnerability Analysis Guidelines.* World Food Program: Rome.

WFP. (2014). *Frequently Asked Questions.* http://www.wfp.org/hunger/faqs

WFP. (2016). *What Causes Hunger?* https://www.wfp.org/hunger/causes

Wheeler, T. and von Braun, J. (2013). Climate Change Impacts on Global Food Security. *Science* 341: 508-513.

Wolde Giorgis, D. (1989). *Red Tears: War, Famine, and Revolution in Ethiopia.* Red Sea Press: Trenton.

Wolde Mariam, M. (1986). *Rural Vulnerability to Famine in Ethiopia – 1958-1977.* Practical Action Publishing: Bourton on Dunsmore.

Woldomeskel, G. (1989). The Consequences of Resettlement in Ethiopia. *African Affairs* 88(353): 359-374.

Wolf-Powers, L. (2014). Understanding Community Development in a "Theory of Action" Framework: Norms, Markets, Justice. *Planning Theory & Practice* 15(2): 202-219.

World Bank. (2006). *Ethiopia: Managing Water Resources to Maximize Sustainable Growth: Water Resources Assistance Strategy.* World Bank: Washington.

World Bank. (2008). *World Development Report 2008: Agriculture for Development.* World Bank: Washington.

World Bank. (2011). *World Development Report: Conflict, Security, and Development.* World Bank: Washington.

World Bank. (2012). *DataBank* databank.worldbank.org

World Bank. (2015). *World Development Report: Mind, Society, and Behavior.* World Bank Group: Washington.

World Bank. (2016). *Ethiopia.* http://data.worldbank.org/country/ethiopia

World Bank. (2018). *DataBank* databank.worldbank.org

World Bank. (2020). Ethiopia. http://data.worldbank.org/country/ethiopia

Wossen, T., Di Falco, S., Berger, T. and McClain, W. (2016). You Are Not Alone: Social Capital and Risk Exposure in Rural Ethiopia. *Food Security* 8: 799-813.

Wubeneh, N. G. and Sanders, J. H. (2006). Farm-level Adoption of Sorghum Technologies in Tigray, Ethiopia. *Agricultural Systems* 91: 122-134.

Yami, M. (2016). Irrigation Projects in Ethiopia: What Can Be Done to Enhance Effectiveness Under 'Challenging Contexts'? *International Journal of Sustainable Development and World Ecology* 23: 132-142.

Yanguas, P. (2018). *Why We Lie About Aid: Development and the Messy Politics of Change*. Zed: London.

Yelemtu, F. G. (2014). *The Social Life of Seeds: An Ethnographic Exploration of Farming Knowledge in Kibtya of Amhara Region, Ethiopia*. Doctoral Thesis submitted to the Department of Anthropology, Durham University.

Yewhalaw, D., Hamels, S., Getachew, Y., Torgerson, P. R., Anagnostou, M., Legesse, W., Kloos, H., Duchateau, L. and Speybroeck, N. (2014). Water Resources Developments in Ethiopia: Potential Benefits and Negative Impacts on the Environment, Vector-borne Diseases and Food Security. *Environmental Review* 22(4): 364-371.

Yilma, Z., Mebratie, A., Sparrow, R., Abebaw, D., Dekker, M., Alemu, G. and Bedi, A. S. (2014). Coping with Shocks in Rural Ethiopia. *Journal of Development Studies* 50(7): 1009-1024.

Yosef, T., Mengistu, U., Mohammed, Y. K., Kefelegn, K. (2013). Camel and Cattle Population Dynamics and Livelihood Diversification as a Response to Climate Change in Pastoral Areas of Ethiopia. *Livestock Research for Rural Development* 25(9): 1-10.

Young, J. (2008). Impact of Research on Policy and Practice. *Capacity* 35(4): 1-9.

Yu, B. and Nin-Pratt, A. (2014). Fertilizer Adoption in Ethiopia Cereal Production. *Journal of Development and Agricultural Economics* 6(7): 318-337.

Yusuf, S. (2019). *Drivers of Ethnic Conflict in Contemporary Ethiopia*. ISS: Addis Ababa.

Zenawi, M. (Undated). *African Development: Dead Ends and New Beginnings Preliminary Draft*.

Zinn, H. (2002). *You Can't Be Neutral on a Moving Train*. Beacon Press: Boston.

AUTHOR BIO

Logan Cochrane is an Associate Professor at HBKU (College of Public Policy), Assistant Professor at Carleton University (Global and International Studies) and Adjunct Professor at Hawassa University (Institute for Policy and Development Research). He has authored over 100 publications, around half of which are peer-reviewed journal articles. In 2021 he co-edited the book *The Transnational Land Rush in Africa* and in 2019 he edited the book *Ethiopia: Social and Political Issues*.

www.ingramcontent.com/pod-product-compliance
Lightning Source LLC
Chambersburg PA
CBHW020529270326
41927CB00006B/501